Kentucky Lake Reservoir Cemeteries

Volume 2

James L. Douthat

Heritage Books
2024

HERITAGE BOOKS

AN IMPRINT OF HERITAGE BOOKS, INC.

Books, CDs, and more—Worldwide

For our listing of thousands of titles see our website
at
www.HeritageBooks.com

A Facsimile Reprint
Published 2024 by
HERITAGE BOOKS, INC.
Publishing Division
5810 Ruatan Street
Berwyn Heights, MD 20740

Originally published 1988
Mountain Press
Signal Mountain, Tennessee

International Standard Book Number
Paperbound: 978-0-7884-9126-9

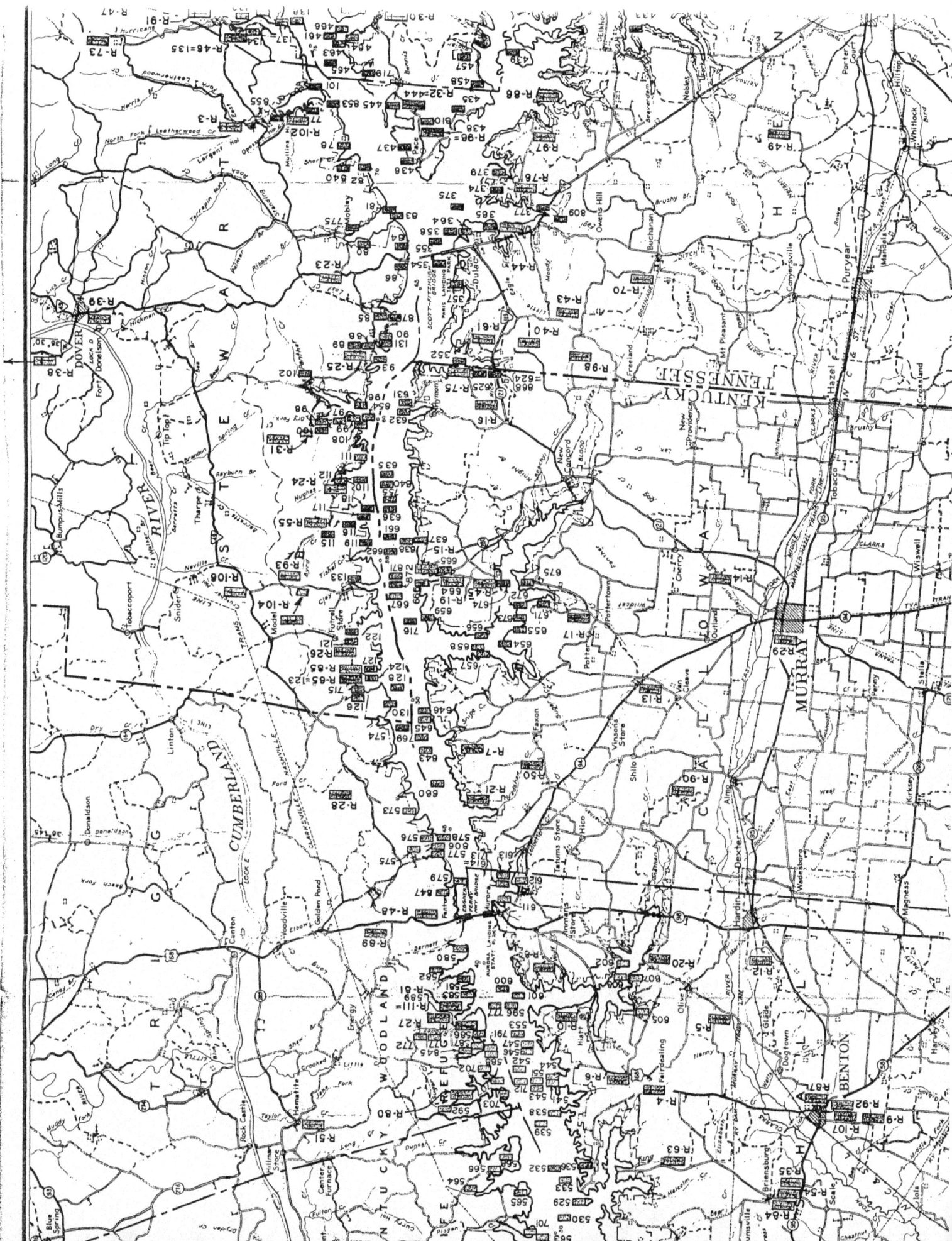

INTRODUCTION

The first grave removals required by construction of the Kentucky project was made in 1937, when it became necessary to relocate a cemetery at the site of a quarry. The regularly scheduled reservoir program was begun in August 1942 and was completed, except for a few graves, in December 1943. The work was done under the supervision of Fred W. Wendt, who acted as superintendent of grave removal operations for the project.

Reconnaissance surveys were made in order to locate all cemeteries in and adjacent to the impoundage area which might be affected by flooding, wave action, construction activities or the inundation of access routes. A total of 914 cemeteries were located and indexed. Detail studies were then made to determine which cemeteries would be directly affected and which isolated cemeteries could not be provided subsititute access comparable to that originally used.

Plane-table surveys were made of the existing cemeteries which would be directly affected or isolated, and of sites chosen for new cemeteries and reburial areas in existing cemeteries – a total of 397 surveys.

A total of 3390 graves were moved and 578 monuments were relocated. Disinterments were made from 120 cemeteries and 113 reinterment cemeteries were used. Remains from two graves were disinterred and turned over to undertakers for reburial in a distant cemetery at the request of the nearest relatives.

The arrangement of this book is by the counties. At the beginning of each county, there is a listing of the cemeteries covered. The file information and plat, if available, is given in numerical order of the cemetery. The file information is taken from the collected files of the Tennessee Valley Authority Office in Chattanooga. There are files on each cemetery, remain forms files and field notes taken in the field at the time of each survey. These are combined to give the information enclosed.

Most of the information from the files is given. We do not include the "Cause of Death" in every cases. Most of the time, this is not known and usually, it is guess work on the informant. Relocation information is not always given either. In the case of "Unknown" burials, it is not necessary. The information given is designed for the serious genealogical researcher. Information is given with that in mind.

James L. Douthat

Signal Mountain, TN
1988

KENTUCKY LAKE RESERVOIR CEMETERIES

* *

T A B L E   O F   C O N T E N T S

* *

BENTON COUNTY, TN CEMETERY REMOVALS

No.   Cemetery Name   Land Map Tract
* * *

No.	Cemetery Name	Land Map	Tract
461	Askew Cemetery	116	5779
463	Askew-Slaves Cemetery	115	5802
466	Askew-Slaves Cemetery	116	5782
475	Akers Cemetery	121	5694
506	Bradley Cemetery	188	C
458	Evans Cemetery	87	3845
483	Farmer Cemetery	136	5513
484	Farmer Cemetery	136	5499
507	Hatley Cemetery	166	5238
474	Irish Cemetery	121	5714
719	Indian Cemetery	115	5791
861	Indian Cemetery	180	5869
457	Liberty Cemetery	87A	3965
477	Lowry Cemetery	131	5532
503	Langly-Fry Cemetery	180	5876
821	Lone Grave	130	5562
733	Melton Cemetery	136	5521 F
501	McDaniel Cemetery	180	5865
485	No Name Cemetery	141	5024
465	No Name White Cemetery	115	5792
482	Phifer Cemetery	132	5945
464	Ralls Cemetery	115	5807
502	Whitfield-Pavatt Cemetery	180	5870

BENTON COUNTY, TENNESSEE

Grave Removal Cemeteries

Cemeteries listed below are either not affected by the lake waters or future access will be provided by relocated roads.

No.   Cemetery Name   Land Map Tract

* * *

No.	Cemetery Name	Land Map	Tract
488	Arnold Cemetery	142	1
860	Arnold Cemetery	142	5
470	Beaton	97	3958F
*498	Baker-Walker Cemetery	168	D
*511	Baker's Chapel Cemetery	108	Marginal
728	Bullock Cemetery	131	5535F
823	Bruce Cemetery	167	3
865	Bloodworth Cemetery	109	A
*473	Crooked Creek Cemetery	121	5728
*490	Chalk Level Cemetery	164	5305
*505	Cantrell Cemetery	188	6069F
*510	Colored Cemetery	109	Marginal
*512	Cedar Grove Cemetery	112	Marginal

* *

805	Cole Cemetery	151	6776
456	Dorch Cemetery	88	2869F
*493	Dalton Cemetery	168	5229F
836	DePriest Cemetery	180	E
*500	Eagle Creek Cemetery	180	6841F
*481	Forrest-Wheatley Cemetery	131	E
*491	Ford Cemetery	164	5310F
*513	Greer Cemetery	111	Marginal
460	Herndon Cemetery	117	5692F
*495	Hatley, Uncle Ned Cemetery	166	6518F
*496	Hatley-Ross Cemetery	167	Marginal
*494	Jackson Cemetery	168	5219
822	Johnson Cemetery	165	6196
455	Leegan Cemetery	88	3801
462	Lick Creek Cemetery	117	5675
472	Lindsey Cemetery	126	Marginal
487	Lone Grave	142	5114
*489	Lashlee Cemetery	151	6779F
*499	Luper Cemetery	166	3250F
750	Luper Cemetery	168	5225F
795	Liberty Cemetery	167	1
815	Lindsey Cemetery	105	Marginal
454	Medlock Cemetery	88	3898F
486	Maiden Cemetery	142	5113
*504	Manley's Chapel Cemetery	187	6079
734	Melton Cemetery	136	4
799	Mitchell Cemetery	152	6756F
841	No Name Cemetery	164	5306
874	No Name Cemetery	180	E
*497	Old Gossett Cemetery	167	Marginal
*508	Old No Name Cemetery	167	Marginal
747	Old Bethleham Cemetery	150	G
469	Pierce Cemetery	96	3642
*509	Pleasant Grove Cemetery	111	Marginal
480	Reynolds Cemetery	106	3759F
748	Robertson Cemetery	150	6744F
468	Robertson Cemetery	96	Marginal
476	Rushing Cemetery	127	5460F
459	Stockdale Cemetery	117	5676
857	Slave Cemetery	109	3890F
859	Un-named Cemetery	111	Marginal
471	Willow Cemetery	105	A
*467	Wynn Cemetery	126	5652
478	Wheatley Cemetery	131	A
479	Warmack Cemetery	106	3755F
492	Wyley Cemetery	164	5301
*720	Wilson Cemetery	121	5736F

* = Present access affected, but future access provided by relocated roads.

* *

#457 LIBERTY CEMETERY

Located on Land Map 87A, Tract GIR-3965, above elevation 450, 51 graves. The cemetery was active and well kept. Access by the old Big Sandy-Mouth of Sandy Road was flooded. Remain permits were executed on 46 graves. The remaining 5 graves could not be identified or no one could be found who would request that they be moved or left undisturbed. No further action was necessary.

No.	Name of deceased	Age	Date of death	Information given by...

* *

No.	Name of deceased	Age	Date of death	Information given by...
1.	Evans infant		1908	Mary Francis Evans, m
2.	Unknown			
3.	Basil Ray Evans		1938	Thelma Evans, mother
4.	Evans infant			Ms Ludie Evans, mother
5.	Merrell infant		1913	Mamie Merrell, mother
6.	Florence Walker		1917	Mary Francis Evans, sis
7.	Sarah Merrell		1920	"
8.	Frank Williams		1918	Emma Williams, wife
9.	Betty Henderson		1918	Georgia Odom, daug.
10.	Lonie Henderson		1908	Ms W.M. McSwain, sister
11.	Henderson infant			" - aunt
12.	Merrell infant			" - aunt
13.	Merrell infant			" - aunt
14.	Margrett Henderson		1903	" - daug.
15.	William Henderson		1899	" - daug.
16.	Loreta Rhodes		1905	Mitchel Rhodes, son
17.	Henderson infant		1912	Georgia Odom, sister
18.	Pierce infant			Ms W.M. McSwain, aunt
19.	Unknown			
20.	Beulah Haley			"
21.	Mrs. Ed Haley			"
22.	Means infant			Eula Mae Markham, cousin
23.	Clara V. Hutchison		1910	Ms E.H. Hutchinson, M
24.	Mary Ann Hutchison		1913	Ms Annie Christopher, d
25.	Jim Hutchison		1925	" - daug.
26.	Lela Simpson		1925	Henry Simpson, husband
27.	Mrs. A. E. Dehart			H. S. Dehart, son
28.	J. A. Dehart			" - son
29.	Lionel Farris		1910	Lula Farris, mother
30.	Unknwon			
31.	Jim Farris			Audie Mae Askew, wife
32.	J. M. Farris		1934	Lula Farris, wife
33.	George Moon		1920	Kate Buie, daug
34.	Martha Moon		1940	" - daug
35. - 36.	Moon infant			Odie Moon, father

* *

37.	Mattie Evans	1925	Earnest Evans, husband
38.	Hershel Evans	1927	" - father
39.	Clyde Markham	1919	T. C. Markham, father
40.	Beulah Mae Farris	1941	L. R. Farris, father
41.	Christine Evans	1931	Hurlie Evans, father
42.	Shirley W. Penson		Ms F.A. Penson, mother
43.	Evans infant	1927	J.A. Evans, g/parent
44.	Evans infant		" - g/parent
45.	Marcell Evans	1924	" - parent
46.	Moris Lemonds	1937	G. L. Lemonds, father
47.	Francis Nell Farris	1938	L. R. Farris, father
48.	Delton Merrell		Ed Merrell, father
49.	Penson infant	1910	Odell Penson, mother
50.	Penson infant	1912	" - mother
51.	Penson infant		" - mother

See Plat Map #457

#458 EVANS CEMETERY

Located on Land Map 87, Tract GIR-3845, above elevation 380, 88 graves. The cemetery was active and well kept. Access by 15 foot county road was flooded. Remain permits were executed on 82 graves. The remaining 6 graves could not be identified or no one could be found who would request that they be moved or left undisturbed. No further action was necessary.

No.	Name of Deceased	Age	Date of Death	Information given by...
1.	Oliver infant	unk	unk	Wade Oliver
2.	Beulah Martin	unk	1922	Eliza Martin, mother
3.	George Martin	unk	unk	Eliza Martin, wife
4.	Culpepper infant			Roger Culpepper, bro
5.	Culpepper infant			Roger Culpepper, bro.
6.	Nova Culpepper			Roger Culpepper, son
7.	W. R. Culpepper			Roger Culpepper, son
8.	Culpepper infant			Roger Culpepper, uncle
9.	Tad Culpepper			Roger Culpepper, bro.
10.	Ethel Culpepper		1910	Eliza Martin, sister
11.	Susan Culpepper		1918	Eliza Martin, daug.
12.	Balum Culpepper			Eliza Martin, daug.
13.	Callie Culpepper			Elizabeth Culpepper, mot
14.	DeHart infant			Lizzie DeHart, mother
15.	W. T. Toombs	29	1910	Lizzie DeHart, wife
16.	Mrs. Isaac Watkins			Harmon Watkins, son
17.	Isaac Watkins			Harmon Watkins, son

* *

18.	Brown infant			Ms E.E. Brown, mother
19.	Alvin Herndon			Janie Herndon, wife
20.	Herndon infant			Janie Herndon, mother
21.	Herndon infant			Janie Herndon, mother
22.	Mary Pierce			Ms E.E. Brown, daug.
23.	Franklin Pierce			Ms E.E. Brown, daug
24.	Grainger infant			Melvina Grainger, mother
25.	John Grainger			Melvina Grainger, wife
26.	Tom Evans			Claudie Evans, wife
27.	Evans infant			Claudie Evans, mother
28.	Evans infant			Claudie Evans, mother
29.	Herndon infant			Janie Herndon, mother
30.	Rhoda Evans			Luther Evans, son
31.	Lena Evans		1914	Luther Evans, bro.
32.	Henry G. Shultz			Luther Evans, b-in-law
33.	Alice Shultz			Luther Evans, bro
34.	Gertie Rhodes			Osa Rhodes, husband
35.	Evans infant			W. E. Evans, father
36.	Annie Evans			W. E. Evans, husband
37.	Mary Hampton			A. M. Hawley, father
38.	Hawley infant			A. M. Hawley, father
39.	Hawley infant			A. M. Hawley, father
40.	Sallie Hawley			A. M. Hawley, husband
41.	Gray infant			Mollie Gray, mother
42.	Gregor un-identified			
43.	Richard Merrill			Ray Perkins, g/son
44.	Alice Merrill			Ray Perkins, g/son
45.	Merrill infant			Ray Perkins, bro.
46.	Merrill infant			Ray Perkins, bro
47.	Nettie Evans	5	1905	Freeman Evans, bro.
48.	Evans infant			Freeman Evans, bro.
49.	Nancy Evans	38	1905	Freeman Evans, son
50.	Tom Evans			Katie Evans, wife
51.	Evans infant			Norman Evans, father
52. - 54.	Evans infants			James Evans, father
55.	Arthur Evans			James Evans, father
56.	Frank Evans			James Evans, father
57.	Lovie Evans			James Evans, father
58.	Martha Evans			James Evans, father
59.	Elias Evans			James Evans, son
60.	Celia Evans			James Evans, son
61.	Merrill infant			A. R. Perkins, nephew
62.	Merrill infant			A. R. Perkins, nephew

6

Benton County, Tennessee

* *

No.	Name	Age	Date	Information given by...
63.	John Culpepper			W. E. Evans, nephew
64.	Unknown			
65.	Louisa Williams			Mary Evans, daug.
66.	Unknown			
67.	Williams infant			J. R. McSwain, uncle
68.	Williams infant			J. R. McSwain, uncle
69.	Lula McSwain			J. R. McSwain, bro.
70.	Robert McSwain			J. R. McSwain, bro.
71.	Maggie J. McSwain			J. R. McSwain, son
72.	M. J. McSwain			J. R. McSwain, son
73.	Merrill un-idenfied			
74.	Luke Merrill			
75.	Mrs. Luke Merrill			
76.	Bertha Barnes			Ms Virgil Vaughn, sister
77.	Vernon Barnes			Ms Virgil Vaughn, sister
78.	Raymond Barnes			Ms Virgil Vaughn, sister
79.	Freddie Barnes			Ms Virgil Vaughn, sister
80.	Flora Barnes			Ms Virgil Vaughn, daug.
81.	Bob Barnes			Ms Virgil Vaughn, daug
82.	Henry Fitch Patrick			Charlie Fitch Patrick, b
83.	Lena Fitch Patrick			" – bro
84.	Ed Fitch Patrick			" – son
85.	Amanda Fitch Patrick	24	1911	" – son
86.	Ed Fitch Patrick			" – bro
87.	James Fitch Patrick			" – bro
88.	Unknown – colored lady			

See Plat Map #458

#461 ASKEW CEMETERY

Located on Land Map 116, tract GIR 5779, below elevation 359, 12 graves. This was an inactive and neglected cemetery containing twelve graves and three monuments. All graves and monuments were moved to Stockdale Cemetery R-30. Removal operations were completed May 15, 1943.

No.	Name	Age	Date of Death	Information given by...
1.	Unknown Askew	unk	unk	Mrs. Tennie Outlaw
2.	Grace Askew	60	1864	Ms Tennie Outlaw, g/d
3.	David A. Askew	73	1880	Ms Tennie Outlaw, g/d
4.	Thomas A. Askew	18	1856	Ms Tennie Outlaw, neice
5. - 9.	Unknown Askew			
10.	Askew child	infant		
11. - 12.	Unknown			

See Plat Maps #461

* *

#464 RALLS CEMETERY

Located on Land Map 115, Tract GIR-5807, above elevation 379, 19 graves. The cemetery was inactive and badly neglected, only one burial having been made in 19 years. Access by Wynn's Ferry Road was flooded. Five graves and two monuments were moved to Ramble Creek Cemetery R-37 on March 16, 1943. Remain permits were executed on three graves. The remaining graves could not be identified or no one could be found who was interested in having them moved. No further action was necessary.

No.	Name	Date of Death		Information given by...
* * * * * * * * *		* * * * * * *		* * * * * * * *
1.	Ralls infant	infant	1903	James E. Ralls, father
2.	Nettie Ralls	38	1914	" - husband
3. - 7.	Unknown			
8.	Martha Ralls	unk	unk	" - husband
9.	Green B. Ralls	45	1867	" - son
10.	Nancy Ralls	35	1863	O. E. Lockman, g/s
11. - 16.	Unknown			
17.	Freddie Lockman		unk	" - bro.
18.	Angeline Lockman		unk	" - son
19.	Oliver B. Lockman		1932	" - son

See Plat Map #464

#465 ASKEW SLAVE CEMETERY

Located on Land Map 115, Tract GIR-5802, below elevation 375, number of graves uncertain. This was an old neglected slave cemetery containing no monuments or markers. Slight depressions are the only indications of graves. No one could be found to request that the graves be moved. No action was necessary.

See Plat Map #465

#466 ASKEW SLAVE CEMETERY

Located on Land Map 116, Tract GIR-5782, below elevation 359, number of graves uncertain. This was said to be an old slave cemetery, but the burial area had been in cultivation and there was no evidence of graves. No action was necessary.

* *

#467 WYNN CEMETERY

Located on Land Map 125, tract GIR - 5652, 58 graves.

No.	Name of deceased	Age	Date of Death	Information given by...
1.	Robins infant			Ms Tommie Robbins, mother
2.	Myrtle Johnson	2	1925	Ben S. W. Johnson, f
3.	William H. Robins	95	1938	George Robins, son
4.	Mrs. William H. Robins	60	unk	" - son
5.	Wm. Oliver Robins	9	unk	" - bro
6. - 8.	Unknown			
9.	Lennie Reed Christopher	0	1890	G.S. Christopher, bro
10.	James W. Christopher	2	1884	" - bro.
11.	Unknown			
12.	Earl T. Wynn	1	1939	Virgil Wynn, father
13.	Mrs. Ruby Wynn	unk	1923	" - husband
14. - 19.	Unknown			
20.	Buddy Wynn	unk	unk	V. T. Wynn, bro.
21.	Kate Wynn	9	1922	" - bro.
22.	G. O. Wynn	57	1903	" - son
23.	E. C. Wynn	71	1903	" - son
24.	A. R. Wynn	34	1904	Ms T.J. Stockdale, wife
25.	Minnie Fitzsimmons	23	1921	P.H. Fitzsimmons, father
26.	Mary L. Fitzsimmons	55	1923	" - husband
27.	Sepha Redick & infant	24	1911	R. T. Redick, husband
28.	Ella Spence	62	1941	W.Mack Spence, husband
29.	Will T. Wynn	65	1939	Ms Evert Perry, wife
30.	Henry Wynn	37	1937	Ms Henry Wynn, wife
31.	Cora Ella Wynn	46	1918	Ms Delila Wynn, daug.
32.	A. J. Wynn	unk	1905	Ms Tennie Pettiford, daug
33. - 45.	Unknown			
46.	Maggie Johnson	12	1928	Sam Johnson, father
47. - 58.	Unknown			
?	Mrs. Byrl Wynn	unk	unk	J. T. Wynn, g/chld
?	Byrl Wynn	unk	unk	" - g/chld

See Plat Map #457

* *

#474 IRISH CEMETERY

Located on Land Map 121, Tract GIR-5714, above elevation 395, 59 graves. The cemetery was fairly active but badly neglected. Access by 20 foot county road was flooded. Remain permits were executed on 26 graves. The remaining 35 graves could not be identified or no one could be found who would request that they be moved or remain undisturbed. No further action was necessary.

No.	Name of Deceased	Age	Date of Death	Information given by...

* *

No.	Name of Deceased	Age	Date of Death	Information given by...
1. - 12.	Unknown			
13.	Henry Fitzsimmons	unk	1938	Lawrence Fitzsimmons, s
14.	Mary Fitzsimmons	61	1925	" - son
15.	Harry Fitzsimmons	35	1920	" - bro.
16.	William Fitzsimmons	27	1904	" - bro.
17.	P. H. Cosgrove	88	unk	" - g/son
18.	Catherine Cosgrove	77	unk	" - g/son
19.	Charles Fitzsimmons	unk	unk	" - bro.
20.	Unknown			
21.	Kate Fitzsimmons	unk	1895	" - bro.
22. - 26.	Unknown			
27.	Edward Craney			Annie Craney, s-in-law
28.	Lillian Craney			"
29.	Edmond Craney			"
30.	Frank Craney	47	1874	" - d-in-law
31.	John Horney	55	1864	
32.	Rose Horney	62	1876	
33.	James P. Butler	32	1833	J. G. McKenzie, nephew
34.	Johona Murphy	17	unk	
35.	Ellen Rooch	50	1893	" - nephew
36.	William Butler	79	1905	" - g/son
37.	Annie M. Beaton	50	1918	J. M. Beaton, husband
38.	William Butler	65	1935	J.G. McKenzie, nephew
39.	Katherine Butler	77	1923	" - g/son
40. - 41.	Unknown			
42.	James P. Roach	25	1902	"
43.	Katie Roach	33	1914	"
44.	Agnes Roach	27	1910	
45. - 46	Unknown			
47.	John Murphy	86	1899	
48.	Unknown			
49.	Kate Murphy	unk	1902	

See Plat Map #474

* *

#475 AKERS CEMETERY

Located on Land Map 121, Tract GIR-5694, below elevation 359, 9 graves. The Cemetery was very old, abandoned and neglected, only indication of graves being slight depressions. Remain permits were executed on the graves of two person known to have been buried in the cemetery and no further action was necessary.

See Plat Map #475

#476 RUSHING CEMETERY

Located on Land Map 127, tract GIR-5460F, 19 graves.

No.	Name of deceased	Age	Date of Death	Information given by...
1.	Lizzie Rushing	19	1876	John Rushing, g/son
2.	Robert Rushing	unk	unk	" - son
3.	Effie Rushing	unk	unk	" - son
4.	Agnes Rushing	20	1905	" - husband
5. - 6. Unknown				
7.	H. Rushing	62	1887	J. H. Rushing, g/son
8.	Elizabeth Rushing	55	1890	" - g/son
9.	Joseph Fry	6	1895	W. H. Fry, bro
10.	Ola Fry	0	1900	" - bro
11. - 13. Unknown				
14. - 15. "River Woman and child" - nothing more is known of them.				
16.	Wynn infant	0	1915	Ms Lizzie Brewer, mother
17.	Brewer infant	unk	unk	Frank Brewer, father
18. - 19. Unknown				
?	Bell Reddick			G. F. Rainwater, nephew
?	Frank Rushing	unk	1886	John Rushing, bro

See Plat Map #476

* *

#477 NOBLES (LOWRY) CEMETERY

Located on Land Map 131, Tract GIR-5532, above elevation 408, 59 graves. The cemetery was active, well cared for, and well monumnted. Access by the Big Sandy-Claud Road was flooded. Remain permits were executed on 58 graves. No answer was received to correspondence addresssed to the nearest relative of the person interred in the remaining grave. No further action was necessary.

No.	Name of Deceased	Age	Date of Death	Information given by...
1.	Leonard Merrell	unk	1938	Poshiel L. Merrell, son
2.	Mrs. Lola Merrell			Dora Cole, sister
3.	Coraway Nobles	7	1909	J. L. Nobles, father
4.	Donnally Nobles	2	1907	"
5.	George W. Nobles	27	1904	Rose Farmer, sister
6.	Kate Nobles	7	1887	"
7.	James Nobles	61	1900	" – daug
8.	Mary Jane Nobles	72	1920	" – daug
9.	Rachel I. Melton	59	unk	E. Melton, husband
10.	James R. Waters	65	1901	Nora Waters, wife
11.	Bobbie Lee Cooley	70	1932	Maggie Cooley, wife
12.	Lela Jane Lowry	7	1912	C.L. & Mary Ann Lowry,p
13.	Crosnoe infant			Abbie England, sister
14.	Jeff Lowry	59	unk	Carrie Lowry, wife
15.	Martha Lowry	84	1929	Tom Lowry, son
16.	John J. Lowry	73	1896	" – son
17.	Rachel Lowry	37	1867	Harry L. Lowry, son
18.	Margurette Lowry	0	1868	Tom Lowry, bro.
19.	Lowry infant	0	1867	" – bro
20.	Lowry infant	0	1879	" – bro.
21.	Alice Melton	1	1887	A. J. Melton, father
22.	Milbra Melton	3	1887	"
23.	Roscoe Melton	1	1896	"
24.	Akers infant	0	1880	H. W. Akers, bro.
25.	James E. Lowry	63	1917	C. L. Lowry, son
26.	Emma Lowry	unk	unk	"
27.	Albert Lowry	unk	1896	" – bro
28.	Carlettie Lowry	8	1896	" – bro
29.	Cole infant	0	1937	Mason Cole, father
30.	Hill infant		1941	Irene Hill, mother
31.	Haskell Lowry	1	1928	Willie & Elsie Lowry, p
32.	Sarah J. Lowry	35	1915	" – son
33.	Horace Lowry	62	1934	" – son
34.	Vera Lois Berry	1	1903	M. F. Berry, father
35.	Lloyd Newton Farmer	1	1937	Newt Farmer, father

* *

36.	Farmer infant	0	1941	" - father
37.	Velma Wheatley	0	1913	W. B. Wheatley, father
38.	Willis Brewer	0	1934	John S. Brewer, father
39.	Berry infant	0	1925	Albert Berry, father
40.	Myrtle E. Lowry	1	1904	Carrie Lowry, mother
41.	Bobbie Joe Lowry	0	1934	Robert Lowry, father
42.	Ernie Lowry	40	1936	Ms Hester Lowry, wife
43.	Mollie Lowry	62	1918	Carrie Lowry, sister
44.	Walter Lowry	60	1934	Tom Lowry, bro.
45.	Lowry infant	0	1935	Ms Hester Lowry, mother
46.	Tom Henry Ball	62	1939	Thedies Ball, wife
47.	Newel Rainwater	88	1934	John Rainwater, son
48.	Margarette Rainwater	66	1935	" - son
49.	John Rainwater, Jr.	3	1937	" - father
50.	Ruth Mannon	1	1921	Tilford Mannon, son
51.	Eliza Mannon	61	1925	" - son
52.	Will Mannon	unk	1921	" - son
53.	Ira Mannon	unk	1924	" - bro.
54.	Grover Stagner	unk	1934	Bulah Rainwater, cousin
55.	John Patrick	92	1892	O. C. Patrick, son
56.	Sarah Patrick	87	1933	" - son
57.	R. A. Patrick	71	1924	" - nephew
58.	Cora Lowry	29	1912	Tom Lowry, husband
59.	Martha Patrick	unk	unk	O. C. Patrick, father

See Plat Map #477

#481 OLD WHEATLEY (FORREST) CEMETERY

Located on Land Map 131, tract E, 37 un-identified graves. The location is unknown, but the following is a listing of some of those known to be buried in this cemetery.

No.	Name of deceased	Information given by...
?	John Nobles	John Nobles, g/son
?	Mary Pulley	" - nephew
?	Mrs. John Nobles	" - nephew
?	Mary Wheatley	W. W. Wheatley, nephew
?	Lina Wheatley	" - nephew
?	Charles J. Wheatley	" - g/son
?	Sarah Wheatley	" - g/son

See Plat Map #481

* *

#482 PHIFFER CEMETERY

Located on Land Map NO. 132, Tract GIR-5945, above elevation 385, 52 graves. The cemetery was active, well kept, well monumented. Access by the Camden-Claud Road was flooded.   Four graves were moved to Sugar Creek Cemetery R-95 on June 18, 1943. Remain permits were executed on 44 graves. The remaining four graves could not identified or no one could be found who was interested enough to request that they be moved.

No.	Name	Age	Date of Death	Information glen by...

* *

No.	Name	Age	Date of Death
1.	Emma Phifer	25	1907
2.	Edgar Phifer	1	1902
3.	A. L. Phifer	75	1925
4.	Mary A. Phifer	86	1941
5.	Oll Hartley	58	1933
6.	Margurette Hartley	75	1920
7.	W. C. Hartley	35	1883
8.	Granville Hartley	6	unk
9.	Laur P. Hartley	3	1913
10.	Virtrus Hartley	16	1918
11.	Ed Hartley	41	1922
12.	George Hartley	25	1922
13.	Joseph Sullivan	38	1875
14.	Unknown		
15.	Charles Phifer	6	1882
16.	Nancy McDaniel	30	1900
17.	Elizabeth Phifer	51	1881
18.	John Phifer	76	1889
19.	Mary Ann Phifer	46	1872
20.	Victoria Phifer	31	1884
21.	Sarah Farmer	32	1872
22.	Sylvia Phifer	1	1935
23.	Mintie Phifer	80	1930
24.	Elija Phifer	75	1904
25.	Dan Phifer		unk
26.	Wyley Phifer	infant	unk
27.	Addie Phifer	infant	unk
28.	Edgar Wilson	infant	unk
29.	Lowry infant		1906
30.	Norah Bates	28	1937
31.	Catherine Blanks		unk
32.	Victoria Cagle		unk
33.	Emily Blanks		unk
34. - 35.	unknown		
36.	Phifer infant		1929

* *

No.	Name	Age	Date
37.	Phifer infant		1937
38.	Johnie Rushing	18	unk
39.	Jesse J. Rushing	7	1932
40.	Rogena Rushing	1	1927
41.	Wheatley infant		unk
42.	Wheatley infant		unk
43.	Melva Jane Wheatley	5	1934
44.	Lizzy Phifer	1	1885
45.	Mary C. Phifer	75	1929
46.	H. A. Phifer	83	1938
47.	Phifer infant		unk
48.	Willie Phifer	18	1930
49.	Phifer infant		unk
50.	Phifer infant		unk
51.	Phifer infant		unk
52.	Vica Bates	40	1942

See Plat Map #482

#483 FARMER CEMETERY

Located on Land Map 136, tract GIR-5513, above elevation 382, 68 graves. The cemetery was well kept and well monumented. Access by Camden-Claud Road was flooded. Remain permits were executed on 54 graves. The remaining 14 graves could not be identified or no one could be found who would request that they be moved or left undisturbed. No further action was necessary.

No.	Name of Deceased	Age	Date of Death	Information given by...

* * * * * * * * * * * * * * : * * * * * * * * * * * * * *

No.	Name of Deceased	Age	Date of Death	Information given by...
1.	Hettie Melton	35	unk	D. P. Melton, husband
2.	Unknown			
3.	Pruitt infant			
4.	Alvin Wheatley	unk	unk	Janie Wheatley, wife
5.	Marie Wheatley	infan:	1931	Janie Wheatley, mother
6.	Bertha Cooley	unk	unk	W. E. Cooley, bro.
7.	Henry Clay Cooley			W. E. Cooley, bro.
8.	Richard Cooley			W. E. Cooley, bro.
9.	Nellie Cooley			W. E. Cooley, bro.
10. - 13.	Unknown			
14.	D. M. Farmer	82	1917	Tom Farmer, g/son
15.	Bob Cooley	40	1928	W. E. Cooley, bro.
16.	Richard Whitley	unk	1935	Vanner Phifer, wife
17. - 18.	Cooley infant			W. E. Cooley, bro.
19.	Mary Cooley	60		W. E. Cooley, son
20.	W. C. Cooley	70	1932	W. E. Cooley, son
21.	Elizabeth Farmer	75	1875	Tom Farmer, g/son
22.	George W. Farmer	80	1876	Tom Farmer, g/g/son
23.	Catherine Farmer	43	1843	Tom Farmer, g/g/son
24.	Elizabeth Benton	unk	unk	John Nobles, nephew

* *

25.	Benton un-identifed			John Nobles, g/s
26.	Marie Cooley	20	1935	W. E. & Gather Cooley, p
27. - 30.	Unknown			
31.	William Blanks	75	1939	Mollie E. Blanks, wife
32.	Olive Blanks	39	1935	Esther McCoy, wife
33.	Blanks infant	infant	1923	Esther McCoy, mother
34.	Willie Blanks	7	1916	Mollie E. Blanks, mother
35.	John Farmer	40	1884	Mollie E. Blanks, daug.
36.	D. C. Farmer	9	1877	Mollie E. Blanks, sister
37.	Kitt Farmer	80	1877	Mollie E. Blanks, daug.
38. - 39.	Unknown			
40.	Mollie Hartley			J. W. Hartley, father
41.	Unknown			
42.	Willie Hartley	unk	unk	E. W. Hartley, bro.
43.	Mary E. Hartley	infant	unk	E. W. Hartley, father
44.	Mary Ann Hartley			E. W. Hartley, son
45.	Mary Harrison		1930	Hermon Harrison, husband
46.	Walter Hartley	40	1910	E. W. Hartley, son
47.	Ella J. Hartley		1899	E. W. Hartley, bro.
48.	Lenam Hartley	inf	1898	E. W. Hartley, bro.
49.	Farmer infant			Tom Farmer, bro.
50.	Birty Farmer	unk	1895	Tom Farmer, bro.
51.	T. W. Farmer	39	unk	Tom Farmer, son
52.	Thomas W. Farmer	1	1905	Bruce Farmer
53.	Betty Farmer	60	1926	Tom Farmer, son
54.	Anna D. Ball	infant	1925	Thedies Ball, mother
55.	Tom H. Ball	unk	1928	Thedies Ball, mother
56.	Lillie Chester	36	1917	Tom Chester, husband
57.	Mary Cole	74	1940	Oscar Cole/Ila Dillon, c
58.	John Cole	80	1940	" - children
59.	Novel Cole	5	unk	Oscar & Dora Cole, par.
60.	Unknown			
61.	Olive K. Lawrence	infant	1930	E. H. Lawrence, father
62.	Leon Farmer	unk	unk	Oscar Farmer, father
63.	Farmer infant			Oscar Farmer, father
64.	Odie Gene Farmer	1	1932	Tom & Flora Farmer, par
65.	John Williams	30	1939	Mary Williams, wife
66.	Maggie Blanks	78	1939	W. E. Blanks
67.	Ball infant	infant	unk	Thedies Ball, mother
68.	Ball infant	infant	unk	Thedies Ball, mother
?	Anna Parker	unk	unk	Wyly Parker, g/son

See Plat Map #483

* *

#484 FARMER CEMETERY

Located on Land Map 136, Tract GIR-5499, above elevation 390, 100 graves. The cemetery was very old and badly neglected. Access by farm road leading off 16 foot county road was flooded. Remain permits were executed on eight graves. The remaining 92 graves could not be identified or no one could be found who would request that they be moved or left undisturbed. No further action was necessary.

No.	Name of Deceased	Age	Date of Death	Information given by...

* *

No.	Name of Deceased	Age	Date of Death	Information given by...
1. - 38.	Unknown			
39.	Mary E. Farmer	12	1864	Felt Farmer, nephew
40.	James H. Davidson	unk	1862	E. D. Davidson, g/nep
41.	Lucinda Farmer	2	1851	Felt Farmer, nephew
42. - 59.	Unknown			
60.	Martha E. Farmer	44	1864	Felt Farmer, g/son
61. - 70.	Unknown			
71.	Martha E. Davidson	unk	1871	E. D. Davidson, g/nep
72. - 74.	Unknown			
?	Abe Bleyen			H. Bleyen g/son
?	Sarah Bleyen			H. Bleyen g/son
?	Tom Bleyen			H. Bleyen bro.

See Plat Map #484

#485 NO NAME CEMETERY

Located on Land Map 141, Tract GIR-5024, below elevation 359, 10 graves. No information could be obtained as to who was buried in this cemetery, and the exact locations of the graves were not determined as the burial area had been in cultivation for a number of years. No further action was necessary.

No.	Name	Age	Date of Death	Information given by...

* *

No.	Name	Age	Date of Death	Information given by...
1.	Jim McDaniel	unk	unk	
2.	Mrs. Jim McDaniel	unk	unk	
3. - 10.	Unknown			

* *

#486 MAIDEN CEMETERY

Located on Land Map 142, tract GIR-5111, elevation 405, 22 graves. This is an old cemetery with one small monument other graves marked with rough stones. Burned over, un-cared for, unfenced and abandoned. Last burial 1911. Located 1000 feet north of Camden east valley road on property of Miss Willie Maiden.

No.	Name of deceased	Age	Date of death	Information given by...

* *

No.	Name of deceased	Age	Date of death	Information given by...
1. - 3.	Unknown			
4.	Nannie Dardin	2	1905	Ms J.C. Dardin, mother
5. - 23.	Unknown			
24.	Cockerell			Mrs. Mattie Hardin g/d
25.	Cockerell			" - neice
?	Leona Cockerell			John Summers, bro
?	Dawaie Cockerell		1909	" - uncle
?	Huie Cockerell		1875	" - bro.
?	Byrl Lashlee		1886	" - g/chld
?	Mrs. Byrl Lashlee		1886	" - g/chld
?	Jack Dardin			A. E. Dardin, g/chld

See Plat Map #486

#492 WYELY CEMETERY

Located on Land Map 164, tract GIR-5301, 89 graves. Only two location are known and a few more identified without location of graves.

No.	Name of deceased	Age	Date of Death	Information given by...

* *

No.	Name of deceased	Age	Date of Death	Information given by...
1. - 29.	Unknown			
30.	Kittie Laster	50	1894	Arthur Laster, son
31. - 88.	Unknown			
89.	T. K. Wyley	unk	unk	Mrs. Gay Wyley g/daug
?	Cooley Napier			" - niece
?	Jim Wyley			" - g/daug
?	Mrs. Jim Wyley			" - g/daug
?	John Menzie			Jennie Donninls, sister
?	Mary Menzie			" - sister
?	Walter Menzie			" - sister
?	Charles Menzie			" - sister
?	Georgia Ann Menzie			" - daughter

See Plat Map #492

* *

#501 McDANIEL CEMETERY

Located on Land Map 180, Tract GIR-5865, above elevation 395, 7 graves. The cemetery
was inactive and badly neglected. Access by farm road was flooded. One grave and one
monument was moved to Byrd Hill Cemetery R-36. Remain permits were executed on five
graves, however, the exact location of only two of these graves was known. The
remaining two graves could not be identified or no one could be found who was interested enough to have them moved. No further action was necessary.

No.	Name	Age	Date of Death	Information given by...

No.	Name	Age	Date of Death	Information given by...
1.	Martha S. Byrd		1880	
2. - 6.	Unknown			
7.	L. V. McDaniel		1899	
8.	Byrd infant		unk	
?	Sam DePriest		1890	
?	Caroline DePriest		1898	
?	Linda DePriest		1898	

See Plat Map #501

#502 WHITFIELD - PAVATT CEMETERY

Located on Land Map 180, Tract GIR-5870, above elevation 414, 38 graves. The
cemetery was active and fairly well kept. Access by a 30 foot county road was
flooded. Three graves and two monuments were moved to two reinterment cemeteries on
March 15, 1943. Remain permits were executed on 32 graves. The remaining three
graves could not be identified or no one could be found who was interested enough to
have them moved. No further action was necessary.

No.	Name		Date of Death	Information given by...
1.	Grady Runions		unk	J. A. Runion, father
2.	Linda Whitfield		unk	T.C. & Bessie Whitfield, parents
3.	Birdie Whitfield		unk	"
4.	Whitfield infant		unk	"
5.	J. B. Whitfield		1901	Edd Whitfield, bro.
6.	Thomas J. Whitfield		1908	" - son
7.	Mattie Whitfield		1930	" - son
8. - 9.	Not graves			
10.	Rubin Earl Whitfield	infant	1911	Clether Whitfield, f
11.	H. W. Whitfield		1899	Thomas W. Whitfield, bro
12.	L. A. Whitfield		1898	" - bro
13.	J. B. Whitfield		1897	" - bro.
	W. B. Whitfield		1897	
14.	B. M. Whitfield	1	1899	" - bro
15.	Bardie Whitfield	1	1899	" - bro

Benton County, Tennessee

* *

16.	Jewell Whitfield		1908	" - bro
	Golden Whitfield		1908	
17.	Phillips infant		1939	Marshall Phillips, f
18.	Eunice S. Phillips		1888	H. C. Phillips, g/son
19.	Isaac N. Phillips		1880	" - g/son
20.	Rufus Phillips	36	1896	" - nephew
21.	Hazel Phillips		1921	H.C. & Mary Phillips, p
22.	Delia Mae Stringer	2	1899	H. C. Phillips, cousin
23.	Jessie Stringer	24	1900	" - nephew
24.	Melissa L. Matlock	44	1906	Eunice Sylvis, daug.
25.	J. C. Matlock	25	1918	" - sister
26.	Walter Runions	1	1919	R.W. & Annie M. Runion,p
27.	Bonnie Ann Cox	11	1938	Erie & E.O. Cox, parents
28.	Riley infant		1903	A.L. & Selma Riley, par
29.	Elsie Lynch	2	unk	H. L. Lynch, father
30.	Dorothy Lynch	1	unk	" - father
31.	Betty Mae Lynch	54	1938	" - husband
32.	Lillian Buchanan	2	1918	W. B. Buchanan, father
33.	Minnie Buchanan		1915	" - husband
34.	Mary L. Phillips	6	1926	H.C. & Mary L. Phillips parents
35.	Unknown			
36.	Zula Gravett		1913	W.B. Buchanan, b-in-law
37.	Leeland Buchanan		1918	" - father
38.	Thomas James Whitfield		1942	T.J. Whitfield, father

See Plat Map #502

#503 LANGLEY OR FRY CEMETERY

Located on Land Map 180, Tract GIR-5876, above elevation 392, 41 graves. The cemetery was very old and abandoned. Graves were indicated by depressions. Access by 30 foot county road was flooded by the 375 contour. Remain permits were executed on the graves of 20 persons known to have been buried in this cemetery, although the exact location of only two of them was known. The remaining 21 graves could not be identified or no one could be found who was interested enough to request that they be moved. No further action was necessary.

No.	Name of Deceased	Age	Date of Death	Information given by...

* *

1. - 16.	Unknown			
17.	Hester Stewart	unk	1916	Sallie Cox, mother
18.	Stewart infant	infant	1909	" - mother
19. - 34.	Unknown			
?	Ward infant (two of them)			J. B. Ward, bro.
?	William Ward			" - bro
?	Katie Goodman			A. J. Goodman, g/s

* *

?	Alie Goodman		" _
?	Elizabeth Goodman		" - grandson
?	Goodman infant		" - bro
?	Bill Goodman		" - son
?	Johnie Goodman		" - bro
?	Simpson Goodman		" - nephew
?	John Wesley Langley	1874	Lilley Hatley, daug
?	Florence Langley	1892	" - sister
?	Eliza DePriest		E. L. Bledsoe, nephew
?	Stella Bledsoe		" - bro.
?	Barnie Bledsoe	1916	" - son
?	Walter Bledsoe		" - bro.
?	Charlie Bledsoe		" - bro.
?	Caroline Hill	1900	A. L. Welch, son

See Plat Map #503

#506 BRADLEY CEMETERY

Located on Land Map 188, tract C, above elevation 382, 60 graves. The cemetery was
very old and abandoned, and contained one small monument. Access by Brevard Landing
Road was flooded. Remain permits were executed on 13 graves. The remaining 47 graves
were not identified or no one could be found who was interested enough to have them
moved. No further action was necessary.

No.	Name of Deceased	Age	Date of Death	Information given by...

* *

1. - 17.	Unknown			
18.	Bradley	unk	unk	J. B. Bradley, nephew
19.	Bradley	unk	unk	J. B. Bradley, nephew
20. -21.	Unknown			
22.	Bill Bradley	unk	unk	J. B. Bradley, nephew
23.	Bradley	unk	unk	
24.	Unknown			
25.	Melgena Bradley	60	1871	J. B. Bradley, g/son
26.	Ed Bradley	unk	unk	J. B. Bradley, nephew
27.	Jose Bradley	unk	unk	J. B. Bradley, nephew
28. - 29.	Unknown			
30.	Groves	unk	unk	
31.	Heinie Ruff	unk	unk	Ms Lucy Ruff g/d
32.	Sarah Coble	unk	unk	Ms A. D. Coble, bro.
33.	Becky Ann Morris	unk	unk	J. A. Morris, g/chld
34.	Wesley Morris	unk	unk	J. A. Morris, g/chld
35.	Bradley	unk	unk	J. B. Bradley, nephew

See Plat Map #506

* *

#507 HATLEY CEMETERY

Located on Land Map 166, Tract GIR-5238, above elevation 418, 10 graves. The cemetery contained no monuments or markers. Grave locations were indicated by depressions. Access by 20 foot county road was flooded. Remain permits were executed on all graves.

No.	Name of Deceased	Age	Date of Death	Information given by...
1.	Nancy Tripplett	60	unk	Wm. Lewis, nephew
2.	Jim Tripplett			Wm. Lewis, nephew
3.	Arthur Hatley	3	1901	C. M. Hatley, father
4.	Clarence Hatley	1	1901	C. M. Hatley, father
5.	no grave			
6.	Mrs. John Lewis			Wm. Lewis, son
7.	John Lewis			Wm. Lewis, son
8.	Lewis infant			Tom Lewis, father
9.	Lewis infant			Wm. Lewis, bro.
10.	Lewis infant			Wm. Lewis, bro.
11.	Lewis infant			Tom Lewis, father
12. - 13.	no grave			

See Plat Map #507

#719 INDIAN CEMETERY

Located on Land Map 115, Tract GIR-5791, below elevation 360, number of graves uncertain. This was reported to be an Indian burial ground and to have been moved previously. No action was necessary.

#733 MELTON CEMETERY

Located on Land Map 136, Tract GIR-5521 F, between elevation 378-379, 30 graves. The cemetery was inactive and badly neglected. It contained only one small stone marker. Remain permits were executed on the graves of 25 persons known to have been buried in this cemetery, although the exact location of only 13 of these graves was known. The remaining 5 graves were unidentified or no one could be found who was interested enough to have them moved. No further action was necessary.

No.	Name of deceased	Age	Date of death	Information given by...
1.	Eliza Bates			Doub. Bates, son
2.	Wiley J. Melton		1890	" - father
3. - 19.	Unknown			
20.	Mary A. Melton		1864	A. J. Melton, son
21.	Trecia Melton	75	1884	" - step-son

* *

22.	Ethel Jridbe Melton	72	1885	" - g/s
23.	Lehence Melton	10	unk	Aaron Melton, bro.
24.	Henry Melton	1	1887	" - bro.
25.	Roena Melton	0	1889	" - bro.
26.	Unknown			
27.	Melton infant			Ms Brasy Berry, sister
28.	Joe W. Melton	40	1876	A. J. Melton, bro.
29.	Beatrice Melton	7	1883	Noah Melton, bro.
30.	John Melton	40	1882	" - bro.
?	Joseph Melton			A. A. Melton, g/chld
?	Melton infant			" - father
?	Mrs. Joseph Melton			" - g/child
?	Martha Melton		1866	" - son
?	Bill Cole			"
?	Analize Myers			"
?	Hiriam Warning			Henry Phifer, g/son
?	Charity Warning			" - g/son
?	Lucietia Phifer			" - bro.
?	Ben Holland			T. J. Melton, nephew
?	Jane Cole			A. J. Melton
?	Melton infant			" - bro.
?	Martha Melton			" - bro.

See Plat Map #733

#747 OLD BETHLEHEM CEMETERY

Located on Land Map 150, tract G, with 36 graves.

See Plat Map #747

#748 ROBERTSON CEMETERY

Located on Land Map 150, Tract 6744F.

See Plat Map #748

* *

#821 LONE GRAVE

Located on Land Map 130, Tract GIR-5562, below elevation 359, one grave. This grave could not be identified, however, Mrs. Ida Farmer, the surrounding property owner, requested that it be moved. It is thought this man drown in the river and was buried where he was found. The grave was moved to Sugar Creek Cemetery R-95 on August 16, 1943.

See PLat Map #821

#861 INDIAN CEMETERY

Located on Land Map 180, Tract GIR-5869, below elevation 359, number of graves uncertain. This was reported to be an Indian burial ground, but the area had been in cultivation for several years. No action was necessary.

* *

HENRY COUNTY, TENNESSEE

Grave Removal Operations

Cemeteries listed below are either submerged or access to them is impaired by the lake waters.

No.	Name of Cemetery	Land	Map	Tract

* *

No.	Name of Cemetery	Land	Map	Tract
437	Baker Cemetery		81	3585
439	Bond Cemetery		87	3854
356	Bradford Cemetery		75	2838
364	Bradford Cemetery		74	3175F
436	Bradford Cemetery		78	3073
379	Brannan Cemetery		77	3214
809	Brooks Cemetery		73	3264F
423	Bucy Cemetery		95	4050
435	Culpepper Cemetery		81	2627
357	Dodson Cemetery		71	2847
802	Eastwood Grave		100	Marginal
425	Ellis Cemetery		99	4329F
438	Fairview Cemetery		81	3596
810	Gray Cemetery		81	3329
355	Kenney Cemetery		75	2828
374	Lemonds Cemetery		77	3231F
451	Manleyville Chapel Cemetery		103	4093F
444	Mt. Zion Cemetery		87A	3778
377	Old Soldiers Cemetery		73	3258F
375	Old Slave Cemetery		75	2837
445	Odom Cemetery		82	3634
433	Russell Cemetery		89A	4150
352	Snow Cemetery		69	2526
365	Taylor Cemetery		74	2899
354	Weldon Cemetery		75	2831
440	Whipple Cemetery		96	3659

Cemeteries listed below are either not affected by the lake waters or future access will be provided by relocated roads.

No.	Name of Cemetery	Land	Map	Tract
376	Antioch M.E. Church Cemetery		80	E
863	Alsop Cemetery		82	3285
358	Busey Cemetery		69	Out Side
369	Bradshaw Cemetery		73	D
378	Bucy Cemetery		73	A
384	Bradford		86	4465F
399	Baucum Colored Cemetery		89A	4161F
411	Boothe Cemetery		92	Out Side
412	Boothe Cemetery		99	2
422	Bowden Cemetery		98	3925
428	Burnett Cemetery		99	Out Side

* *

443	Bucy Cemetery	96	3815F
764	Barton Cemetery	69	2535F
803	Beasley Cemetery	100	No Number
*371	Chiloutt Cemetery	74	A
389	Caldwell Cemetery	85	3
441	Clement Cemetery	96	3815F
786	Cox Cemetery	90	4368F
790	Colored Cemetery	84	2
394	Elkhorn Cemetery	89A	D
395	Easley Cemetery	89A	K
353	Ferguson Cemetery	70	2524
396	Foster-Rogers Cemetery	89A	M
403	Friendship Church Cemetery	85	Out Side
448	Francisco #1 Cemetery	109	3884F
450	Francisco #2 Cemetery	109	F
452	Farmer Cemetery	104	Out Side
359	Groome Cemetery	69	2534F
408	Glover Cemetery	91	4375
385	Hopkins Cemetery	86	4470F
391	Hicks Cemetery	85	1
393	Hughs Cemetery	91	4
416	Hill Cemetery	92	Out Side
418	Henry County Pauper Cem.	92	No Number
429	Hallen Cemetery	99	Out Side
430	Hicks Cemetery	101	B
844	Hoylnan, E. W.	77	No Number
798	Indian Cemetery	77	A
417	Jackson Cemetery	91	1
*785	Jackson Cemetery	86	4058F
405	Kendall Cemetery	85	No Number
406	Kendall Cemetery	90	4356F
446	Key Cemetery	102	4193F
409	Lone Grave	94	4228F
779	Lee, C. C.	71	2859F
858	Lowery Cemetery	107	B
361	Moody Cemetery	71	1
366	Moody Cemetery	74	3182F
381	McCraig Cemetery	73	3273F
390	McAllister Cemetery	86	1
398	Manley Cemetery	89A	A
427	Mays Hill Church Cemetery	100	No Number
449	Mizelle Cemetery	111	Out Side
407	Nored-Wright Cemetery	84	Out Side
410	No Name Cemetery	94	No Number
419	No Name Cemetery	93	Out Side
424	No Name Cemetery	95	4069F
434	No Name Cemetery	89A	No Number
787	No Name Cemetery	94	No Number
788	No Name Cemetery	94	No Number
842	No Name Cemetery	103	4100F
846	No Name Cemetery	101	No Number
360	Old Cemetery	71	2860F
363	Oak Hill Cemetery	74	G
388	Old Sulphur Wells Cemetery	85	Out Side

* *

453	Old Carter Cemetery	109	3878F
367	Parker Cemetery	74	2902
368	Point Pleasant Cemetery	73	3841
392	Providence Colored Cemetery	85	Out Side
420	Parker Cemetery	94-1	36
*421	Parker Cemetery	94	6
426	Prove Cemetery	99	21
442	Pleasant Grove Cemetery	95	14
801	Perry Cemetery	100	No Number
864	Porter Cemetery	93	6
*351	Ratteree Cemetery	69	2540F
370	Rice Cemetery	74	3181F
413	Riley Cemetery	99	Out Side
447	Rev. War Veteran	102	4188F
843	Rowden Cemetery	103	No Number
362	Scarbrough Cemetery	74	3185F
387	Sulphur Wells Cemetery	85	Out Side
432	Simmons Cemetery	100	3
852	Slave Cemetery	104	3967F
789	Upchurch Cemetery	84	1
372	Williams Cemetery	73	3252F
373	Williams Cemetery	77	C
380	Woods Cemetery	77	3229F
382	Williams Cemetery	86	22
383	Walker Cemetery	86	4452F
386	Wynns Cemetery	86	27
397	Wright Cemetery	94	2
400	Weeks Cemetery	90	4358F
401	Williams Cemetery	85	Out Side
402	Weeks Cemetery	85	Out Side
404	Weeks Cemetery	89A	L
414	Witch's Cemetery	93	3
415	Wright Cemetery	92	8
431	Whitehead Cemetery	103	1
808	Wilson Cemetery	73	C

*= Present access affected, but future access provided by relocated roads.

* *

#352 SNOW CEMETERY

Located on Land Map - 69, Tract GIR-2528, below elevation 359, 10 graves. This was an active and well kept cemetery. All graves were identified and removal permits executed. The ten graves and two monuments were moved to three reinterment cemeteries on May 5, 1943.

No.	Name of Deceased	Age	Date of Death	Information given by...

No.	Name of Deceased	Age	Date of Death	Information given by...
1.	Mary Alice Watkins	74	1930	Bette Snow, daug.
2.	James F. Watkins	56	1912	" - daug.
3.	Lucind Watkins	82	1909	" - g/daug.
4.	Mary Frank Watkins	2	1898	" - sister
5.	Lucy Floyd Watkins	5	1896	" - sister
6.	Maurice R. Moody	4	1910	Eula Moody, mother
7.	Tom L. Moody	55	1933	" - wife
8.	Columbus Ratteree	40	1910	Lemuel Ratteree, son
9.	Carroll infant	infant	1921	Stella Carroll, mother
10.	Mildred Carroll	3	1914	" - mother

See Plat Map #352

#353 FERGUSON CEMETERY

Found on Land Map 70, tract GIR-2524, elevation 410, three graves. The cemetery is well cared for and surrounded with a new woven wire fence. The last burial was on August 1941.

No.	Name of Deceased	Age	Date of Death	Information given by...
1.	John A. Ferguson	79	1941	Earnest Ferguson, wife
2.	Hardy Ferguson	1	1910	" - mother
3.	Betty Ferguson	1	1900	" - mother

#354 WELDON CEMETERY

Located on Land Map 75, Tract GIR-2831, below elevation 359, twenty-four graves. This was an old inactive cemetery but fairly well kept. Eleven identified and eight unidentified graves and eleven monuments were moved to two reinterment cemeteries. Remain permits were executed on the remaining five graves.

* *

No.	Name of Deceased	Age	Date of Death	Information given by...

* *

No.	Name of Deceased	Age	Date of Death	Information given by...
1.	Robert Alex Moffett	61	1893	
2.	Willie E. Gatlin		1879	
3.	Mary F. Lawrence	17	1787	
4.	H. C. Lawrence	61	1889	
5.	Robert Lee Gatlin			
6.	Charlie Gatlin		1875	
7.	Mary Bell Gatlin		1873	
8.	Ida Weldon	19	1889	
9.	Charles Meigs	18	1877	
10.	Gillian Cook Weldon	84	1876	
11.	Clara McClarin	1	1874	
12.	Edward Weldon	2	1874	
13.	Lillie J. Chenoweth	9	1869	
14.	Jane H. Chenoweth	85	1904	
15. - 22.	Unknown			
23.	Waynick infant		1931	
24.	Dr. A. J. Weldon	73	1905	

See Plat Map #354

#355 KONNEY CEMETERY

Located on Land Map 75, Tract GIR-2828, below elevation 359, 9 graves. This was a very old cemetery; neglected and abandoned. None of the graves could be identified. Mr. R. L. Dunlap, who had some distant relatives buried there requested that all graves be moved. They were moved to Williams Cemetery R-76 on June 2, 1943.

#356 BRADFORD CEMETERY

Located on Land Map 75, Tract GIR-2838, below elevation 353, 6 graves. This cemetery, located in an open pasture, was badly neglected. All graves and one monument was moved to Williams Cemetery R-76. Removal operations were completed on May 15, 1943.

No.	Name of deceased	Age	Date of Death	Information given by...
1.	Rhoda Bradford	57	1848	Mrs. E. C. Pace, neice
2.	Crawford Bradford	unk	unk	" - neice-in-law
3. - 6.	Unknown			

See Plat Map #356

* *

#357 DODSON CEMETERY

Located on Land Map 71, Tract GIR-2847, above elevation 397 feet, one grave. This was will not be flooded, but the access will be, therefore a removal permit was executed and it was moved to Liberty Church Cemetery R-40 on May 29, 1943.

No.	Name of Deceased	Age	Date of Death	Information given by ...
1.	J. W. Dodson	53	1918	Claud Dodson, son

See Plat Map #357

#362 SCARBORO CEMETERY

Found on Land Map 74, Tract GIR-3185F, 84 graves. Badly neglected, 17 graves covered with shells, enclosed with a woven wire fence. Located just north of Highway 76.

No.	Name of Deceased	Age	Date of Death	Information given by...
1.	J. D. Johnson	5	1939	
2.	Mrs. Lucy May Johnson	31	1939	
3.	Chilcut infant			E. Chilcut
4.	Mrs. Nancy Chilcutt			
5.	Jack Chilcutt			
6.	Beatrice Chilcutt			
7.	Williams infant			Frank Williams, father
8.	W. S. Wainscott	52	1941	Ms Frank Williams, daug.
9.	Wainscott (Tiny)			Jim Wainscott, husband
10.	Luella Wainscott			" - father
11.	Helen Wainscott			" - father
12. - 18.	Oliver un-identified			
19.	Antony Ely			Bud Ely
20. - 24.	Unknown			
25.	Mary Chilcutt	12	1912	E. Chilcutt, father
26.	Chilcutt infant	infant	1902	" - father
27.	John Scarborough			Charley Scarborough, nep
28.	Wilson infant			
29.	Lula Bailey			Charley Bailey, husband
30.	A. A. Scarborough	74	1926	Charley Scarborough, son
31.	Mollie Scarborough	52	1903	" - son
32. - 36.	Unknown			
37.	Mr. Cotton			Mrs. E. Chilcutt, daug.
38.	Mrs. Cotton			" - daug.
39. - 40.	Unknown			

* *

41.	Jack Scarborough			Chas. Scarborough, g/son
42.	Mrs. Jack Scarborough			" - g/son
43.	Cynthia Lee			T. A. Scarborough, neph
44.	E. R. Moody	27	1906	
45.	Hiram L. Moody	81	1932	
46.	Alabama Moody	81	1932	
47.	Lillie L. Moody	49	1933	
48.	Mrs. T. A. Scarborough	35	1912	T.A. Scarborough, hus.
49.	Eulan Scarborough			" - father
50.	Hettie N. Scarborough			" - father
51.	Alexander Scarboro	75	unk	" - son
52.	Harriet Scarboro	unk	unk	" - son
53. - 66.	Unknown			
67.	Leroy Prewett	50	1851	
68. - 76.	Unknown			
77.	Harriet Jane Williams	24	1857	
78. - 86.	Unknown			
87.	Charley Alexander			
88. - 94.	Unknown			

#364 BRADFORD CEMETERY

Located on Land Map 74, Tract 3175F, above elevaltion 450, 91 graves. This cemetery was well kept and well monumented. Twenty-one permits were executed on graves in the white section. Four of these were for the graves of persons known to have been buried in this cemetery, but the exact locations of the graves were not known. No information could be obtained as to the identitiy of the remaining 15 graves in the white section. Thirty-one remain permits were executed on graves in the colored section; 15 of these were on the graves of persons known to have been buried in the cemetery, but the exact locations of the graves were not known. No information could be obtained as to the identity of the 24 remaining graves.

No.	Name of Deceased	Age	Date of Death	Information given by...
1.	Sgt. W. F. Chilcutt	75	1904	Jas. Chilcutt, son
2.	Jack Chilcutt	30	1895	" - half-bro.
3.	Earnest Chilcutt	inf	1900	" - uncle
4.	Adeline Chilcutt - wife	20	1900	" - bro.-in-law
5.	Martha Chilcutt			" - son
6.	Unknown			
7.	Dolly Robinson (male)	30	1926	Ms Dick Shackles, sis.
8.	Geo. Oliver	70	1912	
9.	Mrs. Geo. Oliver	65	1912	
10.	Unknown			
11.	R. Gates Nairon	33	1883	R. Gates Nairon, son
12.	Mrs. J. C. Nairon	80	1900	Ms Josie Robertson, m.

* *

13.	Unknown			
14.	Ms Melissa Williams	45		Jack Williams, son
15.	Henry Ross	3	1890	J. C. Ross, bro.
16.	Mrs. J. H. Ross (Izzy)	45	1907	" - son
17.	May Ross	23	1923	" - bro.
18.	Sam Ross	24	1923	" - bro.
19.	J. H. Ross	69	1925	" - son
20.	Mrs. G. C. (Nettie) Ross	25	1925	G. C. Ross, hus.
21.	Mrs. G. C. (Mary) Lemonds	33	1881	D. L. Lemonds, nephew
22. - 25.	Unknown			
26.	Crawford Bradford	80	1868	Ms. E. C. Pace, neice
27.	Turner infant	infant	unk	Albert Turner, father
28. - 36.	Unknown			
?	Ellen Kendall (colored)	70	1920	Will Kendall, bro.
?	Marion Griffin	32	1862	Walter Griffin, son
?	Mrs. Liz Key	74	1901	" - uncle
?	William Key	75	1898	" - uncle-in-law

COLORED SECTION OF THE BRADFORD CEMETERY

1. - 28.	Unknown			
29.	Mrs. Areta Easley	40	1935	Pete Gray, uncle
30. - 32.	Unknown			
33.	Anna Kendall	70	1936	Pete Gray, bro.
34.	Bill Kendell	70	1922	Will Kennell, nephew
35.	Allen Caldwell	100	1917	Pete Gray, son
36.	Liza Gray	75	1898	" - son
37. - 40.	Unknown			
41.	Will Gaines	25	1914	Tom Gaines
42. - 44.	Unknown			
45.	Lenchi Perkins	unk	unk	Geo. Perkins, bro.
46.	Otho Perkins	4	1910	" - bro.
47.	Willie Perkins	20	1925	" - bro.
48.	Nelson Perkins	75	1928	" - son
49.	Ann Perkins	70	1921	" - son
50.	Walter Perkins	35	1929	Francis Whitnell, wife
51.	Joe Perkins	12	1900	" - bro.
52.	Roy Perkins	12	1903	" - bro.
53.	Mrs. Viola May Pino	23	1932	Pete Gray, father
54.	Lou Gray	50	1938	" - husband
?	Gray - infant twins	infant	unk	" - father
?	Gray infant	infant	unk	" - father
?	Gray infant	infant	unk	" - father
?	Tiberius Gray	2	1906	" - father
?	Gray infant	infant	unk	A. B. Gray, father

* *

?	Mary Ann Colman	35	1902	Katie Atkins, sis.
?	Gray infant	infant	unk	A. B. Gray, father
?	Prince Gray	infant	unk	" – father
?	Hattie Gray	unk	1880	" – father
?	Annie Maria Gray	unk	1880	" – father
?	Ellen Gray	unk	1920	" – husband

See Plat Map #364

#365 TAYLOR CEMETERY

Located on Land Map 74, Tract GIR-2899, three graves. These graves were well above the flooded area, but access would be periodically flooded. All graves were identified and together with two monuments, were moved to Parker Cemetery R-44 on May 29, 1943.

No.	Name of Deceased	Age	Date of Death	Information given by...

* *

No.	Name of Deceased	Age	Date of Death
1.	Thomas Taylor	41	1833
2.	Sarah Taylor	51	1852
3.	Taylor un-identified		

See Plat Map #365

#370 RICE CEMETERY

Found on Land Map 10N74, Tract GIR-3181F, elevation 430, six graves. This cemetery is out in woodland, marked only by depressions and one grave by a rough stone.

No.	Name of Deceased	Age	Date of Death	Information given by...

* *

No.	Name of Deceased	Age	Date of Death	Information given by...
1.	Elizabeth J. Rice	89	1922	Sarah Midyett, daug.
2.	Newton J. Rice	47	1870	" – daug.
3.	Thos. Henry Rice	30	1910	" – sister
4.	Andrew J. Rice	20	1905	" – sister
5.	Robert F. Rice	20	1906	" – sister
6.	Lola Bradford	infant		
7.	Jack Bradford	infant		
8.	Gay Bradford	infant		
9.	Bradford infant	infant		

See Plat Map #370

* *

#372 WILLIAMS CEMETERY

Located on Land Map 73, Tract 3252F, 95 graves.

No.	Name of Deceased	Age	Date of Death	Information given by...
1.	Warren D. Williams	11	1937	Clyde Williams, father
2.	John T. Owens	1	1933	Claud Owens, father
3.	Paul V. Williams	36	1941	Elzie Williams, bro.
4.	Mary A. Williams	64	1938	" - son
5.	Daniel A. Williams	70	1937	" - son
6.	Carah Cooper	80	1896	Ed Williams, g/son
7.	Betty Ann Owens	infant	1932	Loyd Owens, father
8.	Levella Owens	2	1931	" - father
9.	Orella Owens	2	1931	" - father
10.	Carnell Owens	4	1931	" - father
11.	Owens infant		1911	Morris Owens, bro.
12.	Bertha Owens	27	1912	" - son
13.	Jas. A. Owens	54	1936	" - son
14.	A. J. Owens	77	1936	Raymond Owens, son
15.	Ms Carie Owens	76	1934	" - sson
16.	Claytus Owens	unk	1939	" - bro.
17.	Lourette Owens	15	1906	" - bro.
18.	John Acy Owens	19	1905	" - bro.
19.	Owens infant		1900	" - bro.
20.	Owens infant		unk	" - bro.
21.	Willie Owens		1900	" - bro.
22.	Unknown			
23.	Minnie Fowler		1910	Robert Fowler - 1/2 bro.
24.	Fowler infant		1890	" - bro.
25.	James Fowler		1908	" - son
26.	Fowler infant		1906	" - father
27.	Maggie Fowler	27	1931	" - father
28. - 29.	Unknown			
30.	J. P. Owens	41	1902	Ms Emma Owens, wife
31.	Doris Owens		1909	" - mother
32.	Anna Lou Owens		1906	" - mother
33.	Corp. J. B. Owens	75	1890	" - niece
34.	Carline Owens	81	1917	Ms Rhett Thomas, daug.
35.	Tommie Owens	1	1875	" - sister
36.	Jim Owens	81	1875	" - niece
37.	Josie Owens			Dee Bishop, son
38.	Sallie Owens			Ms Emma Owens, sister
39.	Col. Robert A. Owens			" - daug.
40.	Mrs. R. A. Owens			" - daug.
41. - 43.	Unknown			

* *

44.	Hettie Anne Williams	67	1940	Ms Mable Buchanon, daug.
45.	J. Pleas Williams	71	1938	" - daug.
46.	Nellie Williams	9	1911	" - sister
47.	Olivia D. Williams	infant	1908	" - sister
48.	Williams infant	infant	1905	" - sister
49.	Williams infant	infant	1903	" - sister
50.	Alvin Shankle	49	1940	Ms Alvin Shankle, wife
51.	Caylord Shankle	infant	1915	" - mother
52.	John Williams			Ed Williams, son
53.	Sis Williams			" - son
54.	Johnnie Williams			" - nephew
55.	Unknown			
56.	W. L. Williams	72	unk	Minnie Williams, g/daug.
57.	Susan Williams	60	1870	" - g/daug.
58.	Unknown			
59.	R. L. Williams	2	1874	Millie Williams, sister
60.	Betty Sue Williams	2	1862	" - sister
61.	Frances Williams	3	1860	Minnie Williams, sister
62.	Cooper un-identified			
63. - 65.	Unknown			
66.	Monroe Wright	87	1927	Ms Ed Wright, daug.
67.	Mary J. Wright	64	1913	" - daug.
68.	Unknown			
69.	Louis Williams	22	unk	Ed Williams, father
70.	Lillian Williams	19		" - father
71.	Virgie Williams	1	unk	" - father
72.	Rupert Williams	2		" - father
73.	Allen Wright	31	1903	Ms Nero Ed Williams, sis
74.	George Lee Wright	55	1926	" - sister
75.	Owen L. Wright	18	1922	" - aunt
76.	Fannie E. Wright	59	1933	" - sister-in-law
77.	Nora Huston	53	1918	" - aunt
78. - 83.	Unknown			
84.	Mrs. F. T. Wallace	64	1940	T.F. Wallace, husband
85.	Pearl Wynn	18	1921	Lige Wynn, husband
86.	Mrs. Belle Atwood	54	1937	Ted Atwood, son
87.	John Atwood (Co D 7th Ohio)	76	1922	" - son
88.	Atwood infant	1	1904	" - bro.
89.	Ruthie Williams	30	1933	Loyd Williams, husband
90.	Joe H. Williams	4	1930	" - father
91.	Wright infant	infant	1903	Charles Wright, father
92.	Early Wright	21	1905	" - father
93.	L. R. Stubblefield	48	1937	Ms L.R. Stubblefield, w
94.	Mrs. Loyd Owens	28	1932	Loyd Owens, husband
95.	Mrs. Nancy Wright	64	1942	Charles Wright, husband
?	Alton Williams	unk	1928	Loyd Williams, father

* *

#375 OLD SLAVE CEMETERY

Located on Land Map 75, tract GIR-2837, at elevation 350, seven graves. This was a very old abandoned cemetery with no indications of graves. No information could be obtained as to the identity of persons buried here. No further action was necessary.

#377 OLD SOLDIERS GRAVE

Located on Land Map 73, Tract GIR-3258F, below elevation 370, three graves. This is reputed to be a burial ground for guerilla soldiers killed during the Civil War. Although, there were no indications of graves and none of the local citizens could furnish any information as to the exact location or identity of the graves. No further action was necessary.

#378 BUCY CEMETERY

Found on Land Map 10N73, Tract GIR-3518F, elevation 435, 9 graves. Located about 1000 feet north of Highway 76. Cemetery is neglected and more or less lost in woods. A few graves marked with rough stones.

No.	Name of Deceased	Age	Date of Death	Information given by...
1.	Susan Bucy	unk	unk	G. E. Bucy, nephew
2.	Mary Bucy	unk	unk	" – son
	Carter Bucy	unk	unk	" – bro.
3.	George Bucy			" – son
4.	Viney Bucy			" – bro.
5.	Fauney Bucy			" – bro.
6.	Wattey Bucy			" – bro.
7. – 8.	Unknown			
9.	Sally Whitworth			Dee, Elvis, Herman and
10.	Whitworth infant	infant		Eula Whitworth, sons and
11.	Whitworth infant	infant		daug.

#379 BRANNAN CEMETERY

Located on Land Map 10N77, Tract GIR-3214, below elevation 362, 7 graves. This was a very old cemetery and none of the graves could be identified. Mr. J. R. Whitworth, property owner, requested that these graves be moved to a neighboring cemetery. All graves were moved to Williams Cemetery R-76 on March 10, 1943.

* *

#382 WILLIAMS CEMETERY

Located on Land Map 86, Tract Grover C. Williams, 49 graves.

No.	Name of Deceased	Age	Date of Death	Information given by...
1.	James A. Williams	72	1933	G.C. Williams, son
2.	Fannie E. Williams	70	1932	" - son
3.	Fred R. Williams	19	1920	" - bro.
4.	Williams infant	infant	1938	Jno. & Opal Williams-pts
5.	Brooks infant	infant	1900	Allie E. Brooks, mother
6.	Annie B. Williams	18	1902	G.C. Williams, bro.
7.	Annie Williams	32	1911	H.W. Williams, husband
8.	Gordon C. Williams	28	1919	Ms Wells Nix, wife
9. - 10.	Unknown			
11.	Walter Rice			Ms Eliza Rice, mother
12.	James B. Rice			" - wife
13.	Williams infant	infant	1911	Jno. & Opal Williams-pts
14.	Mrs. Sallie Walker	37	1840	
15.	Gray infant	infant	1840	
16.	Rufe Lashlee		1914	Ms R.V. Presnell, sister
17.	Rhoda A. Lashlee (w/o Rufe)	46	1891	" - sister
18.	Emeretta T. Hicks	26	1876	Ms W.C. Chenoweth, sis
19.	Bessa May Williams	8	1895	G.C. Williams, bro.
20.	Eisma A. Williams	18	1900	" - bro.
21.	Klester M. Williams	1	1900	" - bro.
22.	Joseph M. Bowles	2	1878	Ms Allie Brooks, sister
23.	Wm. A. Chenoweth	65	1922	Ms W.A. Chenoweth, wife
24.	James H. Williams	80	1908	G.C. Williams, g/son
25.	Williams infant	infant	1927	" - father
26.	P. Annie Williams	75	1900	John S. Cowan, g/g/son
27.	Rufus C. Williams	5	1868	Ms W.C. Chenoweth, sis
28.	Punkey Williams	3	1856	" - sister
29.	Sarah P. Williams	41	1856	" - niece
30.	W. C. Colman	4	1860	"
31. - 32.	Unknown			
33.	Aney Williams	95	1898	G.C. Williams, g/g/son
34.	John H. Williams	79	1877	John S. Cowan, g/g/son
35.	Woodrow Chenoweth	child	1918	C.R. Chenoweth, father
36.	Annie Chenoweth	child	1911	" - father
37.	Clara Chenoweth	infant	1901	Ms W.A. Chenoweth, mtr

* *

No.	Name	Age	Date	Information
38.	Sallie F. Manley	67	1937	John S. Cowan, nephew
39.	F. L. Manley	57	1927	Ms J.A. Clement, 1/2 sis
40.	John S. Cowan	22	1886	John S. Cowan, g/son
41.	John S. Cowan	63	1883	" - nephew
42.	N. H. Cowan - wife	69	1896	" - g/son
43.	Mrs. R. S. Cowan	28	1897	" - son
44.	R. S. Cowan	71	1929	Mary Cowan, wife
45.	Alex Cowan	unk	1931	" - mother
46.	Robert Cowan		1939	" - mother
47.	Ms Ida Culpepper		1919	Ms W.A. Chenoweth, mtr
48. - 49.	Unknown slaves			
?	Culpepper infant	infant	1911	R.L. Culpepper, father
?	Ed Brown		1901	Kate Evans, wife
?	Mary Ella Rice		1911	Ms Eliza Rice, mother
?	Bryan Lashlee		1909	R. G. Lashlee father
?	Ned Lashlee		1909	Ms Eliza Rice, sister

#383 WALKER CEMETERY

Located on Land Map 86, Tract GIR-4452F, 21 graves.

No.	Name of Deceased	Age	Date of Death	Information given by...
* * * * * * * * * * * * *		* * *	* * * * *	* * * * * * *
1.	A. J. Walker	62	1890	W. E. Hopkins, g/nephew
2.	James R. Walker	23	1862	" - g/nephew
3.	James Walker	55	1856	" - g/nephew
4.	Lucy Walker	56	1861	" - g/nephew
5.	D. M. L. Walker	51	1881	" - g/nephew
6.	Unknown			
7.	Whitfield un-identified			
8.	Cynthia Whitfield	60	1897	
9.	Unknown			
10.	Hannah Whitfield	50	1841	
11. - 12.	Unknown			
13.	S. M. (Ms Eli) Shankle	60	1893	W. E. Hopkins, g/son
14.	Eli Shankle	30	1861	" - g/son
15.	Unknown			
16. - 19.	French un-identified			
20.	H. L. Lee (Ms George)	87	1881	W.C. Wimberly, g/son
21.	George Lee	78	1871	" - g/son
?	Hannah Ann Wimberly		1868	W. E. Hopkins, g/nephew

* *

#397 WRIGHT CEMETERY

Mrs. C. P. Caldwell, age 74, has lived here all her life. She remembers a few funerals, many years ago, but was not able to direct us to any exisiting relatives or interested parties.

#399 BAUCUM COLORED CEMETERY

Found on Land Map 89A, elevation 440, 8 graves. This cemetery is found on the land of T. E. Bowles and is out in a cotton field. While it is not being plowed over at this time, all evidence of graves have disappeared and it is now a briar patch. W. F. Bowles, age 62, says there has not been a burial in his recollection. A. M. Burton, who came to the immediate locality in 1881 says there has been no burial since then. He has never heard any suggestion as to who is buried in this cemetery. No further action necessary.

#409 LONE GRAVE

Found on Land Map 94, elevation 415. This is an old forgotten burial place. Mrs. C. P. Caldwell, age 74, owner of the farm and mother of W. C. Caldwell, remembers a paling fence around this one grave. She did not ever know who was buried here.

#413 RILEY CEMETERY

Located on Land Map 99, elevation 450, 9 graves. Old cemetery with one small monument. It is covered with brush and weeds, neglected and inactive but surrounded by a woven wire fence.

#421 PARKER CEMETERY

Located on Land Map 94, Tract GIR-6, elevation 370, 12 graves. This is an old cemetery on the property of Pleas Fitch. It has become part of surrounding woodland. The only evidence that a graveyard was once here is a carpet of ground ivy. W. W. Fitch, age 61, and J. W. Winsett, age 78, both say they have never known a funeral here. No identification was obtained.

#422 BOWDEN CEMETERY

Located on Land Map 98, tract 3925, elevation 390 with two graves. Found in an open field marked with double monument, old and inactive, not fenced, neglected. On a tract of land owned by H. R. Fitch.

No.	Name of Deceased	Age	Date of Death	Information given by...
1.	B. B. Bowden	81	1886	M. L. Bowden, son
2.	Catherine Bowden	60	1864	" - son

* *

#423 BUCY CEMETERY

Located on Land Map 95, Tract GIR-4050, above elevlation 380, 4 graves. This
cemetery was very old, neglected and abandoned. All graves were identified and
remain permits executed. On the property of C. A. Wimberly. A. M., Geo. H. Bucy, and
Ed Couch make periodic trips back to visit the graves and should be contacted. The
graves will not be flooded but will be surrounded on three sides, although the
Medlock-Ford Road can be reached over fairly level land which information should be
given Mr. George Bucy.

No.	Name of Deceased	Age	Date of Death	Information given by...
1.	John M. Bucy		1864	Geo. W. Bucy
2.	Bucy infant	infant	1857	Geo. W. Bucy, bro.
3.	Louvina Bucy		1883	" - bro.
4.	Mary L. Bucy		1863	" - bro.

See Plat Map #423

#424 NO NAME CEMETERY

Located on Land Map 95, Tract GIR-4069F, elevation 440, 16 graves. This cemetery is
lost among fair sized trees and only faint depressions bear witness that graves are
there. Mr. W. L. Medlock, aged 64, says he has known of the graves all his life, but
they were old when he was a boy. No one could give any information as to who is
buried there.

#425 ELLIS CEMETERY

Located on Land Map 99, Tract GIR-4329F, below elevlation 376, 15 graves. This was
a very old, abandoned cemetery. Only two graves could be identified. Mrs. R. T.
Weaks, who had a number of relatives buried in this cemetery requested that the
graves be moved. All graves were moved to Simmons Cemetery R-77 on June 1, 1943.

No.	Name of deceased	Age	Date of Death	Information given by...
1.	Joe Ellis	75	1875	Ms R. T. Weaks, g/neice
2.	Granny Ellis	unk	unk	" - g/g/daug.
3.	- 15 Ellis un-identified			

See Plat Map #425

#427 MAYS HILL CEMETERY

Located on Land Map 100, Tract - marginal, elevation 445, three graves. It is a very
old cemetery and the local citizens have no knowledge of when any burials have taken
place. There are faint signs of two graves, but no stones of any kind. G. E.
Watkins, age 60, who has been in vicinity all his life says the burials go further
back than his memory.

* *

433 RUSSELL CEMETERY

Located on Land Map 89A, Tract GIR-4150, belowe elevation 359, 3 graves. Remain permits were executed on the graves of three persons known to have been buried there, but the exact location of the graves was unknown. No further action was necessary. On the property of R. A. Lee

No.	Name of deceased	Age	Date of Death	Information given by...
1.	Martha Ann Kendall		1839-1856	
2.	Wimberly infant		1903	L. A. Wimberly, father

See Plat Map #433

#435 CULPEPPER CEMETERY

Located on Land May 81, tract GIR-2627, above elevation 386, 30 graves. Eight identified and 20 unidentified graves were moved to three reinterment cemeteries. Remain permits were executed on the two remaining graves. Removal operations were completed June 8, 1943.

No.	Name of Deceased	Age	Date of Death	Information given by...
1.	A. J. Martin	62	1900	W. A. Martin, son
2.	Mrs. A. J. Martin	58	1905	" - son
3.	Mrs. Sarah A. Culpepper	unk	1900	Ms Melviney Grainger, d
4.	Thomas Culpepper	unk	1911	" - daug.
5.	Maggie Culpepper	30	1892	Mavella Myers, daug.
6.	Louis Culpepper	40	1895	" - sister
7.	Will Culpepper	27	1920	" - sister
8. - 22.	Unknown			
23.	J. C. Merrell, jr.	infant	1928	
24.	Merrell infant	infant	1921	
25.	John Hudgins	unk	1902	
26. - 30	Unknown			

See Plat Map #435

* *

#436 BRADFORD CEMETERY

Located on Land Map 78, Tract GIR-3087, below elevation 380, 80 graves. About one half of the graves were below elevation 376. Thirty-nine removal permits were executed by the nearest living relatives. The remaining 41 graves could not be identified, but Mrs. E. C. Pace, the property owner, requested that these graves be moved also. Five reinterment cemeteries were used in removal operations. Eleven monuments were also moved. Removal operations were completed May 15, 1943.

No.	Name of Deceased	Age	Date of Death	Information given by...
1.	Mary Floyd	76	1918	
2. - 5.	Unknown			
6.	Eula Wynn	30	1917	
7.	Unknown			
8.	J. R. Weldon	35	1860-1893	
9.	Harriet Weldon	infant	1880	
10.	Mrs. Francis Wyninger	45	1875	
11.	Unknown			
12.	Mary A. Nichols	68	1853-1921	Ms Wm. P. Pace, sister
13.	Burline Cathey	infant	1925	
14.	James F. Herndon	51	1868-1919	J. W. Herndon, son
15.	Herndon infant	infant	1894	
16.	Herndon infant	infant	1895	
17.	Herndon infant	infant	1897	
18. - 19.	Unknown			
20.	Henry Bradford	50	1811 - 1869	Ms Wm. P. Pace, daug.
21.	Evaline Frances Bradford	66	1829 - 1895	" - daug.
22.	Mr. Hansel	unk	unk	" - g/daug.
23.	Mrs. Hansel	unk	unk	" - g/daug.
24.	Mary Winters	unk	unk	" - neice
25.	Unknown			
26.	Cora Weldon	36	1918	
27.	Unknown			
28.	Lavelle Weldon	1	1906	
29.	Ora E. Weldon	3	1883	Mrs. H. W. Williams, sis
30.	Edwin Eastman Pace	6	1882	Ms Wm. P. Pace, mother
31.	William E. Pace	11	1902	" - mother
32.	William P. Pace	81	1934	" - wife
33.	Pearl Perry	3	1906	Richard Perry, father
34.	T. J. Brown	30	1926	
35.	Harriet Brown	18	1886	
36. - 41.	Unknown			
42.	Izac Newton			Ms H. W. Williams, aunt
43. - 46.	Unknown			
47.	Martha A. Brown	66	1913	

* *

No.	Name	Age	Date	
48.	Unknown			
49.	Everett Weldon	3	1897	
50.	Weldon infant	infant	1906	
51.	Weldon infant	infant	1907	
52.	Unknown			
53.	Madge Ross	14	1909	
54.- 55.	Unknown			
56.	Robert J. Williamson	24	1900	
57.	Mary A. Williamson	21	1901	
58.	G. W. Williamson	30	1918	
59.	Unknown			
60.	Robert Todd	50	1903	Roy H. Todd, g/son
61.	Unknown			
62.	Nancy Todd	79	1920	" - nephew
63.	Mervin Todd	22	1911	
64.	Unknown			
65.	Wyninger infant	infant	1890	
66.	Wyninger infant	infant	1888	
67. - 73.	Unknown			
74.	Weldon infant	infant	1910	
75. - 80.	Unknown			

See Plat Map #436

#437 BAKER CEMETERY

Located on Land Map 81, Tract GIR-3585, above elevation 522, 36 graves. This cemetery was incactive and poorly kept. Seven graves were identified and remain permits executed. Five additional remain permits were executed on the graves of persons known to have been buried in this cemetery, but the exact location of the graves was not known. No information could be obtained as to the identity of the other 24 graves. Located on the property of W. S. Weldon

No.	Name of Deceased	Age	Date of Death	Information given by...
1.	Jim Wynn, Sr.	30	1898	Crawford Wynn, son
2.	Sally Wynn	30	1898	"
3.	Marvin Wynn	6	1898	" - bro.
4.	Jim Wynn	3 ms	1897	" - bro.
5.	Lizzie Wynn	8	1898	" - bro.
6. - 7.	Unknown			
8.	Mandy M. Baker	52	1890	J. E. Odum, g/son
9. - 12.	Unknown			
13.	John J. Cheatham	45	1881	Ella Stricklin, daug.
14. - 31.	Unknown			

* *

?	Bill Todd	70	1918	Roy Todd g/nephew
?	Sarah Todd	ˌ70	1918	"
?	Geo. dickenson		1899	
?	Ed Todd		1901	B. Todd
?	Hattie Todd		1900	"

See Plat Map #437

#438 FAIRVIEW CEMETERY

Located on Land Map 81, Tract GIR-3596, 10 graves. This cemetery was well above the flooded area, but access was flooded. This was an active cemetery, all burials having been made since 1927. All graves were identified and remain permits executed.

No.	Name of Deceased	Age	Date of Death	Information given by...
*	* * * * * * * * * *	* * *	* * * * *	* * * * * * * * *
1.	J. S. Medlock	74	1933	P. A. Medlock, son
2.	Todd infant	infant	1934	Roy & Ella Todd, parents
3.	Mrs. W. A. Weldon	80	1937	C. J. Weldon, son
4.	W. A. Weldon	76	1927	" - son
5.	Ethelda Gene Odom	2 1/2	1920	L. G. Odom, father
6.	Claudine Perry	infant	1938	Olin Perry, father
7.	Perry infant	infant	1931	" - father
8.	Joel Don Salyers	8	1938	F. F. Salyers, father
9.	Salyers infant	unk	unk	" - father
10.	Martin infant		1931	G. C. Martin, father

#439 BOND CEMETERY

Located on Land Map 87, Tract GIR-3854, below elevation 365, 8 graves. This was a very old abandoned cemetery, the last burial being in 1850. Remain permits were executed on all graves, two of which could not be identified.

No.	Name of Deceased	Age	Date of Death	Information given by...
*	* * * * * * * * * *	* * *	* * * * *	* * * * * * * * *
1.	Louisa I. Bond	4	1849	
2.	Joseph Bond	9	1847	
3.	Barbera Bond	61	1841	
4.	Benjamin Bond	60	1840	
5.	John Bond	58	1863	
6.	Jimmie Cowan	3		John S. Conner, nephew
7. - 8.	Bond un-identified			W. F. Bowles

See Plat Map #439

* *

#440 WHIPPLE CEMETERY

Located on Land Map 96, Tract GIR-3649, below elevation 376, 10 graves. This was an old abandoned cemetery. None of the graves could be identified. Mr. B. C. Gibson, the property owner, requested that all the graves be moved out of the flooded area. These were moved to Gilbreth Cemetery R-78 on June 8, 1943.

#441 CLEMENT CEMETERY

Located on Land Map 96, Tract GIR-3657, elevation 400, unknown number of graves. Found in a field which has been cultivated for 25 years on the property of W. D. McSwain, east of the Medlock-Ford Road.

#443 BUCY CEMETERY

Located on Land Map 96, Tract GIR-3657, elevation 390, two graves. Very old cemetery, neglected and abandoned, found in an open field east of Medlock-Ford Rd. There is one small monument in the pasture and the cemetery is un-fenced on the property of W. D. McSwain.

No.	Name of Deceased	Age	Date of Death	Information given by...
1.	Laura Bucy		1866-1867	N.P. & O.H. Bucy, par'ts
2.	Unknown			

#444 MT. ZION CEMETRY

Located on Land Map 87A, Tract GIR-3778. This cemetery was well above the flooded area, but the access would be periodically flooded. It was active and well kept. Two removal permits were executed and the graves and two monuments were moved to Mansel Cemetery R-49 on May 13, 1943. One hundred and seventy-four remain permits were executed. The remaining eight graves could not be identified or no one could be found who was interested in having them moved. Thirty graves, from more seriously affected cemeteries, were reinterred in this cemetery.

No.	Name of Deceased	Age	Date of Death	Information given by...
1.	James C. Cathey		1921	
2.	Margaret Rowlett		1922	
3.	W. S. Grainger		1922	
4.	Martha E. Grainger		1939	
5.	Chandler infant		1918	

* *

6.	Ambrose Lane	1934
7.	William Lane	1916
8.	Bill Pierce	1918
9.	Ida Leagan	1914
10.	Alfred Bailey	
11.	Jennie M. Williamson	1918
12.	James Stanley Martin	1927
13.	Vena Medlock	1932
14.	Hannah Wood Medlock	1926
15.	Hattie Herndon	1928
16.	Laura Todd	1920
17.	Isham Maynard	1900
18.	Mary E. Dunn	1922
19.	Willie V. Medlock	1918
20.	James Monroe Gray	1928
21.	J. T. McDaniel	1920
22.	J. H. McDaniel	1920
23.	Dunn infant	1921
24.	Rhoda McDaniel	1916
25.	Ina Bell Dunn	1919
26.	Stella Gray Dortch	1934
27.	Ada Medlock	1918
28.	Raymond Medlock	1918
29.	Thurman Odom	1917
30.	Minola Wright	1906
31.	May Stricklin	1902
32.	J. J. Odom	1916
33.	Newt Weldon	1927
34.	Sara Bell Weldon	1927
35.	J. W. Weldon	1927
36.	Sandra Locla Evans	1926
37.	Charlie Evans	1940
38.	Pink Bryant	
39.	Travena W. Wood	1938
40.	James S. Wood	1930
41.	Willie Haskel Odom	1928
42.	Ronald F. Odom	1922
43.	W. H. Wynn	1907
44.	Nannie Velma Bailey	1906

* *

45.	Malinda Wynn	unk
46.	Henry Wynn	1899
47.	James Medlock	1904
48.	Zola Lee Medlock	unk
49.	Mollie Ann Henrdon	1930
50.	Celie Evans	1935
51.	John Evans	1918
52.	Evans infant	1913
53.	Gray infants (twins)	1911
54.	Preston Evans	1914
55.	Mrs. Belle Gray	
56.	Eiah Gray	
57.	Mary W. Gray	1911
58.	SAallie Bradford	
59.	Frances M. Evans	1919
60.	Carolyn Hampton	1917
61.	Finis Hampton	1907
62.	Millard Hampton	
63.	Hardy Hampton	
64.	Willis G. Grainger	1925
65.	B. J. Hampton	1925
66.	Annie Christopher	1930
67.	Dallas Alline Hutchinson	1923
68.	Evelyn Swor	1919
69.	Mary G. Swor	1919
70.	Rosaline Todd	1934
71.	Henry Clay Todd	1926
72.	Mrs. Matt Christopher	1917
73.	John Christopher	1916
74.	Lizzie Christopher	1907
75.	Ed Christopher	1912
76.	Mart Christopher	1920
77.	Walker infant	1908
78.	Clarice Walker	1907
79.	Minnie Walker	
80.	Mrs. W. T. Walker	
81.	John Gray	1902
82.	Evela Gray	19834

* *

83.	Balaam C. Gray	1916
84.	Jeff Gray	1919
85.	Cyrus H. Gray	1910
86.	Clinton Eldridge	1930
87.	Irving Watson	1900
88.	Nadine Watson	1931
89.	Mrs. L. V. Merrill	1915
90.	Hampton infant	
91.	Hampton infant	
92.	Hampton infant	
93.	Allison Hampton	
94.	Mattie Hampton	
95.	Catherine Hampton	
96.	Joe Hampton	1939
97.	Sylvia Stagner	1910
98.	Talmadge Stagner	1905
99.	Rosaland Dortch	1918
100.	Naomi McDaniel	1915
101.	Charlene McDaniel	1923
102.	Culpepper infant	1925
103.	Howard Christopher	1926
104.	G. S. Christopher	1925
105.	Bell Wynn Christopher	1915
106.	Sam McFadden	1925
107.	Mrs. J. H. McFadden	1910
108.	J. H. McFadden	1900
109.	E. S. Gray	1922
110.	Lillie Robbins	1923
111.	Ida Robbins	1901
112.	Cynthia Robbins	1908
113.	Mrs. Cornelia Robbins	1906
114.	Thomas Robbins	1904
115.	Darius Robbins	1899
116.	Robbins infant	1908
117.	Lula Weldon	1912
118.	Weldon infant	1913
119.	Mrs. T. J. Weldon	1915
120.	Larkin McFadden	1921

* *

121.	Henry R. McFadden		1905
122.	Royal T. McFadden		1915
123.	Zittie L. McFadden		1916
124.	Melena McFadden		1938
125.	Mrs. W. W. Christopher		1933
126.	W. W. Christopher		1914
127.	Raymond Richardson		unk
128.	Richardson infant		1913
129.	Glady Richardson		1919
130.	Ruth R. McFadden		1936
131.	Helen McFadden		1938
132.	Lula Robertson		1936
133.	Warren D. Robertson		1928
134.	Pauline Underwood	1	1911
135.	Alberta Underwood	infant	1904
136.	Charley Stitts		1901
137.	Minnie Lee Odom & child		1892
138.	Odom infant		
139.	Cyrus Hall Odom		
140.	Eugene Odom		
141.	Verby Odom		
142.	Odom infant		
143.	Lennie Odom		
144.	Lora Bell Odom		
145.	Ida Lee Odom		
146.	no grave		
147.	Granville Evans		1927
148.	Verbie Evans		1927
149.	Vernie Evans		1915
150.	Evans infant		1915
151.	Nell Robbins		1908
152.	Ty Robbins		1916
153.	Mollie Robbins		1925
154.	Floy M. Robbins		1921
155.	John F. Evans		1911
156.	Mollie Wynn		1912
157.	Herbert Wynn		1910
158.	Porter Wynn		1921
159.	Earnie Wynn		1924
160.	Unknonw		

* *

161. - 162. no grave
163. Loyd Odom   1909
164. Wynn infant   1914
165. Wynn infant   1916
166. Unknown

167. Deckard Odom   1931
168. Sally Odom   1924
169. Britty Odom   1907
170. Coriene Odom   1925
171. Virgell Odom   1937

172. Bessie Odom   1931
173. Dick King   1924
174. Ann Phillips   1920
175. Huice Mitcheson   1903
176. Mitcheson infant   1900

177. Bea Lemonds   1927
178. Mrs. J. B. Morris   1934
179. Dinnie C. Morris   1916
180. Medlock infant   1930
181. Evertte Wallace   1929

182. John Wallace   1936
183. Isa Medlock Flowers   1942
184. Hornburger infant

See Plat Map #444

#445 ODOM CEMETERY

Located on Land map 82, Tract GIR-3634, 125 graves. This cemetery was well above
the flooded area, but the access road would be periodically flooded. It was a very
old, abandoned and neglected cemetery; located in an open pasture. Remain permits
were executed on the graves of 41 persons known to have been buried there, but the
dexact location of these graves was unknown. No further action was necessary.

No.	Name of Deceased	Age	Date of Death	Information given by...
?	Hampton infant	unk	unk	Reno Odom
?	Ruth Hampton			
?	Bill Hampton			
?	Leon Hampton			
?	Odom infant	unk	1896	D. F. Odom, father
?	Odom infant	unk	1892	"
?	Martha Brannon	unk	unk	Ms D. F. Odom - g/daug
?	Shelby Robbins			" - daug.
?	Cynthia Ellen Robbins		1892	" - sister

* *

?	Tom Robbins		" - sister
?	Henry Robbins		" - sister
?	Melviney Robbins		" - sister
?	Martha Robbins		" - sister
?	Tom Brannon		" - neice
?	Nancy Robbins		" - neice
?	Mary Morgan		" - neice
?	Bill Odom	1877	J. E. Odom, g/son
?	Adeline Adzadie Todd	1920	B. Todd, husband
?	Vera Todd	1898	" - father
?	Alzadie Todd	1898	" - father
?	Mathy Todd	1898	" - father
?	Becky Ann Cooper		F. C. Cooper, son
?	Hugh Todd		Walter Lee Todd, g/son
?	Tom Todd		" - son
?	Susie Todd		" - son
?	Adzadie Todd		" - bro.
?	John Todd		" - bro.
?	Charlie Todd		" - bro.
?	Joe Todd		" - bro.
?	Annie Todd		" - bro.
?	Emmaline Todd		" - nephew
?	Josephine Hampton		Rena Odom
?	Maggie Hampton		
?	Jack Hampton		
?	Lou Hampton		
?	Ruth Hampton		" - neice
?	Ida May Brewer		" - neice
?	Kate leegon		" - neice
?	Frances Brewer		" - g/daug.
?	Eli Brewer		" - g/daug.
?	Hampton infant		

#451 MANLEYVILLE CHAPEL CEMETERY

Located on Land Map 103, Tract GIR-4093F. The cemetery was well above the flooded area, but the acess road was affected slightly. This was a fairly active cemetery, but poorly kept. Remain permits were executed on 187 graves, only 109 of which could be identified. Removal permits were executed on three graves. These graves were moved to two neighboring cemeteries on June 19, 1943.

No.	Name of Deceased	Age	Date of Death

* *

1.	Margret E. Carter		1920
2.	J. A. Carter		1926
3.	Mildred Carter		1915
4.	Lillian Bessie Hastings	1	1919
5.	Erbie Moody		1924

* *

6.	Newel Moody		1924
7.	Sallie Carter		1905
8.	Lilly Mae Roby		1915
9.	Georgie Roby		1915
10.	Leon Glover		1917

11.	Walter Whitehead, Jr.	infant	1917
12.	Lovett infant		1905
13.	Lovett infant		1910
14.	Herman Lovett		1908
15.	Alex Warren		1928

16.	Ollie Warren		1913
17.	Geroge Jenkins		1930
18.	Mary Jenkins		1923
19.	James William Jenkins	20 ms	1919
20.	Roby Wiseman		1912

21.	Mrs. Minnie Radford		1906
22.	Jennie Radford		1912
23.	Elizabeth Davis		1908
24.	T. M. Davis		1926
25.	Sarah Carter		1910

26.	W. H. Carter		1915
27.	Rosa L. Johnson		1906
28.	Perneaty Smith		1915
29.	M. F. Smith		1917

30. - 31.	Unknown		
32.	Bertha Davis		1919
33. - 34.	Unknown		
35.	Warren infant		1916
36. - 43.	Unknown		

44.	T. E. Throgmorton		1919
45.	E. L. Throgmorton		1917
46.	J. H. Thorgmorton		1905
47.	Serena Pierce		1889
48. - 49.	Unknown		

50.	Henry Taylor		1913
51.	Lorean Bowden		1912
52.	Lela Moody		1904
54.	Unknown		
55.	William Throgmorton		1915

56.	Mrs. William Throgmorton		unk
57. - 58.	Unknown		
59.	Sam Moody		unk
60.	Thomas Moody		
61.	Mrs. Thomas Moody		

* *

62.	Jennie Moody	
63.	George Moody	
64.	Betty Davis	
65.	Marvin Moody	
66. - 71.	Unknown	
72.	Sarah Ann Hankins	1855
73. - 74.	Unknown	
75.	Minerva Lily	
76.	Mary Lily	
77.	Sarah Ann Lily	
78.	Wilson Lily	
79.	Mrs. J. S. Carter	1871
80.	Ira French	1918
81.	Sidney Lily	
82.	Francis Lily	
83.	Nanny Lily	
84.	Lawrence Lily	
85.	Alexander Erwin	
86.	Sarah Ann Erwin	
87.	James P. Erwin	
88.	Therdore Erwin	
89. - 110.	Unknown	
111.	Martha Manley	1822
112.	Rev. John Manley	1831
113.	Eveline Manley	1835
114.	Unknown	
115.	Geraldine Manley	1854
116. - 120.	Unknown	
121.	Mary Williams	
122.	Willis Williams	
123.	Unknown	
124.	Tom Hastings	
125.	Mrs. M. E. Grinn	1899
126.	Mary A. Hastings	1888
127.	J. M. Hastings	1880
128.	Nancy Hastings	1850
129. - 145.	Unknown	
146.	Marion Morton	
147.	Hastings infant	
148.	Augustus Hastings	
149.	Mrs. Mary J. Hastings	1861
150.	Grace Morton	
151.	Dan Smith	
152.	Irena Smith	
153.	Joe B. Smith	

* *

154. Mrs. Joe H. Smith
155. Smith infant
156. Smith infant
157. Unknown
158. Luther W. Smith

159. - 164. Unknown
165. Edna Jenkins
166. Fannie Jenkins
167. Hattie Jenkins
168. William Smith

169. Osia Smith
170. Edna Smith
171. Irena Smith
172. Cuma Wiseman
173. Carroll Wiseman   1855

174. Mary Wiseman   1913
175. Hastings infant
176. Cynthia Ann hastings   1915
177. John H. Hastings   1934
178. W. H. Smith   1913

179. Lenictia Smith   1905
180. Unknown
181. Birdie Louise Martin   1916
182. Ruth McNunn   1889
183. Wiseman infant

184. Wiseman infant
185. Wiseman infant
186. Wiseman infant
187. Mary Smith
188. Smith infant   1900

189. Nolan Myrick   1904
190. Noble Myrick   unk

See Plat Map #451

#374 LEMOND CEMETERY

Located on Land Map 77, Tract GIR-3231F, below elevation 376, 10 graves. All of the graves were marked by rough stone markers; however, only two could be identified. Mr. D. L. Lemond, who had relatives buried here, requested that all the unidentified graves be moved out of the flooded area. Graves were moved to two neighboring cemeteries on June 2, 1943.

* *

No.	Name of Deceased	Age	Date of Death	Information given by...
1.	Calvin Lemond	80	1900	D. L. Lemonds, son
2. -9.	Lemonds un-identified			
10.	Lavada Lemond	15	unk	Ms Josie Lemonds, mother

See Plat Map #374

#785 JACKSON CEMETERY

Located on Land Map 86, Tract GIR-2513, elevation 428, Two graves. This is an old cemetery containing two graves. It is enclosed in a stake fence, neglected and inactive with no monuments. It is found on the property of the Kentucky-Tennessee Conference. Mrs. R. A. McCullough, age 92, says she has heard her father say that some Jacksons were buried here. It has been 90 years or more since these or anyone else has been buried here. She knows nothing of any relatives.

#798 INDIAN GRAVE

Found on Land Map 10N77, Tract GIR-3226F, elevation 390, three graves. Cemetery is said to be that of Indians and is so old that it is only tradition. There is no indication of graves.

#799 C. C. LEE CEMETERY

Located on Land Map 71, Tract GIR-2859F, elevation 400 and one grave. This cemetery is found on the property of C. C. Lee. It is a very old cemetery, out in a pasture and has been plowed over, although two rough stones mark the graves. Mr. R. E. Lee, age 67, has lived nearby all his life and says that graves were there when he was a boy and his father did not know who it was.

#802 EASTWOOD CEMETERY

Located on Land Map - 100, marginal tract. There was no question of isolation or submergence, but the grave was in the way of construction of Relocated Highway #69. A removal permit was executed by the nearest relative and the grave moved to Poplar Grove Cemetery R-41 on March 1, 1943.   This is the grave of an Eastwood child, a half wit who wandered out to the creek and was drowned and buried on what is now the property of A. L. Sprague.

1.   Eastwood child died from drowning, but the age and date are unknown, but it is thought the burial was about 85-90 years ago.

* *

#809 BROOKS CEMETERY

Located on Land Map 73, Tract GIR - 3264F, above 380 elevation, 4 graves. This was a very old abandoned cemetery in an open field. A remain permit was executed on the only identifiable grave. This grave was a Green infant that died in 1926, the child of Earnest and Alie Green. Members of a Brooks family were reputed to have been buried here, however, no one could furnish any information as to who the surviving relatives might be.

#810 GRAY CEMETERY

Located on Land Map 81, Tract GIR-3329, twelve graves. The cemetery was well above elevation 380, but the access road was flooded. It had been abandoned for several years and none of the graves could be identified; however, remain permits were exeucted on the graves of four persons known to have been buried in the cemetery, although the exact location of the graves was not known. On the property of G. C. Robbins.

No.	Name of Deceased	Age	Date of Death	Information given by...
?	Mrs. J. M. Gray	unk	unk	Ed Gray, step-son
?	J. M. Gray	unk	unk	" - son
?	Levi Gray	unk	unk	" - bro.
?	Bud Gray	unk	unk	" - 1/2 bro.

See Plat Map #810

* *

HOUSTON COUNTY, TENNESSEE

Grave Removal Operations

The following cemeteries will be submerged or access to them is impaired by the lake waters.

No.	Name of Cemetery	Land Map	Tract Number
141	Andrews Cemetery	122	3407
877	Arnold Cemetery	120-1	3825
145	Askew Cemetery	123	3478F
135	Bush Cemetery	119	3116F
721	Beecham Cemetery	125	3349
875	Beecham Cemetery	120-1	3819
134	Cherry Cemetery	119	3108
139	Cathey Cemetery	119	Detail #1
811	Conyers Cemetery	119	3108
137	Grafried Cemetery	116	1
138	Grafried Colored Cemetery	116	3043
839	Holmes Cemetery	123	3478F
146	Keel Cemetery	125	3344
722	McAuley Cemetery	125	3355F
800	Mathis Cemetery	119	3103
812	McKnight or Knight Cemetery	120	3364
876	Parker Cemetery	120-1	3829
856	Rye Cemetery	125	3341

The following cemeteries are either not affected by the lake waters or future access will be provided by relocated roads.

No.	Name of Cemetery	Land Map	Tract Number
*136	Bradley Cemetery	119	1
*140	Cane Creek Cemetery	120	3374
813	Day Cemetery #2	120	3372
814	Day Cemetery #1	120	3372
*144	Hill Orchard Cemetery	124	A
825	Hill Orchard Colored Cemetery	124	B
827	Holmes Cemetery	124	H
143	McKinnon Colored Cemetery	120	E
142	Sikes Cemetery	120	3499F
826	Wilson Cemetery	124	3446F

* = Present access affected, but future access provided by relocated roads.

* *

#134 CHERRY CEMETERY

Located on Land Map 119, Tract GIR-3108, .elevation 400, three graves. This cemetery is found 150 feet north of the Hurrican Road on the property of Mrs. Mae Bush in some woods.

No.	Name of Deceased	Age	Date of Death	Information given by...
1.	John Bush	50	1935	Mrs. John Bush, wife
2.	Frank Bush	21	1918	" – mother
3.	Annie E. Bush	unk	unk	" – mother

See Plat Map #134

#135 BUSH CEMETERY

Located on Land Map 119, Tract GIR-3116F, above elevation 380, 14 graves. This was an active and well kept cemetery. All graves were identified and remain permits executed.

No.	Name of Deceased	Age	Date of Death	Information given by...
1.	Eunice Taylor			J. R. Taylor, father
2.	Bush infant			Russ Bush, father
3.	N. T. Bush	50	1907	Ms N.T. Bush, wife
4.	Rebecca Agy			Guyles Agy, father
5.	Wilburn C. Agy			" – father
6. – 8.	Lindsey infants			Johnnie Loerch, mother
9.	Loerch infant			Bruce Loerch, father
10.	Beulah Ann Loerch			E. D. Loerch, father
11.	Loerch infant			" – father
12.	Lucy Loerch	87	1939	" – son
13.	John Loerch	93	1939	" – son
14.	Mrs. Ollie Loerch	51	1940	" – husband

See Plat Map #135

#137 GRAFRIED CEMETERY

Located on Land Map 116, Tract No. 1, below elevation 359, 42 graves. This was an active but poorly kept cemetery. All graves and six monuments were moved to three reinterment cemeteries. Twenty-six of the graves could not be identified, but Gene Askew, who had a number of relatives buried here requested that all unidentified graves be moved. Removal operations were completed on June 5, 1943.

* *

No.	Name of Deceased	Age	Date of Death	Information given by...

* *

No.	Name of Deceased	Age	Date of Death	Information given by...
1.	G. J. Grafried	infant	1875	Fred Grafried, bro.
2.	Dolly Grafried	infant	1887	"
3.	John Grafried Askew	infant	1918	Gene Askew, father
4.	W. F. Grafried	85	1928	Fred Grafried, son
5.	Mary Bauer Grafried	81	1934	" – son
6.	Mary Bivins	1	1929	Ms Henry Bivins, mother
7.	Scott infant	infant	1935	Griffin Scott, father
8.	Scott infant	infant	1938	" – father
9.	Jane Blackwell	26	1934	J.P. Blackwell, husband
10.	Boswell un-identified			
11.	George Boswell	unk	unk	
12.	Askew un-identified			
13.	Sallie Askew	65	1835	C.D. Askew, g/son
14.	Josiah Askew	70	1832	" – g/son
15.	John Mathis	23	1875	Elbert Mathis, son
16. – 23.	Askew un-identified			
24.	Unknown			
25.	Reve Largent	infant	1927	Bill Largent, father
26.	Unknown			
27.	Scott infant	infant	1928	Griffin Scott, father
28.	Scott infant	infant	1932	" – father
29. – 42.	Unknown			

See Plat Map #137

#138 GRAFRIED COLORED CEMETERY

Located on Land Map 116, Tract GIR-3043, below elevation 359, 70 graves. This was a very old abandoned slave cemetery. None of the graves could be identified. Since the interned were known to have been slaves of the Askew family, Gene Askew requested that all be moved out of the flooded area. All graves were moved to the Askew Colored Cemetery R-53. Removal operations were completed on April 9, 1943.

See Plat Map #138

#139 CATHEY CEMETERY

Located on Land Map 119, Tract No. 1 below elevation 360, 47 graves. This was a poorly kept and inactive cemetery, only two burials having been made in 20 years. Remain permits were executed on 25 graves. Four graves were moved to two reinterment cemeteries on June 14, 1942. The remaining 18 graves could not be identified and no one could be found who was interested in having them moved.

* *

No.	Name of Deceased	Age	Date of Death	Information given by...
* *	* * * * * * * *	* *	* * * * * *	* * * * * * * * * *
1.	Ethel Mathis		1905	Morris Mathis, bro
2.	Martha Mathis		1895	Elec Mathis, son
3.	Unknown			
4.	Kimbrough infant		1931	Nellie Kimbrough, mother
5. - 6.	Unknown			
7.	Albert Moore		1931	D. H. Moore, bro
8.	James L. Moore		1923	" - son
9.	Manervia Ann Moore		1920	" - son
10.	B. F. Moore		1894	" - bro.
11.	Minnie Moore		1880	" - bro.
12. - 14.	Unknown			
15.	Nancy Moore		1866	Sallie McGee, g/g/daug.
16.	Martha Moore		1875	" - sister
17.	Albert Moore		1875	" - sister
18.	Wiley Moore		1872	" - sister
19.	Macon Moore, Sr.		1872	" - daug.
20.	Macon Moore, Jr.		1882	" - sister
21. - 22.	Unknown			
23.	Christine Garrett		unk	Ms M.L. Pennywitt, daug.
24.	J. C. Sikes		1856	
25.	M. E. I. Sikes		1858	
26.	Nicholas T. Carmack		1856	
27.	Peter J. Carmack		1858	
28.	Emerson E. Carmack		1860	
29.	B. W. Hudspeth	40	1875	Ms J.E. Black, daug.
30.	Street Hudspeth	10	1875	" - sister
31. - 32.	Unknown			
33.	Mariah Loerch	2	1882	E.D. Loerch, bro.
34.	Marion Loerch	2	1892	" - bro.
35.	Daniel Bush		1897	" - g/son
36.	Mariah Bush		1887	" - g/son
37.	Noad Bradley		unk	" - nephew
38.	Dee Bush		unk	" - nephew
39.	Billie Bush		unk	
40. - 47.	Unknown			

See Plat Map #139

#141 ANDREWS CEMETERY

Located on Land Map 122, Tract GIR-2407, above elevation 381, 26 graves. This was a very old abandoned cemetery found on the property of A. F. Weaver. Only one grave was marked. None of the graves could be identified. Mr. A. F. Askew stated that he possibly had some relatives buried in the cemetery, but would not be interested in having them moved.

See Plat Map #141

* *

#145 ASKEW CEMETERY

Located on Land Map 123, Tract GIR-3478F, elevation 380, 42 graves. The cemetery was fenced and well kept. All graves were identified, with the exception of some negro graves located on the outside of the fence, believed to be the graves of slaves. Remain permits were executed on 26 graves. The remaining 16 graves could not be identified.

No.	Name of Deceased	Age	Date of Death	Information given by...

* *

No.	Name of Deceased	Age	Date of Death	Information given by...
1.	David O. Deshler	25	1885	C. D. Askew, uncle
2.	Askew infant		1895	" – father
3.	Lucile Askew	3	1899	" – father
4.	Ida Askew	67	1937	" – husband
5.	Louisa Askew	62	1882	" – son
6.	D. O. Askew	70	1872	" – son
7.	Sallie Askew	60	1854	Homer Askew –1/2 bro.
8. - 10.	Un-identified			C. D. Askew, 1/2 bro.
11.	William Askew	12	1866	" – bro.
12. - 13.	Askew un-identified			" – 1/2 bro.
14.	Charlie Deshler			" – uncle
15.	Askew un-identified			" – uncle
16.	D. O. Askew			Homer Askew, bro.
17.	David O. Askew	59	1904	" – son
18.	Sallie E. Askew	23	1880	" – bro.
19.	Mollie J. Askew	57	1911	" – son
20. - 35.	Unknown			
36.	Wyatt un-identified			G. M. Wyatt, 1/2 bro.
37.	Chris Wyatt			"
38.	Emma Wyatt			"
39.	Robert Wyatt			" – g/son
40.	Mary Wyatt			" – g/son
41.	Unknown Wyatt			" – 1/2 bro.
42.	James A. West	13 dys	1903	

See Plat Map #145

#146 KEEL CEMETERY

Located on land Map 125, Tract GIR-3344, above elevaltion 380, 108 graves. Remain permits were executed on 67 graves, only 46 of which could be identified. Twenty-one of these permits were on the graves of persons known to have been buried here, but the exact location of the graves was unknown. No information could be obtained as to the identitiy of the remaining 41 graves.

* *

No.	Name of Deceased	Age	Date of Death	Information given by...
1.	Joseph C. Hooper	22	1914	Ms Gertie Vick, wife
2. - 12.	Unknown			
13.	A. D. McMillian			Ms A.D. McMillian, wife
14.	Ms Elizabeth Hall		1910	W. R. Hall, son
15.	J. W. Hall		1927	" - son
16. - 17.	Unknown			
18.	Jessie E. McMillian			Ms A.D.McMillian, mother
19. - 21.	Unknown			
22.	John G. Cathey		1876	Josie Weaver, daughter
23.	Rebecca Cathey		1896	" - daug.
24.	Eudora Hazelwood	19	1883	W.W. Hazelwood, son
25.	Charlie Cathey		1900	Josie Weaver, sister
26.	Robert Cathey		1903	" - sister
27. - 28.	Unknown			
29.	Ruby Keel			Ms N. M. Hudson, sister
30.	Waymon Keel			" - sister
31.	Orpha Keel			" - sister
32.	Homer Keel			" - sister
33.	William Keel			" - g/daug.
34.	Elizabeth Keel			" - g/daug.
35.	Robert A. Keel	26	1875	" - nearest
36.	Luella Keel			" - daug.
37.	Richard Keel			" - daug.
38.	Mary Keel and infant	30	1895	Marvin Keel, son
39.	Talmage Keel			" - bro.
40. - 49.	Unknown			
50.	T. B. Thompson	infant	1882	Ms Lena Whittaker, sister
51.	Ward B. Thompson	2	1875	" - sister
52.	Unknown			
53.	Mary J. McMillian	79	1905	Grover McMillian, g/son
54.	Neil McMillian	77	1893	" - g/son
55.	Alfred P. McMillian	43	1900	" - nephew
56.	Dock McMillian	57	1916	" - nephew
57.	A. W. McMillian			" - nephew
58.	Mollie P. Powers			Josie Weaver, nearest
59.	James A. Cook	62	1875	" - nearest
60.	Dorcas Cook			" - nearest
61.	James W. Cook	18	1873	
62.	W. S. Cook	19	1869	
63.	J. L. Cook	5	1882	
65.	Thomas H. Cook	27	1884	
66. - 70.	Unknown			
71.	Parlee McMillian			G. G. McMillian, son

* *

72.	Prentice McMillian			" – son
73.	Virgil McMillian			" – bro.
74.	William P. McMillian	21	1907	" – bro.
75. – 78.	Unknown			
79.	Ann Summers	43	1858	Walter Summers, cousin
80.	Macy S. Summers	2	1841	" – cousin
81.	Udora Summers	1	1858	W. B. Summers, nearest
82. – 96.	Unknown			
97.	Flora Daniel			
98.	Zora Daniel			
99.	Betty Daniel			
100.	Lula Daniel			
101.	Gill infant		1934	Mason Gill, father
102.	Morris R. Hudson		1926	N.M. Hudson, father
103.	Agnes Lucille McMillian & infant		1909	W.R. Hall, bro.
?	Mary Ellison			J.E. Ellison, son
?	Keel infant			Howard Keel, father
?	Dassie Cathey			Mary Cathey, mother
?	Mary Cathey			" – mother
?	Zora Daniel			Carrie Smith, daug.
?	Lula Daniel			Lurt Daniel, son
?	Nancy Manning			Annie Knighting, daug.
?	Gray Infant (2)			Marvin Keel, cousin
?	Betty Daniel			Lurt Daniel, step-son
?	Maggie Jacobs		1915	Ms Sarah Gill, niece
?	Sarah Daniel			" – g/daug.
?	Mildred Marie Gill		1917	H.R. Gill, father
?	Herbert E. Gill		1931	" – father
?	Alfred McMillian			G.C. McMillian, bro.
?	Ada McMillian			" – bro.

See Plat Map #146

#721 BEECHAM CEMETERY

Located on Land Map 125, Tract GIR-3340, above elevation 380, 4 graves. This was an old, abandoned cemetery. All graves were identified and remain permits executed.

No.	Name of Deceased	Age	Date of Death	Information given by...

* *

1.	Mrs. Dora Beecham			Mrs. Ernie Flowers, daug.
2.	Alfred Beecham			" – sister
3.	Walter Beecham			" – sister
4.	Levton Beecham			" – sister

See Plat Map #721

* *

#722 McAULEY CEMETERY

Located on Land Map 125, Tract GIR-3355F, above elevation 380, 31 graves. This was a very old abandoned cemetery, last burial believed to have been over 50 years previously. None of the graves could be identified; however, remain permits were executed on the graves of six persons known to have been buried here, although the exact location of the graves was not known.

No.	Name of Deceased	Age	Date of Death	Information given by...

?	Daniel McAuley			Leon McAuley, g/son
?	Elizabeth McAuley			" - g/son
?	Sallie McAuley			" - nephew
?	McAuley un-identified			" - nephew
?	Claud McAuley		1891	" - bro.
?	Mrs. Isabel Cathey			Walter Cathey, son

#800 MATHIS CEMETERY

Located on Land Map 119, Tract GIR-3103, above elevation 380, two graves. Both graves were identified and remain permits executed.

No.	Name of Deceased	Age	Date of Death	Information given by...
1.	John Mathis		1935	Ms J.T. Mathis, wife
2.	Evelyn Mathis		1932	" - mother

See Plat Map #800

#811 CONYERS CEMETERY

Located on Land Map 199, Tract GIR-3108, below elevation 359, one grave. This was the grave of George Conyers, an adult who died in 1927. The grave was moved to Cane Creek Cemetery R-11 on June 9, 1943.

#812 McKNIGHT OR KNIGHT CEMETERY

Located on Land Map 120, Tract GIR-3364, below elevlation 359, one grave. The grave of Jim Knight age 75, who died in 1915 was moved to Cane Creek Cemetery R-11 on June 9, 1943.

* *

#839 HOLMES CEMETERY

Located on Land Map 123, Tract GIR-3478E, between elevation 373 and 375, 6 graves. This was a very old abandoned cemetery on the property of C. D. Askew, last burial was believed to have been over 100 years previously. W. C. Holmes, whose grand parents and great-grand parents are buried here, requested that all graves be left undistrubed.

See Plat Map #839

#856 RYE CEMETERY

Located on Land Map 125, Tract GIR-3341, above elevation 380, two graves. Both graves were identified and remain permits executed.

No.	Name of Deceased	Age	Date of Death	Information given by...
1.	Samuel Cunningham		1898	Ed Cunningham, son
2.	Martin L. Cunningham		1897	" - bro.

See Plat Map #856

#875 BEECHAM CEMETERY

Located on Land Map 120-1, Tract GIR-3819, above elevation 380, 3 graves. The cemetery was fenced and well kept. The graves were moved to Beecham Cemetery R-113.

No.	Name of Deceased	Age	Date of Death	Information given by...
1.	Johnny Hubert Beecham	38	1939	Ms Emma Whitehead, mot
2.	Robert Beecham	65	1939	" - wife
*25.	Reve Largent	infant	1927	

* = This grave was moved by TVA, from Grafried Cemetery No. 137 on June 3,1943.

See Plat Map #875

* *

#876 PARKER CEMETERY

Located on Land Map 120-1, Tract GIR-3829, above elevation 380, one grave. A remain permit was executed on the grave.

No.	Name of Deceased	Age	Date of Death	Information given by...

* *

| 1. | Polly Joyce Parker | 7 ms | 1939 | J.R. Parker, father |

#877 ARNOLD CEMETERY

Located on Land Map 120-1, Tract GIR-3825, one grave, above elevation 380, but access was flooded. The grave of Victoria Arnold who died in 1935, was fenced and well cared for and a remain permit was executed by W. H. Arnold, her husband.

Humphrey County, Tennessee

* *

GRAVE REMOVAL OPERATIONS

Cemeteries listed below are either submerged or access to them is impaired by the lake waters.

No.	Cemetery Name	Land Map	Tract
45	African Methodist Church Cem.	143-4	6716
37	Box Cemetery	137	Detail #1
873	Baker Cemetery	128	9587
740	Crockett Cemetery	143	6688
849	Cumack, Washington Cemetery	143-5	5367
50	Gould Cemetery	144	Detail #1
31	Haley Cemetery	125	5982
33	Hooper Cemetery	129	5610
739	Hopson, G. W. Cemetery	143-5	5364
862	Holland Cemetery	130	5554
58	Johnsonville Cemetery	143	6694
23	Kelly Cemetery	185	Detail #2
36	Lucas Cemetery	139	5089
43	Lucas Cemetery	140	5124
65	Larkin Cemetery	161	6204
71	Lone Grave	170	6151
724	Lashlee Slave	128	5577
726	Luten Cemetery	129	5603
727	Luten Colored Cemetery	129	5608
30	Marberry Cemetery #1	143	5184
44	Marberry Cemetery #2	143	Detail #3
63	Massey Cemetery	148	Detail #3
725	Mason Cemetery	128	5576
14	Neblett Cemetery	159	6799
42	Napier Cemetery	140	Detail #3
48	Nels Anderson Cemetery	143-5	6727
49	No Name Cemetery	143	5174
52	No Name Cemetery	143	5174
792	Primm Cemetery	157	6546
41	Old Reynoldsburg Cemetery	140	Detail #5
*870	Old Soldiers Cemetery		Out Side
804	Phiffer Cemetery	128	5579
46	Rollins Cemetery	143	6690
729	Reeves Cemetery	133	Detail #1
869	Ragan Cemetery	143-5	6726
738	Sutton Cemetery	143-4	5426
35	Union Chapel Cemetery	135	5472
751	Van Hook Cemetery	171	Detail #1
47	Wells Cemetery	143-5	6901
51	Winters Cemetery	144	5207F
741	Williams Cemetery	143-5	5365

* Not affected by the lake waters, but in the way of the relocation of a portion of the N.C. & St. L. Railroad.

* *

7	O'Donnley Cemetery	173	B
29	Old Cemetery	169	6048
782	O'Gwin Cemetery	147	F
832	Pruett Cemetery	177	No Number
20	Page-Ladd Cemetery	159	6808F
25	Pruitt Cemetery	157	I
*64	Plant Cemetery	148	Detail #2
753	Paoe Cemetery	185	H
5	Rogers Cemetery	147	G
12	Roberts Cemetery	175	E
40	Rogers Cemetery	140	Detail #1
746	Rogers Cemetery	146	E
829	Rushing Cemetery	176	No Number
781	Sanders Cemetery	147	A
1	Scarbrough Cemetery	161	6222
21	Scarbrough Cemetery	161	6205
9	Shannon Cemetery	175	D
3	Simpson Cemetery	147	C
74	Simpson Cemetery	147	E
54	Steptoe Cemetery	156	K
62	Stribling Cemetery	156	Out Side
*759	Sullivan Cemetery	134	B
820	Stanfield, Hoson	159	6805F
*38	Turner Cemetery #1	139	Detail #4
*39	Turner Cemetery #2	139	Detail #7
67	Tatum Cemetery	161	B
4	Wells Cemetery	147	D
*34	Wassan Cemetery	139	Detail #3
59	Warren Cemetery	156	D
13	Williams Cemetery	174	C
53	Wyley Colored Cemetery	149	Detail #1
*735	Waddell Cemetery	139	Detail #5
749	Walker Cemetery	160	6398F
*816	Waggoner Cemetery	148	Detail #1
830	Wright Cemetery	177	A
28	Young Cemetery	162	Out Side
60	Yarbrough Cemetery	156	E
70	Yarbrough Cemetery	161	A

* = Present access affected, but future access provided by relocated road.

** = No cemetery exists at this location; possibly confused with Cemetery #723.

* *

Cemeteries listed below are either not affected by the lake waters or future access will be provided by relocated roads.

No.	Cemetery Name	Land Map	Tract
15	Anderson Cemetery	179	A
17	Arrington Cemetery	183	B
22	Blue Creek Cemetery	185	A
737	Batson Cemetery	139	Detail #1
742	Box Cemetery	144	B
744	Burnham Cemetery	146	F
745	Burnham Cemetery	146	G
833	Bakerville Colored Cemetery	178	A
834	Bone, Geo. S.	178	2
835	Brown Cemetery	178	P
61	Corbett Cemetery	156	Out Side
69	Crockett Cemetery	161	Out Side
828	Crockett Cemetery	173	6875F
730	Cooley Cemetery	135	Detail #2
819	Cude Ceemetery	159	3
906	Dobbins Cemetery	185	7957M
73	Estes Cemetery	155	Detail #1
8	Fowler or May Cemetery	173	6874-F
11	Foster Cemetery	159	8
16	Fowlkes Cemetery	172	B
24	George Cemetery	157	6567F
57	Guinn Cemetery	156	H
10	Hobbs Cemetery	158	13
**32	Hooper, E. D.	129	5609
723	Hooper, E. D.	128	5598F
*736	Holmes Cemetery	139	Detail #2
752	Hamm Cemetery	185	C
19	Jones, Sam	172	A
27	James, Jessie	156	Out Side
6	Link Cemetery	158	15
68	Link Cemetery	161	A
756	Lewis Cemetery	156	J
16	Miller Cemetery	159	B
26	Mays Cemetery	146	A
66	Morris Cemetery	161	Detail #1
*731	McGee Cemetery	135	C
732	McEurtrie Cemetery	135	E
743	McAdoo Cemetery	145	C
760	Marberry Cemetery	140	Detail #4
794	Mays Colored Cemetery	157	J
*817	Massey Cemetery	148	6351F
818	Miller, W. S.	158	14
866	Miller Cemetery	148	Out Side
2	Nelson Cemetery	147	B
55	No Name Cemetery	156	6333F
56	No Name Cemetery	156	Out Side
72	No Name Cemetery	169	6048
831	No Name Cemetery	177	No Number

* *

#11 FOSTER CEMETERY

Found on Land Map 159, Tract No. 8, 81 graves. The information found on this cemetery are those found in the Field Book #MS 10473. The Cemetery was not affected by the lake and therefore, little other information will be found in the TVA records.

No.	Name of Deceased	Age	Date of Death	Information given by...

* *

No.	Name of Deceased	Age	Date of Death	Information given by...
1. - 3.	Unknown			
4.	James H. Hall			Ms W.T. Jones - dau.
5.	Minerva Hall			" - dau.
6.	Hall infant			" - sister
7.	Hall infant			" - sister
8.	Unknown			
9.	Delilah Brown Foster	50	1883	Ms L.L. Shipp - g/dau.
10.	Minnie B. Foster	7	1886	" - sister
11.	Malissa Foster	39	1885	" - dau.
12.	Marshald Foster	61	1899	" - dau.
13.	Rue Maybery		1906	Fred Maybery - father
14.	William L. Tate	48	1897	Ms W.S. Miller - dau.
15.	Early Mae Jones	11 dys	1897	" - aunt
16.	Evie Jones	22 dys	1902	" - aunt
17. - 18.	Unknown			
19.	W. T. Spicer	32	1892	Ms Jake Tubbs - sister
20.	Thomas H. Spicer	9	1892	" - aunt
21. - 29.	Unknown			
30.	Merrell infant	infant	1906	
31.	Unknown			
32.	Bamme Dortton			Ms Anderson Warren - s
33. - 45.	Unknown			
46.	David Ghant			Verner Anderson - nep
47.	Bertha Ghant			" - nephew
48. - 81.	Unknown			

* *

#14 NEBLETT CEMETERY

Located on Land Map 159, Tract GIR-6799, above elevation 380, 77 graves. This was an active but poorly kept cemetery. Remain permits were executed on 70 graves. The remaining seven graves could not be identified or no one could be found who was interested in having them moved.

No.	Name of Deceased	Birth or Age	Date of Death	Relative(s)

* *

Information taken from Field Book MS-10473

No.	Name of Deceased	Birth or Age	Date of Death	Relative(s)
1.	Jessie Barnhill	25	1919	
2.	Sarah Barnhill	56	1915	R. Barnhill - husband
3.	Reeves Barnhill	70	1917	
4.	Barnhill infant	3	unk	
5.	Thomas J. Lawson	3	1896	Ms A.L. McClure - cousin
6.	Clarence D. Lawson	4	1899	" - cousin
7.	J. F. Lawson			
8.	Mrs. J. F. Lawson			
9.	Shaver infant			
10.	Jimmy Hathey	80	unk	
11.	Parthenia M. Blackwell	43	1909	" - relationship unk.
12.	Laura F. Blackwell	68	1939	
13.	H. J. Blackwell	63	1939	
14.	Neoma L. Watts	58	1934	
15.	Roy D. Watts	40	1931	
16. - 18.	Watts infant			Walk Watts - father
19. - 20.	McClure infant			
21.	Mrs. Alice McClure	45	1928	
22.	Betty O'Guin	71	1939	
23.	George G. O'Guin	62	1923	
24.	Albert N. O'Guin	11	1919	
25.	Boyd O'Guin	19	1916	
26.	H. M. McIlwain	76	193	Mildred Morris - g/dau.
27.	Sallie K. McIlwain	65	1806	" - g/dau.
28.	Alma M. Woffard	69	1908	
29.	Samuel W. Woffard	67	1901	
30.	Betty Kelly		1900	
31.	Mrs. Woffard		1887	
32.	Woffard infant			
33.	Clara E. Woffard		1885	

* *

34.	Marshall S. Woffard	4	1918	Ms M.S. Woffard - mother
35.	Grick Woffard	10	1910	" - mother
36.	J. F. Woffard	10	1918	" - mother
37.	Bertie D. Woffard	15	1918	" - mother
38.	Lula Woffard			Leslie Woffard - bro.
39.	Woffard infant			" - bro.
40.	Woffard child	4	unk	" - bro.
41.	Lula Woffard	38	1921	" - son
42.	William D. Woffard	59	1930	" - son
43.	Mrs. Lucille Dungan	30	1939	
44.	Ann R. McNeblett	49	1870	Ann Morris - g/dau.
45.	Sterling McNeblett	41	1859	" - g/dau.
46.	Mollie McIlwain	2	1861	
47.	McIlwain infant		1862	
48.	McIlwain infant		1865	
49.	Napier infant		1904	
50.	Nolie McIlwain	1	1900	
51.	Sterling Neblett	1	1861	
52.	George P. Neblett	55	1871	
53.	Mary B. Neblett	52	1896	
54.	Dorris Lee Mosely	2	1937	
55.	Sam Watts			Marvin Watts - son
56.	Mrs. Sam Watts			" - son
57.	Jessey B. Woffard	23	1926	Ms M.S. Woffard - mother
58.	M. S. Woffard	50	1930	" - wife
59.	Richard T. Duncan	infant	1935	" - g/mother
60.	Nannie J. Watts	72	1937	
61.	Pleas H. Watts	69	1934	
62.	Irena H. Watts	78	1913	Walk Watts - son
63.	E. Watts	75	1924	" - son
64.	M. C. Watts	18	1886	" - bro.
65.	John E. Huddleston	40	1878	
66.	Watts infant		1870	
67.	Willie Forister	infant	1876	
68.	- 71. Unknown			
72.	Matilda Forister	61		
73.	Virgie Forister	1	1881	
74.	Charlie Forister	6	1881	
75.	- 76. Unknown			
77.	doubtful grave			

See Plat Map #14

* *

#23 KELLY CEMETERY

Located on Land Map 185, Tract No. 2, below elevation 362, 36 graves. This was a very old abandoned cemetery. Only one grave could be identified. Removal permits were executed on all graves. R. B. Kelly, the owner of the property executed removal permits on all the unidentified graves. All graves were moved to McKeel Cemetery No. 101. Removal operations were completed on September 3, 1943.

No. Name of Deceased   Age   Date of Death   Information given by...
* *

1.   Wesley Seats   unk   unk   George Seats - g/g/son
2. - 36. Unknown

See Plat Map #23

#30 MARBERRY CEMETERY #1

Found on Land Map 143, Tract No. 1, above elevation 380, 15 graves. This is an active and fairly well kept cemetery. All graves were identified and 13 remain permits executed. No answer was received to correspondence concerning the disposition of the two remaining graves.

No. Name of Deceased   Age   Date of Death   Information given by...
* *

* = Information taken from the Field Book MS-641

No.	Name of Deceased	Age	Date of Death	Information given by...
*1.	Mrs. Hester G. Clark	83 yr 9 ms 6 dy	July 15, 1938	Jennie Nichols, daug.
2.	John Marberry		1920	" - daug.
3.	Leslie Nichols		1926	" - mother
4.	Carl Nichols		1928	" - mother
*5.	J. W. Nichols	56 yrs 27 dys	Jan 2, 1932	" - wife
6.	Ollie Stewart		1918	Cal Stewart - father
7.	Louie Stewart		unk	" - father
8.	Tenoie Stewart		unk	" - father
*9.	Lenard Rex Stewart	10 yrs 6 ms 22 dys	2 May 1940	A. J. Stewart - father
*10.	Nichols infant		22 June 1940	M.B. Nichols - father
*11.	Mary Sue Nichols	b. 8 Mar 1930	14 Apr 1930	
12.	Bell Marberry		Unk	Jennie Nichols - sister
13.	Stewart child		unk	Cal Stewart - father
14.	Stewart child		unk	" - father
15.	William Crowell		1920	John P. Crowell - father

See Plat Map #30

* *

#31 HALEY CEMETERY

Located on land Map 1255, Tract GIR-5982, elevation above 380, 25 graves. This was an active and fairly well kept cemetery. Remain permits were executed on all graves. One of these permits was on the grave of a person known to have been buried here, but the exact location of the grave was unknown.

No.	Name of Deceased	Age	Date of Death	Information given by...
1.	R. L. Binkley	infant	1921	Nathan Binkley - father
2.	N. J. Binkley	infant	1917	" - father
3.	H. L. Binkley	infant	1922	" - father
4.	Mrs. J. H. Haley	43	1917	J. H. Haley - husband
5.	Clady Viola Haley	15	1915	" - father
6.	G. W. Evans	87	1930	" - step-son
7.	Mrs. Minerva Evans	86	1932	" - son
8.	Hebert Sykes	23	1922	F. W. Sykes - father
9.	McMillon infant	infant	1931	Belfild McMillon - ft
10.	Nancy Rose Warden	infant	1923	Nannie Warden - mother
11.	Lonnie J. Lattimer	20	1923	Ms Erie Myers - mother
12.	Tom Breeden	74	1930	Sam Breeden - son
13.	Ms Tom Breeden	71	1938	" - son
14.	Wm. Arnold Binkly	infant	1941	Ronell Binkley - father
15.	Elizabeth Binkley	59	1933	Nathan Binkley - son
16.	Walter Lee Binkley	57	1928	" - son
17.	E. Edward Binkley	19	1928	" - bro.
18.	Roy Carter	infant	1939	Dorothy Davidson - mother
19.	Wynn infant		1932	Sam Wynn - father
20.	Junior Davidson	3	1933	C. W. Davidson - father
21.	Willie Joe Davidson	infant	1941	Malcolm Davidson - father
22.	Thomas McMillan	55	1939	Pearl McMillan - wife
23.	Louise McMillan	80	1934	Ms. G.1. Robbs - daug.
24.	Thomas McMillan	75	1933	" - dau.
?	Billy Joe Davidson	unk	1941	Malcolm Davidson - father

See Plat Map #31

* *

#33 HOOPER CEMETERY

Located on Land Map 129, Tract GIR-5610, above elevation 380, 43 graves. This was an active and well kept cemetery. Remain permits were executed on 27 graves. The remaining 16 graves could not be identified or no living relative could be found.

No.	Name of Deceased	Age	Date of Death	Information given by...

* *

No.	Name of Deceased	Age	Date of Death	Information given by...
1.	Hooper infant	infant	1899	Ms H.H. Hooper - mother
2.	Unknown			
3.	A. B. Hooper	92	1932	H. H. Hooper & Stella H.
4.	Mrs. A. B. Hooper	82	1932	Askew - children
5.	Lucile Hooper	2	1891	" - bro. & sister
6.	Beulah B. Griffin	7	1896	Ms Carrie Griffin - mo.
7.	Ross Thomas			Ms Ross Thomas - wife
8.	Gilbert B. Griffin	50	1914	Carrie Griffin - wife
9.	Melinda Griffin	65	1900	" - dau.-in-law
10.	J. A. Lankford	62	1916	Alice Lankford - wife
11.	Blanche Jones	40	1927	G. B. Jones - husband
12.	Jessie Glenn Daniel	11	1917	Ms Chas. Daniel - mother
13.	Willie Jones	60	1926	Ms H.H. Hooper - sister
14.	Mary E. Jones	82	1910	G. B. Jones - g/son
15.	Billie Jones	82	1902	" - g/son
16.	Otho Thompson	unk	unk	W.H. Thompson - father
17.	Lottie Thompson	2	1906	" - father
18.	Unknown			
19.	Alice Hooper		1866	H.H. Hooper - bro.
20.	Bettie Hooper		1868	" - bro.
21.	Carrie Hooper		1890	" - bro.
22.	Unknown			
23.	Parker - un-identified	47	1858	
24.	Bula Carlew	3	1873	
25.	N. C. Hooper	58	1872	H. W. Hooper - son
26. - 27.	Unknown			
28.	George H. Madden	11	1893	E. R. Madden - father
29. - 31.	Unknown			
32.	Hadley H. Hooper	36	1922	H.H. Hooper - bro.
33.	Sara G. Hooper	31	unk	" - bro.
34.	Hooper infant	infant		" - uncle
35. - 37.	Unknown			
38.	Lote Garland			
39.	Clent Hambret			
40.	Unknown			

* *

41.	George Thompson	unk	1920	W.H. Thompson - father
42.	Lessie Horner Thompson	20	1927	J.R. Horner - father
43.	Lottie Thompson	77	1923	T.C. Thompson - son
?	Michael Shaver		1900	Clyde Shaver - bro.

See Plat Map #33

#34 WASSON CEMETERY

Located on Land Map 139, GIR-5103, 24 graves. This cemetery is located about one-fourth mile north east of the county road on property of Mrs. S.F. Perry's heirs. It is fenced and in fair condition.

No.	Name of Deceased	Date of Birth	Date of Death
1.	Gladys Hargrove	21 Apr 1920	21 Apr 1920
2.	Alma Jewell Lipps	23 July 1924	24 July 1924
3.	Sallie D. Wasson w/o J.F.	25 Apr 1847	3 Oct 1914
4.	J. F. Wasson	3 Aug 1844	3 July 1915
5.	John L. Thompson	23 July 1847	7 Oct 1918
		husband of Olivia A. Smith	
6.	Unknown		
7.	D. Byron Rose	22 Nov 1833	5 Apr 1872
		son of N & E Rose	husband of S.D. Rose
8.	Mary T. Smith	2 Dec 1851	7 Apr 1871
		bn of M.S. & S.E.D. Smith	
9.	Mortimer J. Smith	25 July 1845	22 Apr 1870
		son of M.S. & S.E.D. Smith	
10.	Elizabeth Smith	14 Mar 1792	28 Oct 1848
		mother of M. Stephen Smith	
11.	M. Stephen Smith	3 Sep 1807	7 Nov 1865
		husband of S.E.D. Smith	
12.	S. E. D. Smith	7 Aug 1813	27 Oct 1875
		wife of M. S. Smith	
13. - 15.	Unknown		
16.	Hallie I Smith		7 Oct 1872
		dau. of Q.C. & Mary Smith	
17.	Louisa G. Smith	11 May 1860	26 Aug 1861
		dau. of M.S. & S.E.D. Smith	
18.	Celestia B. Smith	7 Nov 1857	27 Oct 1858
		dau. of M.S. & S.E.D. Smith	
19.	Trianna Smith	14 Jan 1844	14 Jan 1844
		dau. of M.S. & S.E.D. Smith	

* *

20.	Olevia V. Smith	11 Apr 1839	14 Oct 1843
		dau. of M.S. & S.E.D. Smith	
21.	William A. Smith	14 Dec 1833	17 Aug 1851
		son of M.S. & S.E.D. Smith	
22.	John T. Smith	14 Mar 1835	2 July 1861
		son of M.S. & S.E.D. Smith	
23.	Flavius Josephus Smith	16 Aug 1848	4 June 1889
		son of M.S. & S.E.D. Smith	
24.	Elmer Thomas	7 June 1882	25 Nov 1884
		dau. of C.J. & T.A. Thomas	

#35 UNION CHAPEL CEMETERY

Located on Land Map 135, Tract GIR-5472, above elevation 380, 141 graves. This was an active but poorly kept cemetery. Six graves and five monuments were movd to three reinterment cemeteries. Eighty-five remain permits were executed. The remaining fifty graves could not be identified or no one could be found who was interested in having them moved. Removal operations were completed on August 9, 1943.

No.	Name of Deceased	Age	Date of Death	Information given by...

* *

No.	Name of Deceased	Age	Date of Death
1.	Unknown		
2.	Charlie Whitten	infant	1917
3.	Charles L. McGee	42	1935
4.	Frank J. McGee	12	1905
5.	Wesley Littleton		1923
6.	No Grave		
7.	Littleton infant	infant	1923
8.	Mrs. Emma Littleton		1924
9.	Unknown		
10.	Nix infant		1916
11.	Patterson infant		1918
12.	Landice Bryant		1918
13.	R. S. Knight		1879
14.	Everett Knight		1883
15.	Martha T. Knight		1885
16.	Mrs. M. C. Knight		1896
17.	Knight infant		1896
18.	Rev. R. T. Knight		1905
19.	Maggie Knight		1908
20. - 21.	Unknown		
22.	Aston Cooley		1918
23.	Lena M. Cooley		1901
24.	D. A. Cooley		1905
25.	Leon Cooley		1914
26.	Mattie Cooley		1911

* *

27.	Harold Cooley	1916
28.	Wynn infant	1905
29.	John Carrell	1894
30.	James Henry Cude	1926
31.	Mrs. J. H. Cude	1908
32.	Sarah H. Cude	1878
33.	Francis E. Lancaster	1875
34.	Jessie E. Cude	1918
35. - 38.	Unknown	
39.	Mrs. James Cotham	unk
40.	James Cotham	unk
41. - 42.	Unknown	
43.	Williams infant	1900
44.	Lucindy Williams	1919
45.	W. M. Williams	1890
46.	W. F. Williams	1917
47.	Paul McKeel	1893
48.	Thomas Colyer	1902
49.	Mary Davidson	1923
50.	Mrs. W. H. McCord	1890
51.	Luda E. Holland	1918
52.	John W. Holland	1923
53.	Mrs. John W. Holland	1939
54.	Maud Holland	1939
55.	William Bolton	1885
56.	Mrs. William Bolton	unk
57.	Dollie Carter	1878
58.	Mrs. J. M. Carter	1880
59.	J. M. Carter	1880
60.	Mrs. Beck Flannery	1881
61. - 70.	Unknown	
71.	Mary L. Blazer	1904
72.	Thomas Blazer	1918
73.	W. R. Holland	1941
74. - 76.	Unknown	
77.	Cassus N. Bonnerman	1875
78.	Unknown	
79.	Annie Pierpont	1898
80.	Larkin Pierpont	1910
81. - 82.	Unknown	
83.	Cooley infant	1902
84.	Cooley infant	1895
85.	Margrett Cooley	1856
86. - 87.	Unknown	
88.	David E. Cooley	1937

* *

89.	Mrs. D. D. Cooley		1932
90.	D. D. Cooley		1895
91.	Marie M. McKeel		1900
92.	Marjorie Binkley		
93.	John Cooley		1882
94.	George Albert Binkley		
95.	Mrs. Anna Binkley		
96.	R. T. Hall		
97.	Ruby May Hall		
98. - 99.			
100.	Charolett Lattimer		1932
101.	Noel Ellis	10	1919
102.	Ellis infant	infant	1911
103.	Mrs. J. E. Ellis		1906
104.	J. E. Ellis		1863
105. - 107.	Unknown		
108.	M. M. Cooley		1875
109.	Unknown		
110.	Alfred Holland		1907
111.	Paul Martin		1904
112.	Mrs. Leah M. Holland		1904
113.	Martha Herrington		unk
114.	Catherine Tucker		1908
115.	Tucker infant twins		1912
116.	W. R. Flannary		unk
117. - 118.	Unknown		
119.	Mrs. R. W. Cooley		1869
120.	R. E. Cooley		1868
121.	Cooley infant		unk
122. - 126.	Unknown		
127.	Margaret Jewel York		1911
128.	Martin infant		1885
129.	Martin infant		1880
130.	Martin infant		1882
131.	Martin infant		1879
132.	Nannie E. Martin		1934
133.	Eddie F. Martin		1936
134.	Unknown		
135.	J. T. Vetter		1918
136.	Willie Ray Littleton		1900
137.	Stella Gray Littleton		1905
138.	Roberta Mae Rainey		1920
139.	Mayce Rebecca Littleton		1933
140. - 141.	Unknown		
?	Colley infant		1912

* *

#36 LUCAS CEMETERY

Located on Land Map 139, Tract GIR-5089, located between elevation 379 and 381, 4 graves. This was an active and fairly well kept cemetery. All graves were identified and removal permits were executed. The graves and two monuments were moved to Wyley Cemetery No. R-60 on June 11, 1943.

No.	Name of Deceased	Age	Date of Death	Information given by...

* *

No.	Name of Deceased	Age	Date of Death
1.	Nimrod Lucas	22 Apr 1905	20 Oct 1921
2.	Willie Dewey Lucas	12 Sept 1898	15 Dec 1918
3.	Lou Ella Lucas	1877	Jan 1929
4.	John Lucas	1851	Jan 1929

Information was received from Coleman Lucas, son of John and Lou Ella Lucas and brother to Nimrod and Willie Dewey Lucas.

See Plat Map #36

#37 BOX CEMETERY

Located on Land Map 137, Tract No. 1, elevation 380-388 feet, 17 graves. Seventeen remain permits were executed. Four of these permits were on the graves of persons known to have been buried here but the exact location of the graves was unknown.

No.	Name of Deceased	Age	Date of Death	Information given by...

* *

No.	Name of Deceased	Age	Date of Death	Information given by...
1.	Mason Box	20	1883	Betty Tomlinson, cousin
2.	Henry A. Box	23	1864	" - niece
3.	Washington H. Box	30	1864	" - niece
4.	Box infants (2)		1874	" - sister
5.	Mason Box	56	1861	" - niece
6.	Elizabeth M. Box			" - g/daug.
7.	Lee Box	infant	1875	M.A. & E.W. Box, pts
8.	Laural Box	6	1875	" - parents
9.	David O. Box	1	1872	" - parents
10.	Mason Box	infant	1878	" - parents
11.	Nancy Mitchell Box	72	1882	Betty Tomlinson, niece
?	Dan A. Stewart	60	1910	Don A. Stewart - son
?	Ed Stewart	18	1910	Cal Stewart - bro.
?	Willie Stewart	24	1895	" - bro
?	Willis Hughs			Dr. Mary H. Elliott, dau
?	Ida Hughs	infant	1895	" - sister
?	Tom Stewart	18	1898	Cal Stewart - bro

* *

#38 TURNER CEMETERY #1

Located on Land Map 139, Detail #4, two graves, above elevation 380 feet, therefore, no identification of graves and data relative to kinship was obtained. dThe cemetery is found one-half mile west of a thirty foot county road on the property of C.W. Turner and A. V. Anderson. The following information was taken from Field Book #MS 640.

No.	Name of Deceased	Date of Birth	Date of Death
1.	James H. Turner	11 Oct 1834	23 Aug 1907
2.	Alice F. Turner	7 June 1854	31 Oct 1916

See Plat Map #38

#39 TURNER CEMETERY #2

Located on Land Map 139, Detail #7, 4 graves, above elevation 380. No identification of graves and data relative to kinship was obtained. The following does appear in Field Book MS-640 as taken from metal or stone grave markers.

No.	Name of Deceased	Date of Birth	Date of Death
1.	Susie D. Turner	25 June 1899 dau. of Mollie Turner	13 Sep 1906
2.	Henry Turner		27 Sep 1923
3. - 4.	Unknown		

See Plat Map #39

#41 OLD REYNOLDSBURG CEMETERY

Located on land Map 140, Tract No. 5, betwen elevation 371 - 385, 163 graves. This was a very old abandoned cemetery, containing 97 white and 66 colored graves. None of the graves could be identified. Mrs. Julia Goodwin, who had a number of relatives buried here, asked that all the graves be moved out of the affected area. All white graves were moved to Hill Orchard Cemetery R-83, and alld the colored graves to Gragg Cemetery R-94. Removal operations were completed April 2, 1943.

No.	Name of Deceased	Age	Date of Death	Information given by...
1. - 163.	Unknown			
?	Caroline Leach	60	1900	Walter Young - nephew
?	Dinah Young	80	1880	" - g/son
?	Henry Young	60	1890	" - g/son
?	Eddie Allen	18	1900	Boyd Allen - bro.
?	Belle Allen			" - bro.
?	Betty Wells	39	1892	" - bro.
?	Lonnie Wells	38	1932	John Wells - bro.
?	Henry Wells	65	1910	" - son

* *

#42 NAPIER CEMETERY

Located on Land Map 140, Tract No. 3, above elevation 380, 44 graves. This was an active but poorly kept cemetery. Remain permits were executed on 29 graves. One removal permit was executed, and the grave was moved to Ebenezer Cemetery R-100 on June 15, 1943. The remaining 14 graves could not be identified or no one could be found who was interested in having them moved.

No.	Name of Deceased	Age	Date of Death	Information given by...

* *

No.	Name of Deceased	Age	Date of Death
1.	Betty Lou Collins		1937
2.	James Horton Hughes		1939
3.	Ruby Hughes		1930
4.	Garfield Smith		1933
5.	Leonard Smith		1936
6.	Webster Smith		1912
7.	Nancy E. Smith		1916
8.	Bessie Webb		1918
9.	Smith infant twins		1925
10.	Smith infant		1927
11.	Smith infant		1934
12.	Unknown		
13.	Sadie Smith		1921
14.	Smith infant twins		1913
15.	Smith infant		unk
16.	Smith infant		1905
17.	Smith infant		1912
18.	Ida May Smith		1909
19.	Smith infant		1910
20.	Callie Smith		1910
21.	Smith infant		1907
22.	Florence Smith & child		1911
23.	Etter Smith		unk
24.	Max Standridge		1935
25.	Lewis Standridge		1927
26.	Gamble infant		unk
27.	J. L. Nix		1922
28.	Mary Ellen Nix		1920
29.	Mildred Stewart	1	1935
30.	Robert Dailey		1926
31.	Dailey infant		1933
32.	Jim Wyly		unk
33.	Tom Wyly		unk
34. - 38.	Unknown		
39.	Missie Eyly Lucas		1854
40. - 44.	Unknown		

See Plat Map #42

* *

#43 LUCAS CEMETERY

Located on Land Map 140, Tract GIR-5124, above elevation 380, 6 graves. This was a fairly active but poorly kept colored cemetery. All graves were identified and remain permits were executed.

No.	Name of Deceased	Age	Date of Death	Information given by...
1.	Harvey infant			Ms Bertha McWilliams - mo
2.	Alice Lucas		1905	Will Lucas - uncle
3.	Jane Ann Mason		1907	" - son
4.	Harriet Burgy		1907	" - g/son
5.	Griffort Burgy		1890	Nora Webb - dau.
6.	Susie Reagon		1912	Myrtle Wells - dau.

See Plat Map #43

#44 MARBERRY CEMETERY #2

Located on Land Map 143, tract No. 3, all above elevation 380, 6 graves. This was a very old abandoned cemetery. All graves were identified and remain permits executed.

No.	Name of Deceased	Age	Date of Death	Information given by...
1.	F. M. Marberry	unk	1896	Lucian Marberry - son
2.	Robinson Marberry			" - bro.
3.	Willie Marberry			" - bro.
4.	Ollie Marberry			" - bro.
5.	George Marberry			" - cousin
6.	Marberry infant	unk	unk	" - cousin

See Plat Map #44

* *

#45 AFRICAN METHODIST CHURCH CEMETERY

Located on Land Map 143-4, Tract GIR 6716, Elevation 380, 108 graves. This was an active but poorly kept colored cemetery, found on the Johnsville Colored Church property. Only 32 graves could be identified. Remain permits were executed on 94 graves. Sixty-two of these permits were on the graves of persons known to have been buried there but the exact location of the graves was unknown. No information could be obtained concerning the remaining 14 graves.

No.	Name of Deceased	Age	Date of Death	Information given by...
1. - 6.	Unknown			
7.	Tom Nelson	unk	unk	Edgar Nelson, nephew
8. - 9.	Unknown			
10.	Mrs. George Madison			Jim Wheeler, cousin
11.	George Madison			" - cousin
12.	Will Madison			" - cousin
13. - 15.	Unknown			
16.	Lucy Thomas		1905	Oro Grundy, niece
17.	Unknown			
18.	Allen Tubbs		1937	Ms Lizzie Tubbs, wife
19.	Albert Lomax		1936	Hubert Lomax, bro.
20.	Lou Marble		1928	Belle Long & Mollie Wheeler, sisters
21. - 25.	Unknown			
26.	Philis Long		1928	Oliver Long, husband
27.	James Phillips		1932	Earnest Phillips, son
28. - 29.	Unknown			
30.	Erlie Long		1936	Oliver Long, father
31.	Velma Wells		1936	Mary Wells, mother
32.	Molly Long		1934	Oliver Long, father
33.	Box infant		unk	T. B. Box, father
34.	Box infant		1930	" - father
35.	Box infant		1931	" - father
36.	Box infant		1934	" - father
37.	Barbara J. Box		1938	" - father
38.	Arthur Leon		1929	
39.	Burton Howard		1937	Maggie Howard, wife
40.	Charley Harvey		1928	Bertha McWilliams, step-d
41.	Dora Lucus		1935	" - daughter
42.	Albert Moore		1938	Tennessee Phillips, g/d
43. - 45.	Unknown			
46.	Andrew Green		1939	Lillian Green, wife
47.	George Wells		1940	Gertrue Anderson, sister
48.	Jewell Fortner		1932	George & Ora Grundy, pts
49.	Calvin Long		unk	Belle Long, sister
50. - 51.	Unknown			

* *

52.	Margrett Howard	1941	Maggie Howard, mother
53.	Monroe Bunch		
54.	Mrs. Monroe Bunch		
55. - 69.	Unknown		
70.	Ida Smith	1931	Bill Smith, son
71.	Howard Smith	1935	" - son
72. - 80.	Unknown		

The following graves could not be located:

?	Miranda Long	unk	Belle Long, g/d
?	Nancy Long		" - daug.
?	Lennie Long		" - sister
?	Georgia Taylor		" - sister
?	Joshua Cooper	1900	E. W. Cooper, g/son
?	Agnes Cooper	1910	" - g/son
?	Freddie Cooper	1918	" - father
?	Agnes Cooper	1910	" - father
?	Belle Cooper & infant	1911	" - husband & father
?	Gertrude Goodlow	1901	" - bro
?	Josh Cooper	1900	" - nephew
?	Clarence Cooper	1907	" - nephew
?	Ella Goodlow	1894	" - son
?	Richard Goodlow	1909	" - step-son
?	Hobart Box	1937	Coy & T.B. Box - bros.
?	Peter Box	1936	" - sons
?	Elizabeth Box	1917	" - sons
?	Almetta Box	1918	" - bros
?	Elec Box	1917	" - bros
?	Iaie Box	1920	" - bros
?	Edward Long	unk	Belle Long & Mollie
?	Edgar Long		Wheeler, sisters
?	Andrew Long		" - sisters
?	Florida Westfield	1880	Jim Wheeler, bro
?	Gilbert Westfield		" - stepson
?	Almetta Long		" - uncle
?	Ella Westfield	1890	" - half-bro.
?	Grundy infant	1902	Geo. & Ora Grundy, pts
?	Alsie Grundy	1883	George Grundy, son
?	Wiley Young	1920	Walter Young, son
?	Dinia Young	1890	" - bro.
?	Georgia Young	1922	" - son
?	Aurther Young	1907	" - bro.
?	Sam Young	1907	" - bro.
?	Lucy Long	1887	Oliver Long, bro
?	Lucy Long	1927	" - son

* *

?	Oran Long	1930	" - son
?	Oliver Long, Jr.	1929	" - father
?	Maudy McWilliams	unk	Alvin McWilliams, bro.
?	Helen McWilliams	1934	" - bro.
?	Julia McWilliams	1928	" - son
?	Ada Rhodes	1910	" - bro.
?	McWilliams infant	unk	" - bro.
?	Henry McWilliams	1900	" - son
?	George McMullen	1898	Robert Lewis, bro.
?	Dora McMullen	1895	" - bro.
?	Joridan McMullen	1913	" - step-son
?	Caroline McMullen	1900	" - son
?	William Coleman	1880	Ms Robert Lewis, sister
?	Overton Lewis	1899	" - mother
?	George Lewis	1891	" - mother
?	Blanche Lewis	1890	" - mother
?	Lewis Corns	1904	" - mother
?	Sam Coleman	Unk	" - step-daug.
?	Nancy Coleman	unk unk	" - daug.
?	Harriet Phifer	1902	Maggie Allen - daug.
?	Jonnie Phifer	1904	" - sister
?	Jerry Phifer	1900	" - daug.
?	Leslie Howard	1923	Maggie Howard - mother
?	Albert Howard	1925	" - mother
?	Tennessee Moore	1912	Tennessee Philips - g/d
?	Mary Williams	1910	Henry Williams - step-son
?	Rachel Williams	1875	" - son
?	Alec Williams	1900	" - son

#46 ROLLINS CEMETERY

Located on Land Map 133, Tract No. 1, above elevation 380, 9 graves. This was a very old abandoned cemetery. Remain permits were executed on the graves of four persons known to have been buried here, but none of the graves could be identified.

No.	Name of Deceased	Age	Date of Death	Information given by...

* *

?	Joe Walker			T. B. Box
?	Molly Walker			
?	Beatrice Walker			
	Al Walker			

* *

#47 WELLS CEMETERY

Located on Land Map 143-5, Tract GIR-6901, between elevation 380 - 400, 31 graves.
This was a fairly active but poorly kept cemetery, only six graves of which could
be identified. Eleven remain permits were executed. Five of these permits were on
the graves of persons known to have been buried here, but the exact location of the
graves was not known.

No.	Name of Deceased	Age	Date of Death	Information given by...

* *

No.	Name of Deceased	Age	Date of Death	Information given by...
1. - 20.	Unknown			
21.	Dorthy Wells		1932	James Wells - father
22. - 23.	Unknown			
24.	Felmer Edwards		1925	Girtrue Anderson - wife
25.	Robert Wells		1920	John Wells - bro.
26.	Julian Wells		1928	" - father
27.	Unknown			
28.	Laura Wells		1930	" - son
29.	Della Wells		1930	" - husband
30.	Unknown			
?	Vina Page		1923	Gertie Anderson - step-d
?	Nancy Page		1920	" - step-dau.
?	Lucy Page		1913	" - g/g/dau.
?	Babe Gentry Wells		1930	" - niece
?	Green Page		1925	" - g/g/dau.

See Plat Map #47

#48 NELS ANDERSON CEMETERY

Located on Land Map 143-5, Tract GIR-6727, above elevation 380, 19 graves. This is
an active but poorly kept colored cemetery. All graves were identified and remain
permits executed.

No.	Name of Deceased	Age	Date of Death	Information given by...

* *

No.	Name of Deceased	Age	Date of Death	Information given by...
1.	Richard Williams		1922	Birtie Wells - sister
2.	Francie Williams		1927	" - sister
3.	Girtie Williams		1927	" - sister
4.	Mary Williams		1926	" - sister
5.	Frank Williams		1925	" - daug.
6.	Marendy Anderson		1905	Elmer Anderson - g/son
7.	Lizzie Williams		1916	Birtie Wells - dau.
8.	George Anderson		1905	Elmer Anderson - sister
9.	William Goodlow		1900	" - g/son
10.	Henry Williams		1914	Birtie Wells - sister

* *

11.	Williams infant	1905	" - sister
12.	Anderson infant	1905	" - aunt
13.	Hattie Anderson	1915	Emily Anderson - sister
14.	Frank Anderson	1923	" - sister
15.	Wardell Anderson	1933	" - sister
16.	Earnest Anderson	1928	" - sister
17.	Mollie Anderson	1925	" - dau.
18.	Nels Anderson	1935	" - sister
19.	William Anderson	1941	" - dau.

See Plat Map #48

#49 NO NAME CEMETERY

Located on Land Map 143, Tract GIR-5174, above elevation 380, 4 graves. Robert Lewis, aged colored man, remembered two men having been buried here about 70 years previously, but did not recall the names of these men. There were four depressions at this spot, but it is doubtful if there are more than two graves. No further action was necessary.

It is thought that the names of the two buried here are Joe French and Joe Lee.

#50 GOULD CEMETERY

Located on Land Map 144, tract No. 1, between elevation 380-381, 4 graves. Access was flooded. This was an active and well kept family cemetery. All graves, with monuments were moved to Wyley Cemetery R-60 on June 11, 1943.

No.	Name of Deceased	Age	Date of Death	Information given by...

1.	A. Grisby Gould	13	1921	Ella M. Gould - mother
2.	Gould infant	infant	1907	" - mother
3.	Virginia Gould	3	1929	Ella M. Gould - g/mother
4.	G. G. Gould	77	1940	" - wife

See Plat Map #50

#51 WINTERS CEMETERY

Located on land Map 144, Tract GIR-5207F, all above elevation 380, 3 graves. All graves were identified and remain permits were executed.

No.	Name of Deceased	Age	Date of Death	Information given by...

1.	Violet Cagle	36	1930	J. Cagle - husband
2.	Winters infant	infant	1920	Walter Winters - father
3.	Winters infant	infant	1920	" - father

* *

#52 NO NAME CEMETERY

Located on Land Map 143, Tract GIR-5174, above elevation 380, two graves. According
to Robert Lewis, aged colored man, of Johnsonville, TN, a number of guerilla
soldiers were buried here during the Civil War. He also stated that several of the
graves wre moved after the war. None of the graves could be identified, and no one
could be found who was interested in having them moved.

#58 JOHNSONVILLE CEMETERY

Located on Land Map 143-4, Tract GIR-6694, above elevation 380, 28 graves. This was a
fairly active, but poorly kept cemetery. Remain permits were executed on 19 graves.
Ten of these permits were on the graves of persons known to have been buried here,
but exact location of the graves was unknown. The remaining nine graves could not be
identified or no living relative could be found.

No.	Name of Deceased	Age	Date of Death	Information given by...
1.	Unknown			
2.	Bedford Branch	40	1930	Ed Branch – nephew
3.	Unknown			
4.	Brigham infant			Ms Eller Graham – mother
5.	Brigham infant			" – mother
6.	Evans infant			Ms Curtis Reynolds – mo
7.	Albert Brigham	1	1928	Sam Brigham – father
8.	Ford Gould Brigham	1	1930	" – father
9.	James M. Davidson	26	1932	Ms Ola Stricklin – dau.
10.	Mrs. James M. Davidson			Ms Sam Stricklin – dau.
11.	Ruth Davidson			" – aunt
12. – 19.	Unknown			
20.	Ida J. Troutman	18	1864	J.T. & M.L. Winfrey – pts
21.	John T. Green	44	1912	
22. – 28.	Unknown			
?	Martin Gossett			John Gossett – son
?	Rachel Gossett			" – son
?	Allen Gossett			" – bro.
?	Sallie Gossett			" – bro-in-law
?	Virginia Gossett			" – bro.
?	Gossett infant			" – bro.
?	Wyandotte Johnson		1881	A.M. Johnson – bro.
?	Armistead M. Johnson		1879	" – bro.
?	Mae West Johnson		1878	" – bro.
?	Hazelwood Johnson		1880	" – bro.

* *

?	Lucien Balsh	1918	Ms Eva Nalley – wife
?	Charles Balsh	1919	" – dau.-in-law
?	Eddie Everett Martin	1907	" – sister
?	Lyra Faye Martin	1900	" – sister
?	Wyley Martin	1899	" – sister
?	C. A. Heath	1900	Reid Heath – son

See Plat Map #58

#63 MASSEY CEMETERY

Located on Land Map 143, Tract No. 3, above elevation 380, 6 graves. All graves were identified and remain permits executed. A monument is located at the former grave of a person whose body was moved from this cemetery to Fulton, Kentucky in 1902.

No.	Name of Deceased	Age	Date of Death	Information given by...

* *

1.	Mary E. Massey		1878	Jim D. Massey – nephew
2.	John Massey		1901	" – son
3.	Betty Massey		1879	" – nephew
4.	Mrs. Bill Massey		1882	" – g/son
5.	Bill Massey		1901	" – g/son

See Plat Map #63

#65 LARKINS CEMETERY

Located on Land Map 161, Tract GIR-6204, elevation 369, 15 graves. This was a very old abandoned cemetery. Remain permits were executed on all graves, only two of which could be identified. Thirteen of these permits were on the graves of persons known to have been buried here, but the exact location of the graves was unknown.

No.	Name of Deceased	Age	Date of Death	Information given by...

* *

1. - 13.	Unknown			
14.	Margaret Cooley		1875-1876	Wilson A. Larkins – g/son
14.	William T. Cooley		Unk	" – g/son
?	Sam Larkins		1898	" – son
?	Mary Larkins		1868	" – son
?	Sally Larkins		1882-1883	" – step-son
?	James Larkins		1891-1892	" – half-bro.
?	Bud Larkins		1875-1876	" – bro.
?	Missie Larkins		1868	" – bro.
?	Ms Willie O'Guinn		1896	" – bro.
?	Martha T. Larkins		unk	" – bro.
?	Hugh Larkins		1877-1878	" – half-bro.
?	Larkins unidentified		unk	" – nearest

See Plat Map #65

* *

#71 LONE GRAVE

Located on Land Map 170, tract GIR-6151, 1 grave. This grave was on the river bank, and below elevlation 359. The grave could not be identified, but E. C. Denslow, the property owner requested that it be moved out of the flooded area. The grave was moved to Ebenezer Cemetery R-100 on June 15, 1943.

#723 E. D. HOOPER CEMETERY

Located on Land Map 128, Tract GIR-5599, two graves. Found one mile east of the Clydeton-Danville Road on the property of E. D. Hooper in an open pasture. One of the graves has a small house over it.

No.	Name of Deceased	Age	Date of Death	Information given by...
1.	Coleman Mulley Hooper	infant	1918	C.F. Hooper – father
2.	Robert Wheeler	infant	1934	Henry Wheeler – father

#724 LASHLEE SLAVE CEMETERY

Located on Land Map 128, Tract GIR-5577, below elevation 399, 30 graves. This was a very old abandoned cemetery. None of the graves could be identified. O. W. Lashlee, a member of the Lashlee family who owned a number of slaves buried in the cemetery, requested that the graves be moved out of the flooded area. All graves were moved to Hill Orchard Cemetery R-83. Removal operations were completed April 6, 1943.

#725 MASON CEMETERY

Found on Land Map 128, Tract GIR-5576, above elevation 380, one grave. This was a very old grave, and no one could be found who could identify the grave or was interested in having it moved.

#726 LUTEN CEMETERY

Located on Land Map 129, Tract GIR-5603, above elevation 380, 5 graves. This was an inactive and poorly kept cemetery. Remain permits were executed on four graves. The remaining grave could not be identified.

No.	Name of Deceased	Age	Date of Death	Information given by...
1.	Dorsey W. Luten	33	1889	J. D. Luten – bro.
2.	G. H. Dreaden	22	1910	Tom Dreaden – bro.
3.	W. D. Dreaden	25	1910	" – bro.
4.	Unknown			
5.	Dovie Hooper & infant	unk	1902	James Hooper – hus. & ft

* *

#727 LUTEN CEMETERY

Located on Land Map 129, Tract GIR-5608, below elevation 369, 21 graves. This was an old abandoned colored cemetery. None of the grave could be identified. John Ike Brigham, whose family owned a number of slaves who were buried there, asked that the graves be moved out of the affected area. All graves were moved to Hill Orchard Cemetery R-83. Removal operations were completed April 6, 1943.

No.	Name of Deceased	Age	Date of Death	Information given by...

* *

1. - 21. Unknown

No.	Name of Deceased	Age	Date of Death	Information given by...
?	Ethel Lashlee	infant	1900	Susan Simpson - mother
?	Charles Turner	23	1890	"
?	Lige Griffin	21	1890	"
?	Lige Turner	86	1920	
?	Mary Lashlee	75	1927	Riley Brigham - nephew
?	Tom Lashlee	70	1928	" - nephew
?	Burl Turner	child	1908	Dixie Turner - sister
?	Anna Moe Turner	infant	1908	" - sister
?	Pearlie Turner	infant	1912	" - sister
?	Elliott Turner	child	1900	" - sister
?	Rosie Turner	2	1875	John Ike Brigham - neph
?	Nancy Turner	25	1875	" - nephew
?	Bob Woods	16	1896	
?	Israel Woods	18	1912	
?	Betty Turner	21	1890	
?	Turner children (2)			Lee Turner - father

#729 REEVES CEMETERY

Located on Land Map 133, Tract No. 1, above elevation 380, nine graves. This was a very old abandoned cemetery. Remain permits were executed on the graves of four persons known to have been buried here, but none of the graves could be identified.

No.	Name of Deceased	Age	Date of Death	Information given by...

* *

No.	Name of Deceased	Age	Date of Death	Information given by...
?	Richard Lemox			Ms M.E. Ham - wife
?	Lemox infant			" - mother
?	Mrs. Lemox			" - dau.-in-law
?	Wash Beavers			

#730 COOLEY CEMETERY

This is a very old, overgrown cemetery. Diligent inquiries has failed to find any one connected with those buried here, except to say they are "Cooleys". Cal Cooley, age 84, of Waverly, TN grew up in the neighborhood and knew nothing of those buried here more than they were Cooleys.

* *

#731 McGEE CEMETERY

Located on Land Map 135, Detail C, three graves.

No.	name of Deceased	Age	Date of Death	Information given by...
* * *	* * * * * * * * *	* *	* * * * * *	* * * * * * * *
1.	Mrs. Daisy McGee	30	1920	J. A. McGee - husband
2.	James L. McGee	3	1925	" - father
3.	William J. McGee	2	1926	" - father

#738 SUTTON CEMETERY

Located on Land Map 143-4, Tract GIR-5426, above elevation 380, 13 graves. This was a very old abandoned family cemetery. All graves from No. 5 - 13 inclusive, were intended to have been buried on the property of African Methodist Cemetery, but the exact location of the graves was unknown. Graves No. 1 - 4 inclusive were identified as the graves of members of the Sutton family, but no trace of the relatives could be found. No further action was necessary.

No.	Name of Deceased	Age	Date of Death	Information given by...
* *	* * * * * * * * * *	* *	* * * * * *	* * * * * * * *
1.	Mrs. Joe Sutton			Joe Sutton - husband
2. - 3.	Sutton infants			" - father
4.	Charles Sutton		1864	" - father
5. - 13.	Unknown			

See Plat Map #738

#739 HOPSON CEMETERY

Located on Land Map 143-5, Tract GIR-5364, between elevation 361-362, 9 graves. This was an abandoned and poorly kept colored cemetery. All graves were identified and remain permits executed.

No.	Name of Deceased	Age	Date of Death	Information given by...
* *	* * * * * * * * *	* *	* * * * * *	* * * * * * * *
1.	Long child			Sarah Hopson
2.	Mariah E. Williams			" - daug.
3.	George Williams			" - daug.
4.	Winnie Williams			" - step-daug.
5.	Polly Williams	18	unk	" - sister
6. - 9.	Williams infants			" - aunt

See Plat Map #739

* *

#740 CROCKETT CEMETERY

Located on land Map 143, Tract GIR-6688, above elevation 380, 156 graves. This was an active cemetery but poorly kept. Remain permits were executed on 94 graves. Two of these permits were on the graves of persons known to have been buried here, but the exact location of the graves was unknown. The remaining 62 graves could not be identified or no one could be found who was interested in having them moved.

No.	Name of Deceased	Age	Date of Death	Information given by...
* * * * *	* * * * * * * * * * * *	* * *	* * * * * * *	* * * * * * * * * * *
1. - 3.	Unknown			
4. - 11.	Lamastus un-identified			Pete Lee, nearest
12.	Smith un-identified			
13.	Jacob L. D. Smith		1895	" - nearest
14.	Putman Plant		1901	" - nephew
15.	Martha Plant	unk		" - g/son
16.	L. D. Plant	unk		" - g/son
17.	Charlie Lee		1884	" - bro.
18.	Lee infant		1880	" - bro.
19.	Elizabeth Lee		1885	" - bro.
20.	Fred O'Dell Lee		1892	" - bro.
21.	Harry Lee		1895	" - bro.
22.	Emma Lee		1901	" - bro.
23.	George W. Lee		1939	" - son
24.	Emma C. Lee		1901	" - son
25.	Jennie Lee		1903	" - bro.
26.	Mary W. McKelvy		1906	" - bro.
27.	Freddie Lumphred		1912	Ola Strickland, aunt
28.	Jim Elvington		1912	John Elvington - son
29.	Elizabeth Elvington		1902	" - step-son
30.	Warren infant		1935	R. S. Warren - father
31.	Henry Lee		1905	Pete Lee - nephew
32.	Buster Lee		1902	" - cousin
33.	Mrs. Henry Lee		1912	" - nephew
34. - 35.	Unknown			
36.	Susan Warren		1910	Ms M.D.Elvington, dau
37.	Jessie Warren		1911	" - sister
38. - 39.	Unknown			
40.	Louise Warren			Victoria Warren, mother
41.	Warren infant			" - mother
42.	Warren infant			" - mother
43. - 44.	Unknown			
45.	Robert Elvington		1931	Eva Elvington, wife
46.	Lester Elvington		1894	John Elvington, father
47.	Oneta Elvington		1895	" - father

*   *

48.	Mable Elvington		1897	" - father
49.	Alma Elvington		1898	" - father
50. - 52.	Unknown			
53.	Billy Webb			Will Webb, father
54.	Claude Brown Webb		1911	Ms C.B. Webb, mother
55.	George Herbert Webb		1931	" - mother
56.	Charles B. Webb		1931	" - wife
57.	Grady Alberta Chance		1933	Grady Chance - father
58. - 65.	Unknown			
66.	Nancy Parlee Smith			Ms W. C. Curtis - dau.
67.	Edwards un-identified			Jim Edwards - husband
68.	Edwards infant			" - father
69.	Robert A. Smith			Ms W.C. Curtis - daug
70.	Smith infant			" - mother
71.	Smith infant			" - mother
72.	Florice O. Crawford		1922	Ms John Hassell - sister
73.	Vera M. Crawford		1921	" - sister
74. - 81.	Unknown			
82.	Frank Crafton			Horace Crafton - son
83. - 93.	Unknown			
94.	Omer S. Crafton		1938	" - bro.
95.	Don B. Crafton		1918	Ms Ola Strickland - wife
96.	Davis Crafton		1937	Bettie Crafton - wife
97. - 99.	Unknown			
100.	James Howe	infant	1934	Dick Howe - father
101. - 105.	Unknown			
106.	T. Corbitt		1936	Bettie M. Corbitt - wife
107.	Andrew Jackson Parlee		1920	Ms E.L.Ledbetter - wife
108.	Frankie Sharpe		1918	Malvena Parish - daug.
109.	A. J. Parker, Jr.		1921	Ms E.L.Ledbetter - mother
110.	J. E. Parker			Will Parker - son
111.	Kizzie L. Parker			" - son
112.	Nancy Ann Stricklin		1927	Ethel Townsend - dau
113.	J. M. Bibb		1919	Ms Media Fuller - wife
114.	Sam Stricklin		1931	Ethel Townsend - dau
115.	Cecil Bibb		1920	Media Fuller - mother
116.	Jackson Crockett		1879	W. G. Crockett - g/son
117.	Martha J. Crockett		1884	" - g/son
118.	Mrs. M.J. Winfrey		1899	" - nephew
119.	Harry Crockett		1902	" - bro.
120.	Clay Crockett		1902	" - bro.
121.	Mrs. Adda Crockett		1940	" - son
122.	W. G. Crockett		1913	" - son
123.	Virginia Crockett		1909	" - bro.
124.	Clara Elizabeth Sharpe			Eugene Sharpe - son

* *

125.	John Plant	1916	Amelia Cagle - wife
126.	G. W. Miller	1916	" - dau.
127.	Martha Miller	1910	Ms F.D. Lofton - dau
128.	Unknown		
129.	Cletie Juaneta Chance	1929	Ms E.L. Chance - mother
130.	Lucy Miller	1928	Jim Miller - bro.
131.	Howard Miller	1922	" - father
132.	Hester Miller	1918	" - son
133.	Unknown		
134.	James Miller	1925	" - son
135. - 138. Unknown			
139.	Mary Jane Russell	1911	Ms A.G. Scott - dau
140.	Unknown		
141.	G. W. Russell	1922	" - dau.
142.	Unknown		
143.	Stella Lofton	1899	Walter Lofton - bro.
144.	Harry G. Lofton	1887	" - bro.
145.	Unknown		
146.	Frank D. Lofton	1940	Ms F.D. Lofton - wife
147.	Jerry Lofton		Beadie Lyell - sister
148.	Unknown		
149.	Orson Lofton	1900	Ms F.D. Lofton - mother
150.	Willie Criss	1906	Amelia Cagle - wife
151.	Betty Mae Lofton	unk	Ms F.D. Lofton - mother
152.	Lofton infant twins	unk	" - mother
153.	Howard Lofton	1902	" - mother
154.	Frank Lofton	1901	" - mother
155.	Lofton infant	unk	" - mother
156.	William Clarence Daniel	1942	W.E. Daniel - father
157. - 160. Unknown			
?	Crigg infant	1906	Amelia Cagle - mother
?	Eulah C. Crafton	1917	Ms Ola Stricklin - mother

See Plat Map #740

* *

#741 WILLIAMS CEMETERY

Lcoated on Land Map 143-5, Tract GIR-6365, above elevation 380, 8 graves. This was a fairly active but poorly kept cemetery. All graves were identified and remain permits executed.

No.	Name of Deceased	Age	Date of Death	Information given by...
1.	Manuel Williams		1930	Sarah Hopson - sister
2.	Amanda Williams		1936	" - sister
3.	Cal Smith			T. B. Box - nephew
4.	Chonie Smith			" - nephew
5.	Lila Box			Coy & T.B. Box - g/chld
6.	Jane Cumack			" - nephews
7.	Missie Box			" - nephews
8.	Ann Haynes			" - nephews

#751 VAN HOOK CEMETERY

Located on Land Map 171, Tract No. 1, above elevation 380, 10 graves. This was an old abandoned cemetery. Only one grave could be identified. Remain permits were executed on two graves. One of these permits was on the grave of a person known to have been buried here, but the exact location of the grave was not known.

No.	Name of Deceased	Age	Date of Death	Information given by...
1.	Unknown			
2.	W. B. VanHook		1888	Ms C.B. Wofford - sister
3. - 10.	Unknown			
?	Leslie VanHook		1885	" - sister
?	Dave VanHook			" - father
?	Mrs. Lizzie VanHook			" - mother
?	Allie VanHook			" - sister
?	Doss VanHook			" - sister

#792 PRIMM CEMETERY

Located on Land Map 157, Tract GIR-6546, above elevation 380, three graves. This was an old abandoned family cemetery, now enclosed in a barn lot. All graves were identified and remain permits executed.

No.	Name of Deceased	Age	Date of Death	Information given by...
1.	Billy Primm		1880	J.M. Reeves - cousin
2.	Mrs. Billy Primm		1890	" - cousin
3.	Story infant		1887	Allen Story - bro.

* *

#804 PHIFFER CEMETERY

Located on Land Map 128, Tract GIR 5579, above elevation 380, 3 graves. This was an old abandoned family cemetery. All graves were identified and remain permits executed.

No.	Name of Deceased	Age	Date of Death	Information given by...

* *

No.	Name of Deceased	Age	Date of Death	Information given by...
1.	Beatrice A. Phifer	20	1899	Thomas B. Phifer - bro.
2.	Mrs. D. G. Phifer (w/o #3)	45	1898	" - step-son
3.	T. P. Phifer	68	1913	" - son

#816 WAGGONER CEMETERY

Located on Land Map 148, above 380 elevation, 19 graves. The following information appears only in Field Book MS-645. The graves are all Waggoners, according to Pott Waggoner.

No.	Name of Deceased	Age	Date of Death	Information given by...

* *

No.	Name of Deceased	Age	Date of Death	Information given by...
1.	George W. Waggoner	61		Pott Waggoner - bro.
2. - 3.	Unknown			
4.	Martin A. Waggoner	75	1880	" - nephew
5.	Sallie E. Waggoner	27		
6.	Unknown			
7.	George W. Waggoner, Sr.	62	1873	" - son
8.	Lamira E. Waggoner	45	1882	
9.	Henry Marable Waggoner	70	1940	
10. - 12.	Unknown			
13.	Martin Q. Waggoner	75		
14.	Unknown			
15.	John G. Waggoner	35	1863	
16. - 19.	Unknown			
?	Maggie Waggoner			
?	Henry Waggoner			
?	Will Waggoner			
?	Waggoner infant			" - father

See Plat Map #816

* *

#817 MASSEY CEMETERY

Located on Land Map 148, tract GIR-6351F, 2 graves. These two graves are marked by monuments and the following information came from Field Book MS-645.

No.	Name of Deceased	Age	Date of Death	Information given by...

* *

1.	H. H. Massey	75	1881	
2.	Nancy Massey	72	1881	

#849 CUMACK, WASHINGTON GRAVE

Located on Land Map 143-5, Tract GIR-5367, elevation 365, 1 grave. This was identified as that of Washington Cumack, a colored man, and a remain permit was executed by Coy and T. B. Box, nephews

See Plat Map #849

#862 HOLLAND CEMETERY

Located on Land Map 130, Tract GIR-5554, below elevation 370, 15 graves. This was a very old abandoned cemetery, located in an open pasture. None of the graves could be identified. J. O. Baugus who owned the surrounding property, requested that all the graves be moved out of the flooded area. They were moved to Cragg Cemetery R-49 on March 30, 1943.

No.	Name of Deceased	Age	Date of Death	Information given by...

* *

1. - 15. Unknown

?	Holland infant	infant	1900	Alice Stanfield - sister
?	Minnie Holland	unk	unk	J. H. Holland - bro.
?	Sally Davidson	unk	1890	Alice Stanfield - g/d
?	Davidson un-identified	unk	unk	J. H. Holland - g/s

See Plat Map #862

* *

#869 RAGAN CEMETERY

Located on Land Map 143-5, Tract GIR-6726, above elevation 380, seven graves. This was a fairly active but poorly kept family cemetery. Remain permits were executed on six graves, only three of which could be identified. Three of these permits were on the graves of persons known to have been buried here, but the exact location of the graves was not known.

No.	Name of Deceased	Age	Date of Death	Information given by...
1.	John Reagon		1942	Myrtle Wells - dau.
2.	Hobart Reagon		1937	" - child
3.	Viola Wells		1936	Annie Wells - mother
?	Rosalee Reagon		1922	Myrtle Wells - sister
?	Maria Reagon			" - g/dau.
?	Solomon Reagon			" - g/dau.
?	John Reagon			Lyman Reagon - father

#870 OLD SOLDIERS CEMETERY

Located approximately 3 miles east of the Tennessee River on U.S. Highway No. 70. This cemetery was outside the limits of the reservoir land surveys and was not affected by the lake, but was crossed by the relocation of the L. & N. Railroad. This was a very old abandoned Civil War Soldiers Cemetery, enclosed in a hog lot. None of the graves could be identified. Mrs. Julia Harrison, the property owner, signed a permit requesting that all the affected graves be moved. One hundred and ninety-nine graves were moved to the unaffected part of the cemetery. Removal operations were completed December 19, 1943.

#873 BAKER CEMETERY

Located on Land Map 128, Tract GIR-5587, elevation 380, two graves. Both graves were identified and remain permits executed.

No.	Name of Deceased	Age	Date of Death	Information given by...
1.	James Baker	unk	unk	Mrs. V. M. Lashlee, dau
2.	Christine Baker	unk	unk	" - dau

* *

GRAVE REMOVAL OPERATIONS

Cemeteries listed below are either submerged or access to them is impaired by the lake waters.

No.	Cemetery Name	Land Map	Tract
100	Boyd Cemetery	64	2679F
110	Barnes Cemetery	63	2439
112.	Bailey Cemetery #3	63	2446
115	Byrd Cemetery	61	2224F
116	Bailey Cemetery #1	61	2216
854	Bailey Cemetery	64	2659
855	Brooks Cemetery	83	3094
83	Campbell Cemetery	75	2820
85	Coleman Cemetery	72	2801
96	Campbell Cemetery	64	2654
124	Dilday Cemetery	47	2136
127	Futrell Cemetery	47	2140
84	Gray Cemetery	72	2792
88	Gardner Cemetery	67	2708
97	Gardner Cemetery	64	2675
98	Cardner, A. J.	64	2675
99	Gardner, M. F.	64	2675
101	Gansner or Scarbrough	83	3091
111	Herndon Cemetery	63	2437
130	Heathcock, Pink	47	2169
119	Lone Grave	55	2198
128	Lone Grave	47	2127
78	Mobley Cemetery	79	2968
80	Missionary Baptist Cemetery	76	2983
853	Martin Cemetery	83	3094
86	Negro or Gray Cemetery	72	Detail #6
87	Negro Cemetery	72	2805
775	No Name Cemetery	76	2986
82	Old Cemetery	79	2954
93	Old Cemetery	67	2790
118	Old Cemetery	61	2211
840	Old - No Name Cemetery	79	2965
90	Payne Cemetery	67	2695
102	Phillips Cemetery	64	2674
715	Rushing Cemetery	47	2185F
117	River Gate Cemetery	61	2210
123	Rushing Creek	47	2145
81	Sexton or Old Cemetery	76	2973
89	Taylor Cemetery	67	2730F
131	Taylor Cemetery	67	2731F
121	Vinson Slave Cemetery	51	2118
122	Vinson Cemetery	51	2119
133	Vinson Public Cemetery	55	2203
77	Wynns Cemetery	83	3094
108	Wofford Cemetery	64	2660
126	Williams Cemetery	47	2152

* *

Cemeteries listed below are either not affected by the lake waters or future access
will be provided by relocated roads.

*94	Buchannan Cemetery	64	2651
*95	Boswell Cemetery	64	2653
105	Boswell Cemetery	68	2674
*109	Bailey Cemetery	63	2449F
*132	Brigham Cemetery	61	2220
114	Dill Cemetery	61	B
120	Hendon Cemetery	61	Detail #2
79	Jobs-Sexton Cemetery	76	3188F
*757	Kennerly-Wofford Cemetery	67	2725
75	Leatherwood Cemetery	83	F
*76	Lane Cemetery	83	E
92	Lone Grave	67	2730F
107	Mathis Cemetery	64	Detail #7
718	Marberry Cemetery #3	63	2443
106	Old Cemetery	68	2647F
125	Old Cemetery	47	A
129	Rushing Cemetery	47	C
*91	St. Mary's Cemetery	67	2711
103	Stalls Cemetery	68	Out Side
104	Wofford Cemetery	68	Out Side
*113	Wallace Cemetery	63	Detail #1

* *

#77 WYNNS CEMETERY

Located on Land Map 83, Tract GIR-3094, above elevation 380, 95 graves. This was an old abandoned cemetery, badly neglected. Remain permits were executed on 17 graves. Four of these permits were on the graves of persons known to have been buried here, but the exact location of the graves was not known. The remaining 78 graves could not be identified, or no one could be found who was interested in having them moved. No further action was necessary.

No.	Name of Deceased	Age	Date of Death	Information given by...

* *

No.	Name of Deceased	Age	Date of Death	Information given by...
1.	Thomas Wynn	unk	1821	C.H. Wynn
2. - 38.	Unknown			
39.	Durham infant		1907	Mary Durham - mother
40.	Billy Sullivin		1909	" - dau.
41.	Baucky Durham			
42. - 73.	Unknown			
74.	Jimm Biggins		1884	Wm. Biggins - son
75.	Julia Biggins		1890	" - bro.
76.	Kate Biggins		1894	" - bro.
77. - 95.	Unknown			
?	Granville Herion		1890	Bill Herion - son
?	Minnie Herion		1880	" - bro.
?	Susan Herion			" - bro.
?	Katie Herion		1885	" - son

#78 MOBLEY CEMETERY

Located on land Map 79, Tract GIR-2968, above elevation 380, 125 graves. This was an active and well kept cemetery. Sixty-nine remain permits and five removal permits were executed. Twenty-three of the remain permits were on the graves of persons known to have been buried there, but the exact location of the graves was unknown. The remaining 51 graves could not be identified or no one could be found who was interested in having them moved. D. N. Mobley, the property owner, was concerned with three graves in this cemetery, but refused to execute either a removal or remain permit on the graves. Five graves and five monuments were moved to two reinterment cemeteries. Removal operation were completed June 14, 1943.

No.	Name of Deceased	Age	Date of Death

* *

No.	Name of Deceased	Age	Date of Death
1.	Unknown		
2.	Martin infant		1914
3.	Jerry Martin		unk
4.	Clifton Bass		
5.	Maggie Payne		1901

* *

6.	Martha Martin		unk
7.	Ed Martin		1920
8.	Mrs. Naomi Wofford		
9.	Lester Wofford		1931
10.	Sam Wofford		
11.	George Wofford		1906
12.	Ryan infant		1909
13.	Viana E. Mobley		1914
14.	A. N. Mobley		1915
15.	William C. Mobley		1917
16. - 18.	Unknown		
19.	Elijah Westerman		unk
20. - 21.	Unknown		
22.	Mary A. Goodman		1871
23.	Unknown		
24.	Rebecca Goodman		1872
25. - 29.	Unknown		
30.	Mrs. Mattie Byrd		1926
31. - 46.	Unknwon		
47.	Charlie Moore		1895
48.	O. Westerman		1928
49. - 62.	Unknown		
63.	Albert T. Stockton		1874
64. - 68.	Unknown		
69.	Josie Taylor		1885
70.	Unknown		
71.	Arry Jane Taylor		1913
72.	J. W. Taylor		1933
73.	Mae Satterwhite		1926
74.	Nancy M. Kibble		unk
75.	Flora Kibble		
76.	Martha Henderson		
77. - 84.	Unknown		
85.	California Kibble		unk
86.	James S. Kibble		unk
87.	Thedus Taylor		1935
88.	Unknown		
89.	G. W. Largent	75	1936
90. - 96.	Unknown		
97.	Ann Locke Bass	79	1887
98.	Walter Bass	23	1902
99.	Jethro Bass	85	1920
100.	Alice Hendon Bass	77	1927
101. - 105.	Unknown		
106.	Fannie Myrtle Payne		1920

* *

107.	Unknown		
108.	Owen L. Payne	1931	
109. - 114.	Unknown		
115.	George Daniel	1928	
116.	Ida Daniel	1941	
117.	Unknown		
118.	W. H. Taylor	1926	
119.	Cliff Dortch	1923	
120.	Alberta Dortch	1921	
121.	Harry Graham Dortch	1929	
122.	D. Logan Dortch	1933	
123.	Andrew McDaniel	1926	
124.	Amy Jane Largent	1887	
125.	Benny Largent	1889	
?	George Boswell	1895	Callie Taylor - wife
?	Ella Boswell		
?	Wofford infants (4)		
?	William A. Wofford		
?	Wilbur Gansner		
?	Willie Gansner		
?	Chris Gansner		
?	Benny Gansner		
?	Ella Gansner		
?	Martha Gansner		
?	Annie Oliver		
?	Frank Oliver		
?	Henry Oliver		
?	George Oliver		
?	Oliver infant		
?	Annie Wofford		
?	Abe Phillips		
?	Virgil Phillips		
?	Cory Phillips		

See Plat Map #78

* *

#80 MISSIONARY BAPTIST CHURCH CEMETERY

Located on Land Map 76, Tract GIR-2983, between elevation 376-380, 5 graves. This was an old abandoned cemetery. None of the graves could be identified. W. A. Martin had a number of relatives buried in the cemetery but could not identify the graves. He requested that all graves be moved out of the flooded area. All graves were moved to St. Mary's Cemetery R-25 on Octoer 9, 1942.

No.	Name of Deceased	Age	Date of Death	Information gven by...
1.	J. K. Nolan		1919	J.A. Nolan - nephew
2.	Amanda Ryan	70	1918	Eva Mullins
3.	N. M. Williams	57	1912	Maggie Williams - wife
4.	Coy infant	infant	1916	Richard P. Coy - bro.
5.	Willard Andrews		1915	Annie Andrews - mother

See Plat Map #80

#81 SEXTON CEMETERY

Located on Land Map 76, Tract GIr-2975, seven graves. According to C. C. West, the property owner, there had been no evidence of graves there for the past 15 years as the area had been in cultivation during that time. Remain permits were executed on the graves of six persons known to have been buried here, but the exact location of the graves was not known. No further action was necessary.

No.	Name of Deceased	Age	Date of Death	Information given by...
1.	Matilda Sexton		1887	J.D. Sexton - g/son
2.	Tilghman Sexton		1847	" - g/son
3.	Harrison Sexton		1850	" - nephew
4.	George Sexton			" - nephew
5.	Mary Ellen Sexton			" - nephew
6.	West infant		1898	C.C. West - 1/2 bro.

#89 TAYLOR CEMETERY

Located on land Map 67, Tract GIR-2730F, below elevation 380, 20 graves. This was an old abandoned cemetery, only four graves of which could be identified. Aubrey Rutland, who had a number of relatives buried there but could not identify the graves, executed removal permits on all graves. All graves were moved to St. Mary's Cemetery R-25 on november 12, 1942.

No.	Name of Deceased	Age	Date of Death	Information given by...
1.	Unknown			
2.	Blake Rutland	65	1880	Aubrey Rutland - g/nep
3.	Mrs. Rayford Rutland	58	1860	" - g/g/son
4.	Rayford Rutland	60	1850	" - g/g/son
5. - 20.	Unknown			

* *

#82 OLD CEMETERY

Located on Land Map 79, Tract GIR-2954, below elevation 359, uncertain number of graves. A thorough investigation was made but no one could be found who could point out any grave locations. No further action was necessary.

#83 CAMPBELL CEMETERY

Located on land Map 73, Tract GIR-2820, below elevation 361, 65 graves. This was an inactive and poorly kept cemetery, no burials having been made in over 20 years. Removal permits were executed on all graves. Otto Coldiron, the property owner, executed removal permits on all (44) unidentified graves. Sixty-five dgraves and seven monuments were moved to two reinterment cemeteries. Removal operations were completed October 27, 1942.

No.	Name of Deceased	Age	Date of Death	Information given by...
1.	Billy Crutcher	unk	unk	Walter Crutcher - g/son
2.	Thomas W. Crutcher	1	1857	" - cousin
3.	Charlie Crutcher	2	1872	" - bro.
4.	Osborne Crutcher	17	1889	" - bro.
5.	J. M. Crutcher	48	1898	" - son
6.	Elizabeth Crutcher	72	1915	" - son
7.	Andrew Crutcher	32	1913	" - bro.
8. - 13.	Unknown			
14.	J. R. Young	infant	1922	Nellie Westerman - m
15.	Nancy Burcham	61	1921	" - dau.
16.	Jim Young	61	unk	" - dau.
17.	Charlie Young	unk	unk	" - sister
18. - 22.	Unknown			
23.	Nellie Crutcher	16	1880	T.H. Crutcher - bro.
24.	Betty Crutcher	30	1867	" - son
25.	Shelton Crutcher	50	1887	" - son
26. - 29.	Unknown			
30.	Samuel Scarborough	1	1891	I.F. Scarborough - bro.
31.	M. J. Watkins	51	1878	
32.	David Watkins	40	1851	
33.	Sara Jane Anderson	23	1853	
34.	John T. Anderson	infant	1848	
35. - 62.	Unknown			
63.	Millie Crutcher	80	1888	Walter Crutcher - g/son
64.	Benny Crutcher	1	unk	
65.	Unknown			
?	Emma Crutcher	12	1880	
?	John E. Crutcher	73	unk	

* *

?	Albert N. Crutcher	39	1890
?	Mary Alvis Marberry	unk	unk
?	Dee Marberry	unk	unk
?	George Marberry	unk	unk
?	George A. Marberry	unk	unk
?	Sam Marberry	unk	unk

#84 GRAY CEMETERY

Located on Land Map 72, Tract GIR-2792, above elevation 380, 7 graves. This was an active and well cared for family cemetery. All graves were identified and remain permits executed.

No.	Name of Deceased	Age	Date of Death	Information given by...
1.	James Gray		1869	Jack Gray - g/g/son
2.	Anna Gray		1852	" - g/g/son
3.	A. J. Gray		1893	" - g/son
4.	Rebecca Gray		1928	" - g/son
5.	Gray infant		1915	Ms A.J. Gray - mother
6.	John Gray			Jack Gray - uncle
7.	A. J. Gray		1942	Ms A.J. Gray - wife

#85 COLEMAN CEMETERY

Located on Land Map 72, Tract GIR-2801, above elevation 387, 10 graves. This was an inactive and badly neglected cemetery. Remain permits were executed on all graves. Five of these permits were on the graves of persons known to have been buried here, but the exact location of the graves was not known. No further action necessary.

No.	Name of Deceased	Age	Date of Death	Information given by...
1.	Harriet L. Rutland		1878	Myrtle Higgins - dau.
2. - 9.	Unknown			
10.	Mary Coleman			J.H. Coleman - g/son
?	Peter Coleman			Frank Coleman - g/son
?	Elmus Coleman			" - nephew
?	Luesa Coleman			" - nephew
?	Rebecca Coleman	74	1846	J.H. Coleman g/g/son
?	Robert S. Coleman	76	1852	" - g/g/son
?	William H. Coleman	51	1851	" - g/son

* *

#86 GRAY COLORED CEMETERY

Located on Land Map 72, Tract No. 1, between elevation 377-393, 28 graves. This was an old abandoned cemetery. Only two graves could be identified. H. J. Wofford, had a number of relatives buried there, but could not identify the graves. He requested that all unidentified graves be moved. All graves were moved to St. Mary's Cemetery R-25. Removal operations were completed January 4, 1943.

No.	Name of Deceased	Age	Date of Death	Information given by...

* *

No.	Name of Deceased	Age	Date of Death	Information given by...
1. - 11.	Unknown			
12.	Mrs. S. McButghen	unk	unk	
13. - 18.	Unknown			
19.	Adaline Gray	unk	unk	
20. - 28.	Unknown			
?	Callie Wofford		1887	
?	Cora Wofford		1882	
?	Carrie Alice Wofford		1885	
?	Watson un-identified			
?	Mary Cherry			
?	Nancy Cherry			
?	Martha Palmer			
?	Bill Palmer			
?	Bud Payne			
?	Mary Payne			
?	Reddick Kendall			
?	Sally Ann Cherry			

See Plat Map #86

#87 NEGRO CEMETERY

Located on land Map 72, Tract GIR-2805, between elevation 358-361, 16 graves. This was an old abandoned cemetery. None of the graves could be identified. H. J. Wofford had relatives buried in the cemetery but could not identify the graves. He requested that all graves be moved out of the flooded area. All graves were moved to St. Mary's Cemetery R-25 on January 4, 1943.

#88 GARDNER CEMETERY

Located on Land Map 67, Tract GIR-2728, above elevation 380, 2 graves. Both graves were identified and remain permits executed.

No.	Name of Deceased	Age	Date of Death	Information given by...

* *

No.	Name of Deceased	Age	Date of Death	Information given by...
1.	C. L. Gardner		1933	Ms C.W. Gardner - mother
2.	G. W. Gardner		1929	" - wife

* *

#90 PAYNE CEMETERY

Located on Land Map 67, Tract GIR-2695, between elevation 374-377, six graves. This was an old abandoned cemetery. Removal permits were executed on all graves. A. J. Phillips, who had relatives buried there but could not identify the graves, executed removal permits on four unidentified graves. All graves were moved to St. Mary's Cemetery R-25 on November 12, 1942.

No.	Name of Deceased	Age	Date of Death	Information given by...
1.	Mary Whitford	70	1851	R.L. Whitford
2.	Thomas Payne	48	1851	
3. - 6.	Unknown			

#93 OLD CEMETERY

Located on Land Map 67, Tract GIR-2790, below elevation 359, nine graves. This was an old abandoned cemetery, only one grave of which could be identified. Aubrey Rutland, the property owner executed removal permits on all unidentified graves. All grave were moved to St. Mary's Cemetery R-25 on November 11, 1942.

No.	Name of Deceased	Age	Date of Death	Information given by...
1.	Jimmie Rutland	9	unk	Ms J.S. Niles - sister
2. - 9.	Unknown			

#96 CAMPBELL CEMETERY

Located on Land Map 64, Tract GIR-2654, above elevaltion 387, 16 graves. This was an inactive and neglected cemetery. Four remain permits and four removal permits were executed. The remaining eight graves could not be identified or no one could be found who was interested in having them moved. The four graves were moved to Wofford Cemetery R-23 on March 12, 1943.

No.	Name of Deceased	Age	Date of Death	Information given by...
1.	William J. Edwards	unk	unk	O.H. Edwards - bro.
2.	Unknown			
3.	Archie Stalls			Nellie Pennington - sis
4. - 7.	Unknown			
8.	Joseph Campbell	unk	unk	Cordie Edwards - dau.
9.	Rebecah Campbell	unk	unk	" - dau.
10.	Jim McCutcheon	68	1901	Kate McCutcheon - dau.
11.	Mary Campbell McCutcheon	62	1899	" - dau.
12.	Florence McCutcheon	26	1906	" - sister
13. - 15.	Unknown			
16.	Jack B. McCutcheon	2	1874	" - sister

* *

#97 GARDNER CEMETERY

Located on Land Map 64, Tract GIR-2675, elevation 377, two graves. Both graves were identified and removal permits executed. These infant Gardner children graves were moved to Relocated Boyd Cemetery R-31 on November 11, 1942.

#98 GARDNER, A. J.

Located on Land Map 64, Tract GIR-2675, above elevation 380, single grave. This grave of A. J. Gardner who died in 1890 is buried on the land of N. K. Gorham. It was removed to Relocated Boyd Cemetery R-31 on November 11, 1942.

#99 GARDNER, M.F.

Located on Land Map 64, Tract GIR-2675, above elevation 380, single grave. This grave was identified as Mrs. M.F. Gardner, age 75 who died in 1875 according to her daughter-in-law Mrs. G. W. Gardner, and a remain permit executed.

#100 BOYD CEMETERY

Located on Land Map 64, Tract GIR-2679F, between elevation 376-378, 183 graves. This was an active and fairly well kept cemetery. L. B. Nance donated a site for the purpose of relocating the Boyd Cemetery and the Blue springs Church. This site is approximately one-half mile east of the present cemetery, and on the north side of Relocated road, Project #8-5111. Professional assistance was furnished in laying out and staking the cemetery lots. All graves (183) and 32 monuments were moved to four re-interment Cemeteries. One hundred and seventy-three of these graves were moved to the Relocated Boyd Cemetery R-31. N. K. Gorham, the owner of the original cemetery, executed removal permits on all (60) unidentified graves. Removal operations were completed November 11, 1942.

No.	Name of Deceased	Age	Date of Death
1.	Katie Rowlett	9	1924
2.	Joe P. Rowlett	17	1924
3.	J. H. Rowlett	infant	1912
4.	Geneva May Rowlett	2	1914
5.	Jack Bailey	21	1922

* *

6.	Zeantha Rowlett	21	1908
7.	Mrs. Lottie Anne Rowlett	47	1905
8.	Bumpus infant	infant	unk
9.	Stimpson infant	infant	1915
10.	Unknown		
11.	Effie Jane Welker	64	1918
12.	W. A. Welker	77	1930
13.	Claud Chadwick	52	1936
14.	Chadwick infant	infant	1922
15.	J. W. Nance	50	1906
16. - 18. Unknown			
19.	Alpha Moody	26	1903
20.	Mary Elizabeth Champion	43	1902
21.	J. E. Champion	72	1915
22.	Amanda A. Hoseford	60	1918
23.	Millard Hoseford	3	1920
24.	Louie Hoseford	15	1930
25.	Mabel H. Love	23	1925
26.	Herschel Love	1	1924
27.	Hurley Love	1	1924
28.	N. K. Gorham	76	1931
29.	Minnie Atkins Gorham	47	1906
30.	Tommie A. Gorham	1	1887
31.	Mattie Gorham	infant	1879
32.	Mattie A. Gorham	18	1878
33.	Newton Sidney Gorham	28	1909
34.	Siddie Gorham	52	1883
35.	Mollie Lorene Gorham	infant	1904
36.	Annie Gorham	40	1915
37.	John Gorham	38	1915
38.	Mollie Boyd Gorham	77	1934
39.	J. G. Gorham	63	1915
40.	Unknown		
41.	Sills infant	infant	unk
42.	Floyd Sills	35	1918
43.	Olan Sills	20	1918
44.	Pearl Thomason	28	unk
45.	Mrs. Ada Sills	45	1921
46.	Hardy Sills	54	1930
47.	Roy Sills	35	1930
48.	Troy Sills	37	1933
49.	Gilbert Sills	28	1936
50.	Wilma Doris Kennerly	3	1929
51.	James S. Gorham	2	1874
52.	Unknown		

* *

53.	Mrs. W. J. Sexton	55	1918
54.	Unknown		
55.	Vada Ester Sexton	2	1920
56.	Minnie C. Sexton	32	1931
57.	Willie A. Sexton	38	1937
58.	Unknown		
59.	Caroline Gray Boyd	79	1910
60.	E. J. Boyd	85	1906
61.	Minerva Boyd McCraw	unk	1902
62.	Mollie McCraw	unk	unk
63.	Sills child	child	1900
64.	Emma Gorham	75	1936
65.	R. T. Gorham	83	1938
66.	Lou Newberry	45	1910
67.	Shaver infant	infant	1922
68.	Oel Shaver	infant	1922
69.	Noel Shaver	infant	1922
70.	J. C. Garner	6 ms	1928
71.	Garland Newberry	23	1930
72.	Mary Lou Newberry	infant	1923
73.	J. Lee Thomason	68	1937
74.	Cuba Thomason	8	1913
75.	Ruby Thomason	6 ms	1917
76.	Leroy Thomason	infant	1921
77. - 80.	Unknown		
81.	Moody infant	infant	1926
82.	Thomas H. Crutcher	3	1925
83.	Maxine Greenup	3 ms	1932
84.	Greenup infant	infant	1933
85.	Zebbie Cherry	45	1928
86.	Edwin Cherry	20	1930
87.	Rushing infant twins	infants	1914
88.	Elmer Rushing	1	1909
89.	Burley Rushing	infant	1917
90.	Unknown		
91.	Lucy D. Gatlin	28	1884
92.	Mary M. Gatlin	3 ms	1881
93.	Ephram E. Gatlin	8 ms	1884
94.	Unknown		
95.	Roy Downs	11	1898
96.	Downs infant	infant	1898
97.	Mary E. Downs	35	1899
98.	G. W. Gatlin	64	1886
99.	Mrs. N. L. Gatlin	37	1865
100.	R. S. Gatlin	2	1858

* *

101. E. G. Gatlin	10	1850
102. J. E. Gatlin	2	1849
103. - 107. Unknown		
108. Herndon infant	infant	1881
109. Herndon infant	infant	1881
110. Lee Mitchell	22	1934
111. Mrs. Perry Murray	unk	unk
112. Perry Murray	unk	unk
113. Robertson infant	infant	1933
114. - 117. Unknown		
118. Lawson Wofford	54	1897
119. Unknown		
120. Mary E. Herndon	74	1899
121. Louis Herndon	89	1914
122. Martha Welker	73	1931
123. Virginia Lois Westerman	infant	1934
124. Mildred G. Hoseford	14	1937
125. Basil T. Love	infant	1934
126. Herbert C. Cherry	1	1936
127. - 128. Unknown		
129. Catherine Hoseford	56	1936
130. Hoseford infant	infant	1928
131. Cornell Hoseford	4	1936
132. Wilson Hoseford	1	1899
133. Hester Thomason	90	1927
134. Mary Eaves	70	1937
135. John T. Eaves	80	1938
136. - 143. Unknown		
144. Maude Lane	infant	1937
145. Florida Lane	1	1926
146. Tom Hoseford	37	1907
147. Marion Phillips	75	1902
148. Mrs. Mary Phillips	75	1905
149. Dill Phillips	50	1912
150. Samuel Hoseford	52	1921
151. R. M. Milton	79	1940
152. Dr. Grace	unk	unk
153. Unknown		
154. Crutcher infant	infant	1912
155. Unknown		
156. Cherry infant	infant	1938
157. Unknown		
158. W. J. Sexton	81	1940
159. - 162. Unknown		
163. Mattie J. Morgan	infant	1940
164. Katie Morgan	25	1940
165. - 183. Unknown		

See Plat Map #100

* *

#101 GANSNER OR SCARBROUGH CEMETERY

Located on Land Map 83, Tract GIR-3091, above elevation 380, 161 graves. This was an active and fairly well kept cemetery. One hundred and forty-three removal permits and 13 remain permits were executed. G. F. Gansner, the property owner, executed removal permits on all (126) unidentified graves. The remaining five graves were identified, but no one could be found who was interested in having them moved. One hundred and forty-three graves and ine monuments were moved to four reinterment cemeteries. Removal operations were completed on June 21, 1943.

No.	Name of Deceased	Age	Date of Death

* *

No.	Name of Deceased	Age	Date of Death
1.	Cathey infant		1902
2.	Sam Cathey		1902
3.	Ethel Cathey		1910
4.	Yarbrough child		1937
5. - 9.	Unknown		
10.	Will Cathey		1906
11.	Mattie Cathey		1910
12.	Franklin Angelo Cathey		1906
13.	Herman L. Jones		1910
14.	Sterling E. Jones		1939
15. - 17.	Unknown		
18.	Wynns infant	infant	1851
19.	Winna Wynns	1	1856
20. - 32.	Unknown		
33.	Mrs. Sarah A. Wynns	19	1849
34.	Unknown		
35.	Winniefred Wynns	67	1846
36.	William G. Wynns	35	1845
37. - 43.	Unknown		
44.	Whitehead infant	infant	1929
45.	Westerman infant		1934
46.	Westerman infant		1936
47.	Nancy Westerman	60	1924
48.	Owen Westerman	infant	1929
49. - 51.	Unknown		
52.	Doctor Perigold		
53. - 83.	Unknown		
84.	Eula Bomar		
85.	Unknown		
86.	Dr. J. A. Bomar		
87.	Unknown		
88.	Anna Reed		1897
89.	Gilbert Gray	2	1905
90.	Lucille Bradley	35	1898
91.	Betty Bradley	1	1898

* *

92.	Minnie Bradley	3	1898
93.	Benjamin Franklin Booker	infant	1910
94.	Cortney infant		1902
95. - 161.	Unknown		

#102 PHILLIPS CEMETERY

Located on Land Map 64, Tract GIR-2674, between elevation 376-380, 29 graves. This was an old abandoned cemetery. Only one grave, that of an Edding infant, could be identified. A. J. Phillips, who had a number of relatives buried here, but could not identify the graves, requested that all graves be moved out of the flooded area. All graves were moved to St. Mary's Cemetery R-25 on November 11, 1942.

#108 WOFFORD CEMETERY

Located on land Map 64, Tract GIR-2660, elevation 376, 6 graves.   All graves were identified and removal permits executed. All were moved to Wofford Cemetery R-23 on May 10, 1943.

No.	Name of Deceased	Age	Date of Death	Information given by...

* *

1.	Wofford infant	infant	unk	
2.	Betty Wofford			
3.	Betty Miles			
4.	Sam Wofford			
5.	Mrs. Sam Wofford			
6.	George Wofford			

#110 BARNES CEMETERY

Located on Land Map 63, Tract GIR-2439, above elevation 380, three graves. This was an active, and well kept family cemetery.   All graves were identified and remain permits executed.

No.	Name of Deceased	Age	Date of Death	Information given by...

* *

1.	Emily Futrell Barnes		1913	Ms Eddie Hodges – dau.
2.	J. S. Barnes		1922	" – dau.
3.	J. H. Barnes		1933	Van T. Barnes – son

#111 HERNDON CEMETERY

Located on Land Map 63, Tract GIR-2437, between elevation 378-379, 18 graves. This was a very old abandoned cemetery, no burials having been made in over 60 years. None of the graves could be identified. R. M. Mathis, the property owner, requested that all graves be moved out of the flooded area. They were moved to St. Mary's Cemetery R-25 on November 13, 1943.

* *

#112 BAILEY CEMETERY #3

Located on Land Map 63, Tract GIR-2446, below elevation 359, 11 graves. This was an inactive, but fairly well kept cemetery. All graves were identified and removal permits executed. All graves and nine monuments were moved to Wallace Cemetery R-24, on October 23, 1942.

No.	Name of Deceased	Age	Date of Death	Information given by...

* *

No.	Name of Deceased	Age	Date of Death	Information given by...
1.	M. L. Nolin	51	1879	Ms Dink Kennedy - niece
2.	Lucinda Bailey	78	1884	" - g/dau.
3.	John T. Bailey	72	1868	" - g/dau.
4.	Roxana Melton	5	1872	
5.	J. W. Melton	infant	1865	
6.	M. E. L. Bailey	1	1863	" - niece
7.	Nancy A. Bailey	26	1858	
8.	J. F. Melton	infant	1862	
9.	Esther Lyon	8	1875	T.M. & W.A. Lyons - bro.
10.	T. L. Bailey	unk	unk	Ms Dink Kennedy - niece
11.	J. W. L. Bailey	1	1866	" - niece

#115 BYRD CEMETERY

Located on Land Map 61, Tract GIR-2224, between elevation 378-380, 38 graves. This was an active and fairly well kept cemetery. Removal permits were executed on all graves. J. A. Bailey, who had a number of relatives buried here but could not identify the graves, requested that all (19) unidentified graves be moved. Thirty-eight graves and three monuments were moved to Relocated Bailey Cemetery R-93. Grave removal operations were completed June 10, 1943. Taken from the records of Field Book #MS-639

No.	Name of Deceased	Date of Birth	Date of Death	Information

* *

No.	Name of Deceased	Date of Birth	Date of Death	Information
1.	Evaline Byrd			Minter Byrd
2.	Penelope Byrd			J.A. Bailey
3. - 4.	Unknown			
5.	Rhoda Byrd			Joe Phillips
6.	Cherry infant			Rody Cherry, f
7.	G. W. Byrd	28 Feb 1829	14 Oct 1898	Ms Joe Phillips
8.	Phillips infant	Probably infant child of Mrs. Joe Phillips by former marriage about 1890.		
9.	Ann Eliza Byrd	25 Nov 1846	17 Dec 1908	G.W. Byrd -h
10.	Byrd child			J.A. Byrd - & 1st wife - pts
11.	Mrs. John Ashley Byrd			First wife of J.A. Byrd

* *

12.	John Ashley Byrd		1910	J.A. Bailey
13.	Parker infant			child of Bud and Mary Parker
14.	Dolly Ann Byrd			J.A. Bailey - son-in-law
15.	Annie Lee Bailey	11 Dec 1868	7 Mar 1934	J.A. Bailey,h
16.	Jerome Byrd			Florence Byrd,wife
17.	Jack Byrd	oldest grave in cemetery		J.A. Bailey,n
18.	Mrs. Jack Byrd	oldest grave in cemetery		" - nephew
19.	Byrd infant			child of J.A. Bailey & 1st w
20.	Parker infant			child of Bud and Mary Parker
21.	Ollie Parker (probably)			John Parker,b
22.	Byrd child			G.W. Byrd, f
23.	Parker infant			Shade Parker

* Note: "Mrs. Joseph Phillips of Murray, KY was not contacted. Mr. J.A. Baileey, local resident and relative of Mrs. Phillips supplied all the information. There is a possibility of two or more additional graves, but Mr. Bailey is too feeble to go to the cemetery and identify them.

12 June 1940   H. G. Higgs"

#116 BAILEY CEMETERY #1

Located on Land Map 61, Tract GIR-2216, all graves between elevation 364-382, 60 graves. Thirty-seven removal permits and 19 remain permits were executed. Ten of the remain permits were on the graves of persons known to have been buried in the cemetery but the exact location of the graves was unknown. The remaining four graves could not be identified or no one could be found who was interested in having them moved. Thirty-seven graves and eight monuments were moved to seven reinterment Cemeteries. Removal operations were completed June 10, 1943. The following inform-ation taken from the Field Book #MS-639.

No.	Name of Deceased	Date of Birth	Date of Death	Information by...
1. - 4.	Unknown			
5.	Charles Elkins		1924	Cecil Elkins - son
6.	Anne Bell Elkins	2 Apr 1905	13 Apr 1931	" - husband
7.	Oralee Bailey	child		Jas. A. Bailey - f
8.	Lashlee infant	infant	1909	
9.	Florine Gardner	4 Feb 1906	27 May 1926	H.G. Gardner - hus
10.	Theodore Elkins	d. 1916	child of Charles & Maggie Elkins	
11.	Nannie Ruth Brigham & infant			Vernon Brigham - h
12.	Brigham infant	infant		" - father
13.	Lizzie Parker	2 Aug 1881	8 Nov 1881	d/o G.C. & K.E. Parker
14.	Ramona Jean Bailey	infant	1929	
15.	James Champion	age 30	1904	Dave Champion - u

* *

No.	Name	Age/Birth	Date	Relation
16. - 18.	Unknown			
19.	Dr. W. B. Champion			" - bro.
20.	Unknown			
21.	Charles Bailey			J.A. Bailey - bro
22.	Unknown			
23.	Lillye Rose Burcham			Melvin Burcham - h
24.	John Hall	age 70	1928	
25.	Mrs. Mary Jackson & infant	age 33	1920	J.H. Crutcher - b
26.	Ellen Barrow	age 50	4 Mar 1928	Loyd Barrow - son
27.	Realus Russell		1910	
28.	Mrs. James Taylor			
29.	Lee Ellis Manning		Dec 1925	Mack Manning - f
30.	Mary Hall	73	1920	
31.	G. H. Steele	4 Mar 1879	26 Mar 1920	Ms G.H. Steele - w
32.	Russell child		1931	Lee Russell - f
33.	J. J. Crutcher	65 years	1930	J.H. Crutcher - s
34.	Unknown			
35.	Mrs. Alice Russell		18 May 1934	62 yrs 9 ms 3 dys H. F. Russell - h
36.	Bailey infant	infant	1890	
37.	Roxy Jackson		10 yrs	J.H. Crutcher - u
38.	Odie Moody		1930	
39.	R. E. Moody	5 Nov 1859	18 Oct 1926	Ms G.H. Russell,d
40.	Unknown			
41.	Ida Barrow Hardin		15 Jul 1936	40 yrs 10 ms 29 dy
42.	Ann Eliza Burcham	age 72	1935	
43.	Mrs. Winnie Barrow	age 22	1927	
44.	Unknown			
45.	Mrs. Della Champion	age 48	1897	Dave Champion
46.	Ora Lee Bailey	child	1898	Raymond Bailey - f
47.	Sarah Jane Bailey	age 65	1890	J.A. Bailey - son
48.	Annie L. Peal	1871	1938	J.H. Crutcher - s
49.	Charles Bailey		1910	28 yrs
50.	D. H. Boyle		7 Jan 1940	78 yr 4 ms 5 dys Annie Boyle - wife
51.	Lottie Taylor	child	unk	James Taylor - f
52.	William Bailey	age 85	1888	J.A. Bailey -g/s
53.	Polly Brigham Bailey	age 60	1890	" - g/son
54.	Tom Bailey	age 60	1885	" - nephew
55.	Unknown			
56.	William A. Bailey	age 65	1900	J.A. Bailey - son
57.	M. M. Manning	age 76	1942	
58.	Dave Champion		1941	
59.	Marly Moody		1941	
60.	M. F. Knight	age 70	1895	

* *

?	Lloyd Barnett Elkin	1916	Maggie Elkins -m
?	Eliza Burchan	1935	J.M. Burchan - son
?	Charles E. Elkin	1914	Maggie Elkins - m
?	Champion infant	1900	Oscar Champion - b
?	Tuck Champion	1908	" - bro.
?	Dee Champion	1903	" - son
?	Samuel D. Dill	1904	Ida E. Dill - m
?	Bruce Dill	1906	" - mother
?	George W. Geurin	1908	" - dau.
?	Clemintine Geurin	1906	" - dau.

* Note: "Mr. J. A. Bailey, whose parents and relatives used this cemetery says there were several graves there before he was old enough to remember who or where they were buried. The rectangular area between #16, 9 and 15 was the first burying ground. Most of the graves shown are of last 50 years.
H. G. Higgs"

#117 RIVER GATE CEMETERY

Located on Land Map 61, Tract GIR-2210, 16 graves. This was an old abandoned cemetery and none of the graves could be identified. R. H. Melton, the property owner, requested that all graves be moved out of the affected area. They were moved to St. Mary's Cemetery R-25 on November 13, 1942.

The following information is found in Field Book #MS-639. The grave numbers is uncertain, but the general information agrees with the above official report.

No.	Name of Deceased	Age	Date of Death	Information given by...

* *

1.	Orville Champion (probably)	unk	unk	Ben Champion - bro.
2.	Unknown			
3.	"Bud" Creek (probably)			
?	Orville Champion			
?	Jordan Champion			
?	Laura Champion			

* Note: "Mr. and Mrs. J. W. Brigham, mr. Dave Champion, Mr. W. M. Wilkerson and Mr. J. A. Bailey estimate 35 white graves and 15 colored graves in this cemetery. There is very little evidence of these three graves. Shown by Sively's Survey - cemetery is grown up and there has not been anyone buried there in 30-35 years. The above mentioned people were with Sively on survey and some contacted again.
3 Jun 1940   H.G. Higgs"

#118 OLD CEMETERY

Located on Land Map 51, Tract GIR-2211, below elevation 359, eight graves. This was an old abandoned cemetery, and none of the graves could be identified. Mrs. Dessie Wilkinson, who had relatives buried here but could not identify the graves, requested that all graves be moved out of the flooded area. All graves were moved to St. Mary's Cemetery R-25, on October 22, 1942.

* *

#119 LONE GRAVE

Located on Land Map 55, Tract GIR-2198, below elevation 340, single grave. The burial area had been in cultivation for a number of years, and there was no indication of a grave. No information could be obtained as too who might have been buried there, or the date of burial. However, it is generally accepted among local residents that one or more graves are in this area. No further action was necessary.

#120 HENDON CEMETERY

Located on Land Map 51, Detail #2, 218 graves. The following information is taken from Field Books MS-639 and MS-667.

No.	Name of Deceased	Date of Birth	Date of Death	Information given by
1.	Boatwright			Doss Boatwright
2.	O. W. Cable	1866	1931	Ida Cable - wife
3.	Ida Owen Cable	6 Dec 1906	11 Dec 1909	d/o O.W. & Ida Cable
4.	Cable infant son	19 Jan 1901	24 Jan 1901	s/o "
5.	J. W. Cable	6 Sep 1824	14 Oct 1902	
6.	Unknown			
7.	Angie Cable Hodges	12 Apr 1860	11 May 1918	Ms Richard McNutt-d
8.	John T. Hodges	12 Sep 1855	8 Jun 1885	" - daug.
9.	Pinckney Boyles			Dave Boyles, son
10.	Thomas Boyles			Ms Raymond Bailey gd
11.	Vinson infant	20 Aug 1901	4 Sep 1904	s/o H.C. & S.A.
12.	M. A. Vinson	11 Aug 1858	23 Dec 1891	J.H. Vinson - hus
13.	S. D. Vinson	4 Nov 1881	22 Apr 1893	d/o J.H. & M.A.
14.	Daniel T. Cagle	9 Dec 1862	2 Aug 1878	Jas. Cagle - bro.
15.	A. T. Bilbrey			Walter Bilbrey, son
16.	Mrs. A. T. Bilbrey			" - son
17.	Plomer W. Vinson	1881	1932	Ms M.H. Dill, dau
18.	Nettie W. Vinson	1885	1937	" - dau.
19.	Vinson infant	23 Jan 1911	29 Jan 1911	s/o Plomer & Nettie
20.	Matilda Ann Vinson	18 Feb 1871	19 Feb 1891	d/o B.P. & M. J.
21.	Vinson twin son	22 Sep 1885	22 Sep 1885	s/o J.H. & M.A.
22.	Vinson twin son	22 Sep 1885	22 Sep 1885	"
23.	B. P. Vinson	22 Dec 1839	26 Apr 1918	H.C. Vinson - g/son
24.	Amanda Vinson		9 Feb 1861	22 yrs 1 ms 19 dys
		wife of B. R. Vinson		H.C. Vinson - g/son
25.	J. P. Vinson	13 Nov 1874	6 Oct 1875	d/o B.P. & H.J.
26.	Hariet J. Vinson	28 Nov 1838	21 Jul 1888	w/o B. P. Vinson
27.	Sammie Ella Suddarth	31 Jul 1860	29 Apr 1929	w/o S.D. Suddarth
28.	S. D. Suddarth	14 Feb 1846	5 Mar 1909	John Suddarth - son
29.	Mary Suddarth		5 Jun 1865	51 yrs 4 mos 15 dys
				John Suddarth - g/s
30. - 31.	Unknown			

* *

32.	J. C. Vinson	7 Jun 1834	30 Jun 1909	H.C. Vinson - g/son
33.	James H. Reid	19 Aug 1845	15 Jan 1865	J.D. Reid - son
34.	Mathew M. Reid	14 Mar 1822	1 Mar 1850	" - son
35.	Martha Futrell	22 Feb 1818	21 Feb 1853	w/o S. Futrell &
				d/o H. & P. Vinson
36.	Unknown			
37.	Henry Vinson	9 Jun 1794	21 Aug 1863	
38.	Permelia Vinson	29 Mar 1793	8 Feb 1886	92 yrs 10 mos 9 dys
39.	Sarah Vinson	6 Jan 1858	28 Sep 1862	
40.	Francis E. Sholar	4 Aug 1845	14 Nov 1873	d/o E.J.& Jacqualine
41.	Mary J. Thomas	8 Aug 1847	10 May 1929	w/o A.D. Thomas &
				d/o E. J. & Jacqualine Vinson
42.	Clementine V. Hamlin	1 May 1850	6 Jan 1886	d/o E.J.& Jacqualine Vinson
43.	Eva Cable	15 Aug 1894	2 Sep 1897	d/o E.F. & Rena
44.	Edward Cable	10 Feb 1884	17 Jun 1886	s/o E.F. & Rena
45.	Elmore Cable	27 Feb 1886	16 Jul 1888	s/o E.F. & Rena
46.	E. F. Cable	22 Jan 1854	7 Oct 1899	Clint Cable - son
47.	Joe W. Tishell	1862	1934	Ms J.W. Tishell wife
48.	Frank Tishell	10 Jan 1835	26 Jun 1919	" - dau.-in-law
49.	Rebecca Ann Tishell	17 Apr 1829	24 Aug 1896	"
50. - 59.	Unknown			
60.	A. F. Dilday	28 May 1873	13 Sep 1875	L.A. Dilday - bro.
61.	Mary J. Dilday	23 Aug 1852	11 Mar 1879	w/o R.H. Dilday
62.	M. D. Dilday	10 Feb 1876	12 Jun 1904	L.A. Dilday - bro.
63.	Mrs. Russell			F.L. Russell - son
64.	Unknown (probably child of Elmore Adkins)			
65.	Russell infant			Walter Russell - f
66.	Russell infant			" - father
67.	Russell infant			" - father
68.	Adkins infant			Elmore Adkins - f
69.	Hargrove infant			J.M. Hargrove - f
70.	Hargrove infant			" - father
71.	Hargrove infant			" - father
72.	James Forest Hendon	17 Mar 1852	15 Sep 1869	s/o Sarah Hendon
73. - 77.	Hendon infants			c/o Henry & P.J.
78.	Thomas Hendon	27 Sep 1859	17 Jun 1860	s/o Henry & P.J.
79.	P. J. Hendon	27 Nov 1840	20 Feb 1910	Billy Hendon - son
80.	Henry Hendon	12 Sep 1839	9 Feb 1919	" - son
81.	Sarah Outland			" - nephew
82.	Mrs. T. L. Cook			James Cook - son
83.	Tandy L. Cook		16 Feb 1932	" - son 41 yrs 7 ms 14 days
84.	L. E. Futrell	24 Aug 1919	18 Dec 1919	s/o L.W. & Eula
85. - 99.	Unknown			
100.	Emma Cable Futrell	16 Aug 1862	1 Jan 1915	J.S. Futrell - hus.

* *

101. - 102. Unknown
103. Drucilla Garland

104. John Hargrove
105. Dell Heath Knight
106. Billie Heath   19 Jan 1901   18 Aug 1901   J. H. Heath - father
                                                                J.H. & I.J. parents
107. - 108. Unknown
109. Amy E. Scott   9 Sep 1891   J. H. Scott - hus.

110. Sally Outland   J.B. Futrell - bro.
111. Futrell un-identified
112. McDougal un-identified
113. Mary Elizabeth McDougal   22 Jun 1886   19 Feb 1904   R.P. & Mary parents
114. McDougl un-identified   " - parents

115. - 118. Futrell un-identified
119. Ann Elisabeth Futrell   11 Jul 1876   25 Mar 1877   W.B. & Martha A. pts
120. Ollie Futrell   8 Nov 1869   31 Mar 1886   " - parents
121. Virginia Futrell   16 Apr 1874   2 Jun 1896   " - pts; J.N.
                                                                Futrell - husband
122. C. M Hargrove   Ms C.M. Hargrove -w

123. J. H. Jones   1853   1927   Dixie Williams - sis
124. Eva May Jones   3 Nov 1913   24 Oct 1914   J.H. & O.M. - pts
125. Joohn Wilmer Jones   11 Dec 1915   23 Sep 1935   Dixie Williams -aunt
126. Unknown
127. Henry W. Heath   3 May 1900   15 Jul 1906   J.H. & I.W. - pts

128. Marvin Barnes   2 May 1892   15 May 1893   J.H. & M.A. - pts
129. Rosalie Barnes   23 Sep 1886   12 Jul 1888   " - parents
130. - 131. Unknown McDougal
132. Mary C. McDougla   21 Mar 1853   24 Apr 1917   R.P. McDougal - hus.
133. Unknown McDougal

134. Mary Jane Vinxon   6 Sep 1899   20 Jul 1922   G.S. & Alpha parents
135. Little Tommie Vinson, Jr. 22 Mar 1929   19 Nov 1930   Tommie Vinson - f
136. Lola Vinson   1908   1935   " - husband
137. Adam Garner   Ms Tishie McDougal-s
138. Sills infant   23 Oct 1909   23 Oct 1909   B.B. & P.A. Sills -p

139. Mrs. M. A. Sills
140. Henry G. Futrell   12 Sep 1911   22 Mar 1930   A.C. Futrell - f
141. Fannie Futrell   19 Oct 1897   8 Mar 1929   " - father
142. Annie Elizabeth Futrell   1 Jul 1900   16 Dec 1915   A.C. & R.E. - pts
143. Ollie Lee Futrell   4 Sep 1888   6 Jan 1891   " - parents

144. Dellam Futrell   8 Oct 1890   13 Oct 1890   " - parents
145. Oscar B. Futrell   24 Oct 1886   27 Jul 1888   " - parents
146. R. E. Futrell   31 May 1867   11 May 1923   A.C. Futrell - hus.
147. McDougal un-indentified
148. Hontas Hope McDougal   15 Feb 1919   7 Jul 1919   W.E. & F.McDougal-pt

149. Ronald Earl McDougal   29 Sep 1912   8 Feb 1923   W.E. & F.J. - parent
150. Unknown

* *

151. George Garland		6 Sep 1936	76 yrs
152. Margaret Garland			
153. Ms Ollie Green		6 Sep 1935	40 yrs 4 ms 20 dys
			Jesse Green - hus.
154. - 156. Green infants			Jesse & Ollie - pts
157. Rose May Vinson	29 Jan 1898	25 Aug 1899	W.F. & L.R. parents
158. F. C. Vinson	6 May 1896	10 Feb 1897	" - parents
159. A. D. Vinson	12 Dec 1894	21 Dec 1894	" - parents
160. Little Inor Hodges	12 nov 1886	18 Aug 1888	W.H. & E. J. parents
161. Etna Janie Vinson	14 Feb 1889	30 Sep 1912	W.F. & L.R. parents
162. Alfred Downs	Co D - 50 TN INF - CSA		Ann Downs - wife
163. Rachel Garner			
164. - 165. Green un-identified			
166. - 169. Unknown			
170. McDougal infant	16 Apr 191?	16 Apr 191?	R.S. & D.B. parents
171. R. Stokeley McDougal	1875	1936	Ms R.S. McDougal - w
172. Relus Jackson McDougal	1872	1935	Rayburn McDougal - s
173. G.W. Atkins	19 Mar 1874	1 Jan 1936	Dell Atkins - son
174. Walter Scott			Will Scott - bro.
175. A. B. Scott	26 Sep 1896	6 Nov 1924	" - bro.
176. Unknown			
177. McDougal infant	24 Dec 1912	24 Dec 1912	Ms Starkey Futrell m
178. M. F. McDougal	25 Nov 1880	20 Sep 1917	" - widow
179. Montico Cook	18 Jun 1899	1 Aug 1931	Frank Cook - father
180. B. Elmont Cook	1902	1924	J.F. & S.J. parents
181. Cook infant	1898	1898	" - parents
182. Orval Cook	1917	1918	" - parents
183. Garland infant			John Garland - f
184. Elam Shemwell	15 Jun 1912	15 Jun 1912	Lou & T.M. parents
185. W. H. Fox			Ms Troy Knight - dau
186. Almedia Fox	28 Sep 1865	14 Dec 1913	W.H. Fox - hus
187. Unknown			
188. Joe Cook		8 Aug 1936	64 yrs 7 ms 16 dys
189. Mrs. Joe Cook			Ralph Cook - son
190. Unknown			
191. A.M.H. Frizzell			Ms B.B. Sills - dau.
192. - 193. Unknown			
194. Shaw infant	17 Oct 1927	17 Oct 1927	d/o C.B. Shaw
195. Unknown			
196. Anna Gale McDougal	6 Aug 1923	17 Sep 1923	
197. Euphenia Futrell	1850	1937	J.B. Futrell - son
198. John J. Futrell	1851	14 Jul 1936	85 yrs 2 ms 5 dys
			J.B. Futrell - son
199. Mrs. W. T. Hendricks			Hugh Hendricks - son
200. William T. Hendricks		27 Jun 1928	" - son
201. Oscar Vinson		26 Mar 1940	48 yrs 4 ms 5 days

* *

202.	J. H. Vinson	9 Dec 1859	13 Jan 1940	
203.	Unknown			
204.	W. T. Suddarth	4 May 1882	6 Feb 1938	A. Marion Suddarth f
205.	James S. Futrell	22 Jun 1859	24 Feb 1938	J.S. Futrell - son
206.	Unknown			
207.	Martha Vinson Dick	1866	1938	wife of J.F. Dick,
208.	Naomi A. Sills		11 Dec 1937	83 yrs 10 ms 14 dys
				B.B. Sills - son
209.	Fannie Ann Irvin		23 Jun 1939	1 yr 8 ms - Grace
				Irvin - mother
210.	Willie F. Vinson		15 May 1939	73 yrs 4 ms 19 dys
211. - 212.	Green un-identified			
213. - 217.	Unknown			
218.	Tishey Garner McDougal	1874	1939	Rayburn McDougal - s

#121 VINSON SLAVE CEMETERY

Located on Land Map 51, Tract GIR-2118, above elevation 380, 21 graves. This was an old abandoned slave cemetery. None of the graves could be identified and no one could be found who was interested in having them moved. No further action was necessary.

#122 VINSON CEMETERY

Located on land Map 51, Tract GIR-2119, above elevation 380, number of graves un-certain. This burial area had been in cultivation and there were no indications of graves. Some negro graves were said to be located in the area. Charles Vinson, age 66, was born and raised on the place and only vaguely remembers being shown the location as a small boy.

#123 RUSHING CREEK CEMETERY

Located on Land Map 47, Tract GIR-2145, above elevation 380, 71 graves. This was a fairly active cemetery and fairly well kept. Remain permits were executed on all (65) identified graves. One remain permit was executed on the grave of a person known to have been buried here, but the exact location of the grave was not known. This permit possibly covered one of the six unidentified graves. No further action was necessary. The following information was taken from Field Book #MS-874.

No.	Name of Deceased	Date of Birth	Date of Death	Information given by

* *

1.	Futrell child			Storkey Futrell - f
2.	Futrell child			" - father
3.	Deno Futrell	14 Jun 1887	23 Sep 1917	" - husband
4.	Ollie Knigh			
5.	Crete Knight			Tony Knight - nephew

* *

No.	Name			
6.	Lola Knight			
7.	Walter Downs	18 Feb 1889	16 Apr 1930	Francie Downs - wife
8.	Moncil Knight	30 Aug 1857	16 Jan 1923	Mary J. May Knight,w
9.	Mary J. May Knight	10 nov 1858	2 Oct 1924	Ben F. May - bro.
10.	S. S. Knight	30 Dec 1880	3 Jul 1904	
11.	Stroud Knight	child		Ollie Pague - mother
12.	Orvill Futrell			Onus Futrell - f
13.	O'Kay Rushing		d/o D. and Sarah E. Rushing	
14.	Tabithey Rushing			" - parents
15.	Rushing twins			" - parents
16.	Rushing child			" - parents
17.	Sarah E. Rushing			Arty Rushing - son
18.	Lora Knight			Finne Knight - f.
19.	Amy Knight			" - g/son
20.	Nannie Knight			Rufus Knight (#21) f
21.	Rufus Knight			Ms M. Knight d-in-1
22.	Thomas Knight			
23.	R. V. Knight			
24.	Paulie Knight			" - mother
25.	Colley Knight			" - mother
26.	D. Knight			" - wife
27.	D. R. Futrell	18 Nov 1935	72 yrs 11 ms 24 dys	
		husband of Mary E Futrell (#74)		
				Cozy Lee Doughty - d
28.	Unknonw			
29.	Sarah Echols Knight			Zora Hendon - sister
30.	Pondexter Knight			" - sister
31.	Futrell child			Cozy Lee Doughty - s
32.	Arthur Herman Futrell			" - sister
33.	Andie Futrell			" - sister
34.	John Futrell	husband of Alphey Futrell (#35)		
35.	Alphey Futrell		1909	Ms J.W. Barrow - dau
36.	Futrell child			Robert Futrell - f
37.	Futrell child			" - father
38.	Janey King			A.G. King - father
39.	Lucy King			" - father
40.	King child			P.V. King - father
41.	King child			" - father
42.	Connie King			" - father
43.	Eula King			" - father
44.	W. B. King	husband to Mary King (#45)		M.F. King - son
45.	Mary King	17 Apr 1842	3 Nov 1906	" - son
46.	Kandy King			W.B. & Mary King - pts
47.	Janey King			" - parents
48.	Kate Walker		wife of George Walker #49	
49.	George Walker			
50. - 53.	Unknown			

* *

54.	Lizzie Garland			wife of Jessie Garland #55
55.	Jessie Garland			Fenton Garland – son
56.	Taylor child			Pink Taylor – father
57.	Lottie Knight			Julie Knight #58 mother
58.	Julie Knight			B. Knight – husband
59.	Ashton Knight			" – father
60.	George Fuqua	15 Feb 1875	3 Jul 1909	Seaman Fuqua – bro.
61.	John Fuqua			" – son
62.	John Smith			Kate Smith – dau.
63.	Smith child			" – sister
64.	Niecie Rushing Futrell	mother of #36 & #37		Robert Futrell – hus
65.	Askew un-identified			
66.	Amy Downs			Oliver Downs – g/son
67.	Lorraine Rushing	husband of Theeney Rushing #68		
68.	Theeney Rushing			J.D. Rushing – son
69.	Robert King			M.F. King – bro.
70.	Mary Elizabeth Futrell	1866	1939	wife of D.R. Futrell #37

Note: Other graves are evident but have been destroyed. Mr. J. W. Barrow and other competent persons are positive that three or four graves are within a radius of 30 feet of grave #69.

#124 DILDAY CEMETERY

Located on Land Map 47, Tract GIR-2136, above elevation 380, 81 graves. This was a fairly active and well kept cemetery. Two removal permits and 15 remain permits were executed. The remaining 64 graves could not be identified or no one could be found who was interested in having them moved. Two graves and one monument were moved to Murray City Cemetery on November 14, 1942. Information found in Field Book MS-895.

No.	Name of Deceased	Birth	Date of Death	Information given by...

* *

1.	Mary Etta Dilday	1844	1924	Lon Dilday – son
2.	R. H. Dilday	1850	1915	" – son
3. – 4.	Unknown			
5.	Minnie May Locke	1867	1869	
6.	Mary Jane Vinson	1842	1863	
7.	Abie Ross			
8.	Lurue Bass			
9.	West Bass			
10.	Augusta Bass			
11. – 14.	Unknown			
15.	Russell infant	infant	1914	
16.	Dr. A. D. Russell	1876	1935	
17. – 53.	Unknown			
54.	Outland infant	infant	unk	

* *

No.	Name	Birth	Death	Information
55. - 59.	Unknown			
60.	Ruff Downs		1894	Ms Wess Fugua - wife
61.	Will Downs		unk	Ms Walter Miller - wife
62. - 66.	Unknown			
67.	J. F. Barrow	1869	1924	
68.	Ethel Barrow	1880	1916	
69.	Barrow infant		unk	
70.	Bertie B. Barrow	1902	1916	
71. - 72.	Unknown			
73.	W. K. Barrow	1834	1879	
74.	Blanche E. Barrow	1842	1907	
75.	Robert L. Hicks	1869	1898	
76. - 78.	Unknown			
79.	Mary Louise Barrow		1930	Oscar Barrow - father
80. - 81.	Unknown			

#126 WILLIAMS CEMETERY

Located on land Map 47, Tract GIR-2152, above elevation 380, seven graves. All were identified and remain permits executed.

No.	Name of Deceased	Birth	Death	Information given by...
1.	J. S. Williams	1837	1882	Esther Allen - dau.
2.	Isabella Williams	1839	1925	" - dau.
3.	Anderson Williams	1880	1885	" - aunt
4.	Irving Williams		1885	Age 2 yrs " - aunt
5.	Williams infant		1885	
6.	N. A. Dilday	1856	1889	" - dau.-in-law
7.	Lola Belle Dilday		1888	" - aunt - 8 ms

#127 FUTRELL CEMETERY

Located on Land Map 47, Tract GIR-2140, between elevation 368-372, 14 graves. All graves were identified and removal permits executed. Fourteen graves and two monuments were moved to two reinterment cemeteries. Removal operations were completed October 22, 1942.

No.	Name of Deceased	Age	Date of Death	Information given by...
1.	Jane Fakes	unk	unk	
2.	Pocohontas Knight	infant	unk	
3.	Barrow infant	infant	1893	
4.	Alden Futrell	unk	unk	
5.	Knight infant	unk	unk	

* *

No.	Name	Date of Birth	Date of Death
6.	Bud Knight	unk	unk
7.	James E. Futrell	24	1852
8.	Isaac Futrell	25 Dec 1796	25 Aug 1836
9.	Levicy Futrell	unk	unk
10.	J. Knight	unk	Unk
11.	Stokley Futrell	5	unk
12.	Francis Knight	unk	unk
13.	Virginia Knight	unk	unk
14.	Neoma Clark	unk	unk

#128 LONE GRAVE

Located on Land Map 47, Tract GIR-2127, elevation 320, single grave. It was reputed to be the grave of an unidentified negro, whose body was found in the river near this site. There was no evidence of a grave and no further action was necessary.

#130 PINK HEATHCOCK CEMETERY

Located on Land Map 47, Tract GIR-2169, elevation 380, single grave. This grave of Pink Heathcock, age 15 who died in 1893 of typhoid, and monument were moved to Futrell Cemetery R-28 on March 4, 1943.

#131 TAYLOR CEMETERY

Located on land Map 67, Tract GIR-2731F, above elevation 380, 3 graves. All graves were identified and remain permits executed. Information taken from Field Book #MS-895.

No.	Name of Deceased	Date of Birth	Date of Death	Information given by
1.	J. M. Taylor	26 Oct 1832	12 Feb 1916	Fanny Lancaster – d
2.	Maranda Taylor	2 Jun 1829	7 Jan 1908	" sister
3.	Thedus Taylor		1902	age 24

* *

133 VINSON PUBLIC CEMETERY

Located on Land Map 55, Tract GIR-2203, above elevation 380, 26 graves. This was a fairly active but poorly kept cemetery. Remain permits were executed on 25 graves. No relatives of the person interred in one grave could be located.   No action was necessary.

No.	Name of Deceased	Age	Date of Death	Information given by...

* *

No.	Name of Deceased	Age	Date of Death	Information given by...
1.	J. L. Seawright		1900	E.O.Seawright - son
2.	Seawright infant		1878	" - bro.
3.	Claudie G. Vinson		1885	Annie M. Vinson - mother
4.	Moston C. Vinson		1899	" - wife
5.	Unknown			
6.	Lillie C. Vinson		1900	" - mother
7.	Eleana June Vinson		1906	C.D. Vinson - father
8.	Vinson infant		1936	" - father
9.	John P. Thomas		1898	Lucy P. Roper - sister
10.	Roper infant			" - mother
11. - 14.	Unknown			
15.	Louisa J. Seawright		1903	E.O. Seawright - son
16.	E. J. Vinson		1907	Annie M. Vinson - d-in-1
17. - 26.	Unknown			

#715 RUSHING CEMETERY

Located on Land Map 47, Tract GIR-2185F, between elevation 371-372, 10 graves. This was an old abandoned cemetery.   Four removal permits and 6 remain permits were executed. Four graves were moved to Rushing Cemetery R-85 on May 10, 1943.

No.	Name of Deceased	Age	Date of Death	Information given by...

* *

No.	Name of Deceased	Age	Date of Death	Information given by...
1.	Billie Rushing	unk	unk	
2.	Betsy Rushing			
3.	Unknown			
4.	Lucy Rushing			
5. - 8.	Unknown			
9.	Peter Rushing			
10.	Unknown			

#775 NO NAME CEMETERY

Located on Land Map 76, Tract GIR-2986, above elevation 380, two graves. This was an old abandoned cemetery. No information could be obtained as to who might have been buried here, and no one could be found who was interested in having them moved.

* *

#840 OLD CEMETERY

Located on Land Map 79, Tract GIR-2965, above elevation 380, two graves. The graves could not be identified and no one could be found who was interested in having them moved. No further action was necessary.

#853 MARTIN CEMETERY

Located on Land Map 83, Tract GIR-3094, between elevation 378-380, 24 graves. This was an old abandoned cemetery. None of the graves could be identified. W. A. Martin had a number of relatives buried in the cemetery but could not identify the graves. He requested that all graves be moved out of the flooded area. All graves were moved to St. Mary's Cemetery R-25 on October 9, 1942.

#854 BAILEY CEMETERY

Located on Land Map 64, Tract GIR-2659, above elevation 380, 8 graves. This was an old, abandoned, slave cemetery. No burials having been made in over 65 years. None of the graves could be identified and no one could be found who was interest in having them moved. No further action was necessary.

#855 BROOKS CEMETERY

Located on Land Map 83, Tract GIR 3094, elevation between 368-377, 133 graves. This was a very old, abandoned, colored cemetery. Only six graves could be identified. Alice Conyers, a colored woman, had a number of relatives buried in the cemetery, but could not identify the graves. She requested that all the graves be moved out of the flooded area. The graves and six monuments were moved to St. Mary's Cemetery R-25. Grave removal operations were completed April 15, 1943.

No.	Name of Deceased	Age	Date of Death

* *

No.	Name of Deceased	Age	Date of Death
1. - 23.	Unknown		
24.	Evans Humbel	17	1888
24. - 35.	Unknown		
36.	Starkis Irvin	11	1886
37. - 40.	Unknown		
41.	Thomas Moody	18	1868
42.	Ella Moody	18	1889
43.	Johnny Perry	9	1889
44. - 47.	Unknown		
48.	Chaney Woods	17	1887
49. - 133.	Unknown		

* *

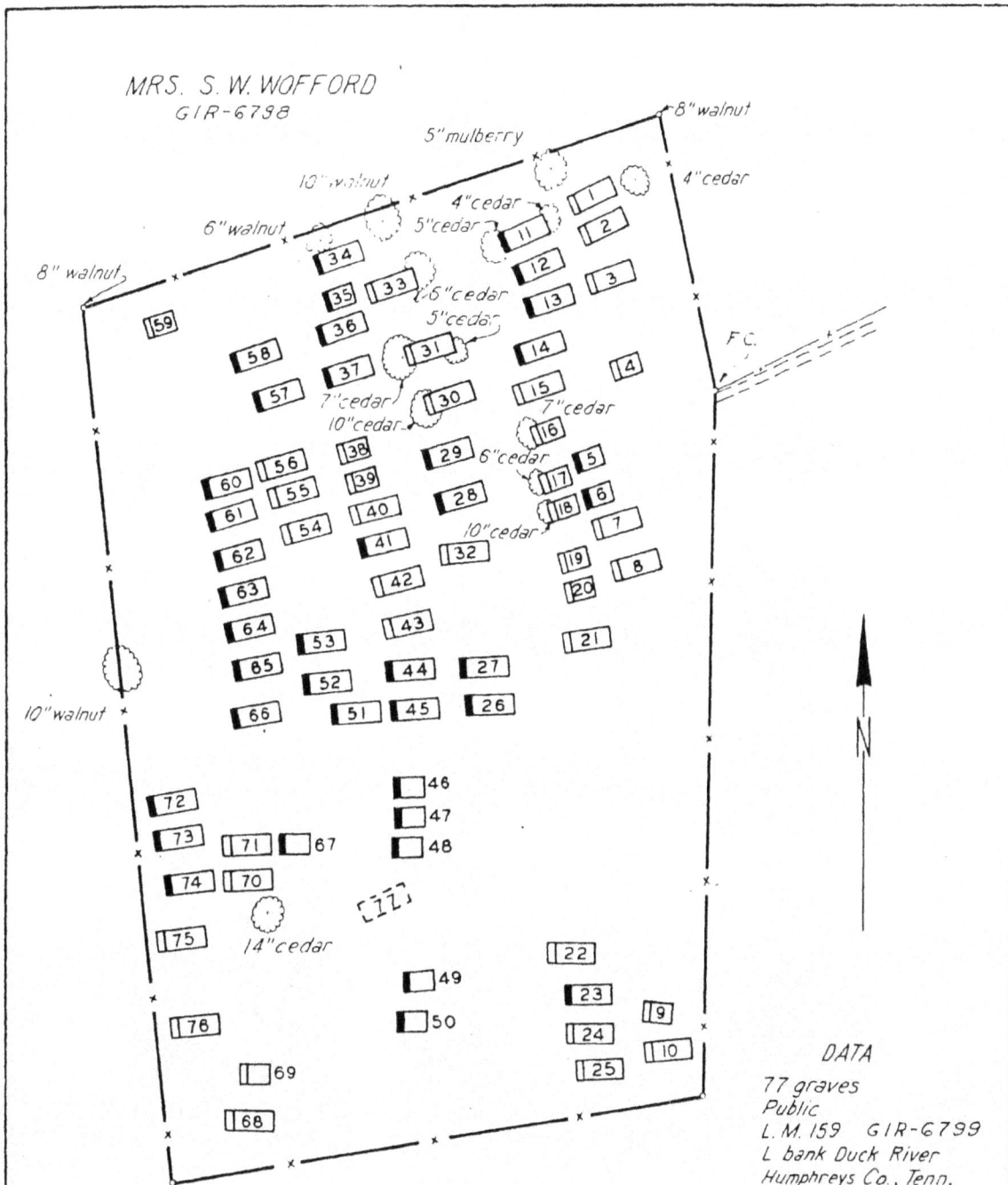

MRS. S. W. WOFFORD
GIR-6798

5"mulberry

8"walnut

10"walnut

4"cedar

4"cedar

6"walnut

34

5"cedar

1

11

2

35   33

12

6"cedar

13

3

8" walnut

59

36

5"cedar

58   31

14

57   37

14

7"cedar

30

15

10"cedar

16

7"cedar

38   29   6"cedar   5

60   56   39

17

61   55   28   18   6

62   54   40

7

63   41   10"cedar

32   19

8

64   42

20

65   53   43   21

85   52   44   27

66   51   45   26

FC.

N

72

46

73   71   67   47

74   70   48

75

???

14"cedar

49

22

76   50

23   9

24

10

69   25

68

Note: Above Elev. 400

DATA

77 graves
Public
L.M. 159 GIR-6799
L bank Duck River
Humphreys Co., Tenn.
P.T.S. 8MS 432A808-14

LEGEND

■ Graves with monuments and names

▯ Graves marked but unnamed

▯ Graves unmarked and unnamed

⌐¬ Questionable graves

CEMETERIES

NEBLETT
CEMETERY

NO.
14

KENTUCKY RESERVOIR
TENNESSEE VALLEY AUTHORITY
MAPS AND SURVEYS DIVISION

SCALE OF FEET

CHATTANOOGA 5-22-42 MGT-432A1003

* *

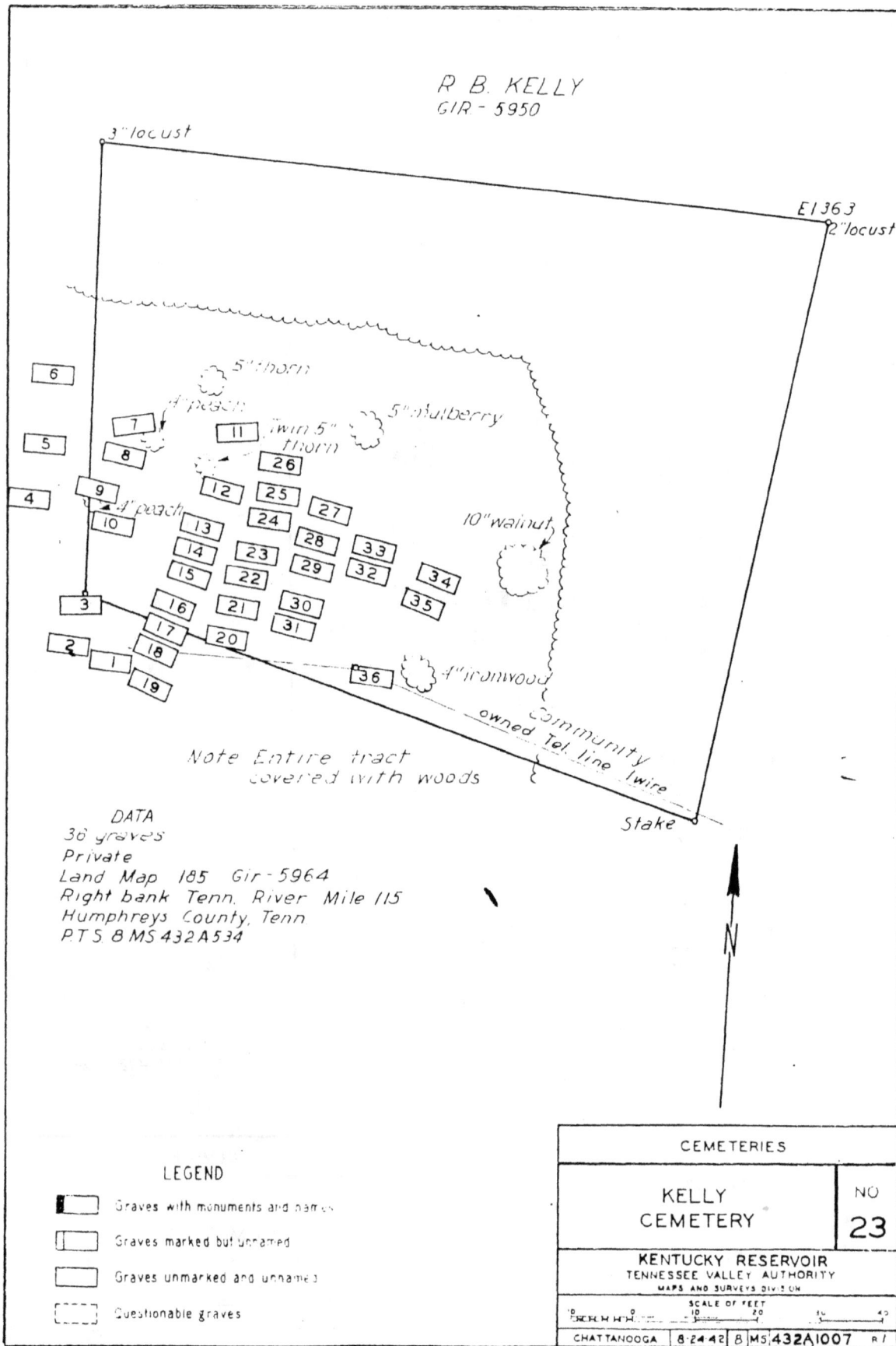

R B. KELLY
GIR - 5950

3"locust

E1363
2"locust

6

5"thorn

4"peach

5"mulberry

7

11 Twin 5"
thorn

5

8

26

4

9

12 25 27

10 4"peach

10"walnut

13 24 28 33

14 23 29 32

15 22

34

3

16 21 30

35

17 20 31

2

18

1

36 4"ironwood

19

Community
owned Tel. line Iwire

Note Entire tract
covered with woods

Stake

DATA
36 graves
Private
Land Map 185 Gir - 5964
Right bank Tenn. River Mile 115
Humphreys County, Tenn
P.T.S. 8 MS 432 A 534

N

LEGEND

Graves with monuments and names

Graves marked but unnamed

Graves unmarked and unnamed

Questionable graves

CEMETERIES

KELLY
CEMETERY

NO
23

KENTUCKY RESERVOIR
TENNESSEE VALLEY AUTHORITY
MAPS AND SURVEYS DIVISION

SCALE OF FEET

CHATTANOOGA 8-24-42 8 MS 432 A 1007 R.1

* *

HESTER CLARK
GIR - 5184

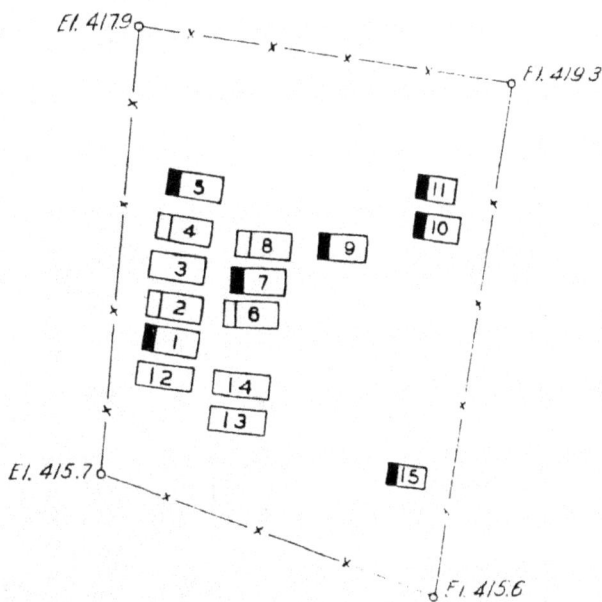

DATA
15 graves
Private
Land Map 143
Right bank Tennessee River Mi. 69
Humphreys County, Tennessee
PTS 8NS432A 808-30

LEGEND

- ▮ Graves with monuments and names
- ▯ Graves marked but unnamed
- ☐ Graves unmarked and unnamed
- ⊡ Questionable graves

CEMETERIES		
MARBERRY #1 CEMETERY		NO 30
KENTUCKY RESERVOIR TENNESSEE VALLEY AUTHORITY MAPS AND SURVEYS DIVISION		
SCALE OF FEET		
CHATTANOOGA 9-18-41	8 ES 7	50AI-30 R1

* *

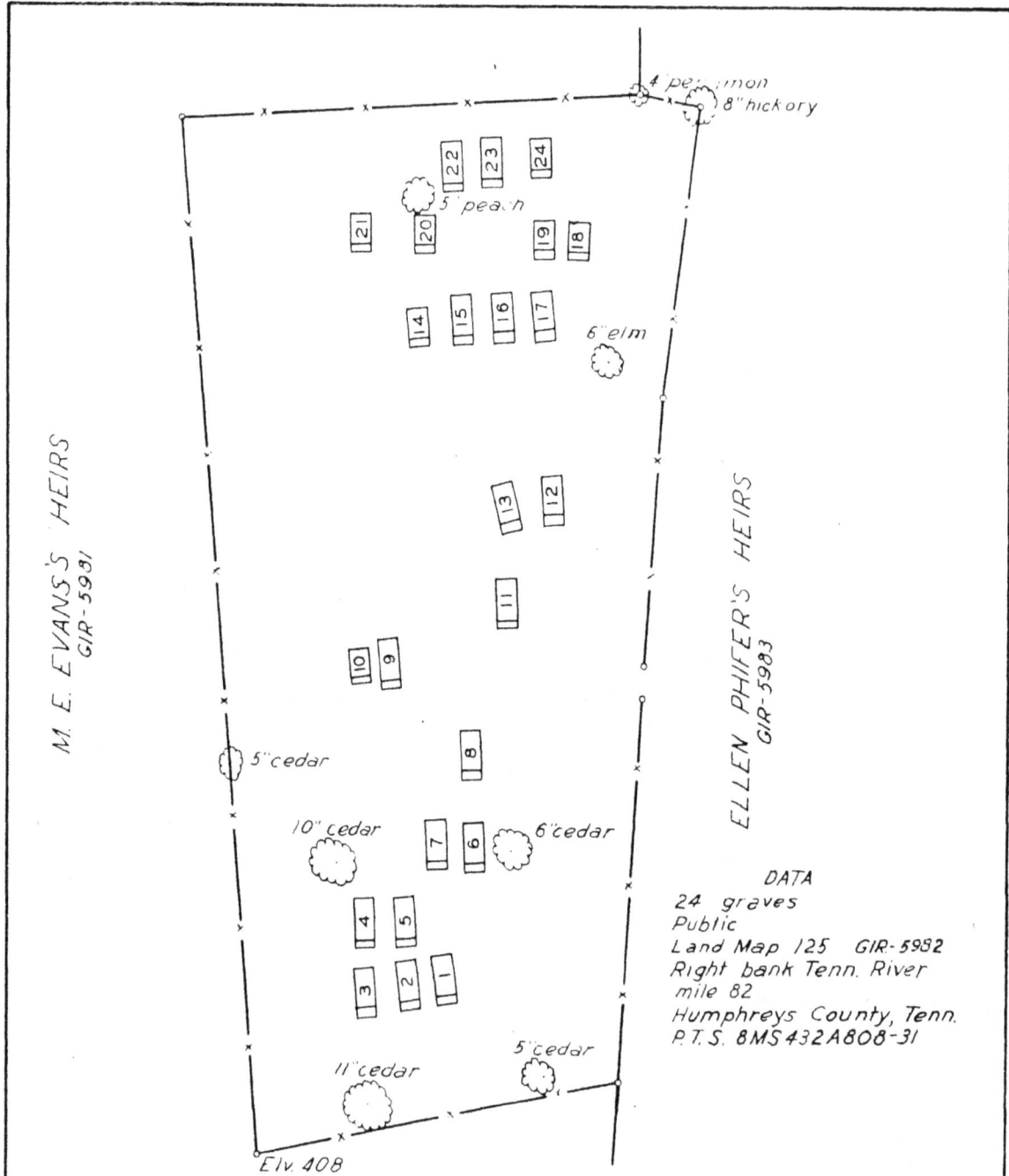

4" persimmon
8" hickory

22 23 24

21 20 5" peach 19 18

14 15 16 17

6" elm

13 12

11

10 9

8

5" cedar

10" cedar 7 6 6" cedar

4 5

3 2 1

5" cedar

11" cedar

Elv. 408

M. E. EVANS'S HEIRS
GIR-5931

ELLEN PHIFER'S HEIRS
GIR-5983

DATA
24 graves
Public
Land Map 125   GIR-5932
Right bank Tenn. River
mile 82
Humphreys County, Tenn.
P.T.S. 8MS 432A808-31

N

LEGEND

Graves with monuments and names

Graves marked but unnamed

Graves unmarked and unnamed

Questionable graves

CEMETERIES	
HALEY CEMETERY	NO. 31

KENTUCKY RESERVOIR
TENNESSEE VALLEY AUTHORITY
MAPS AND SURVEYS DIVISION

SCALE OF FEET

CHATTANOOGA   6-23-42   432A986

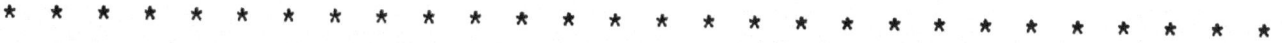

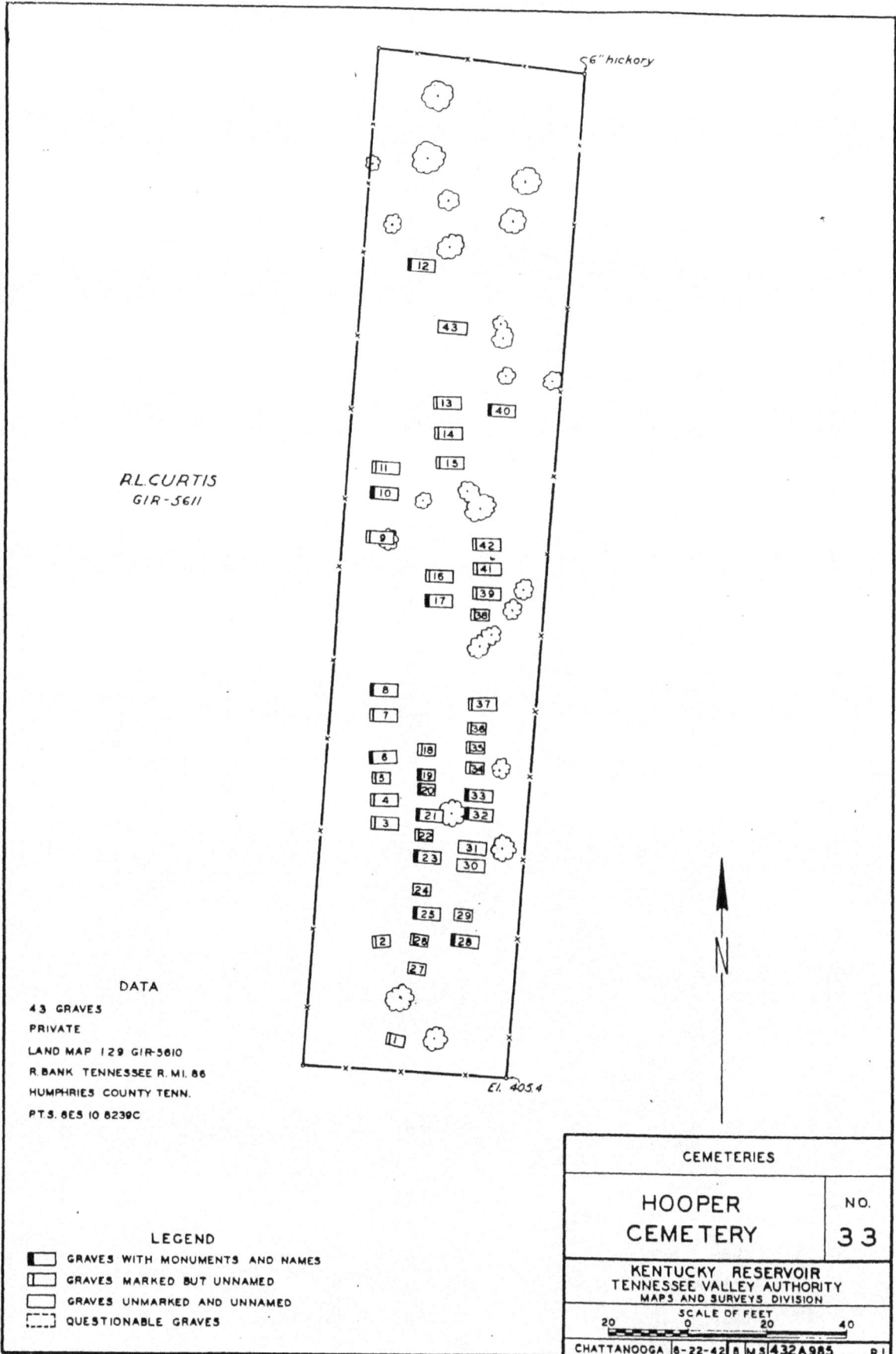

R.L.CURTIS
GIR-5611

6" hickory

DATA

43 GRAVES

PRIVATE

LAND MAP 129 GIR-5610

R.BANK TENNESSEE R. MI. 86

HUMPHRIES COUNTY TENN.

P.T.S. 8E5 10 8239C

N

LEGEND

- GRAVES WITH MONUMENTS AND NAMES
- GRAVES MARKED BUT UNNAMED
- GRAVES UNMARKED AND UNNAMED
- QUESTIONABLE GRAVES

El. 405.4

CEMETERIES	
HOOPER CEMETERY	NO. 33
KENTUCKY RESERVOIR TENNESSEE VALLEY AUTHORITY MAPS AND SURVEYS DIVISION	

SCALE OF FEET

20 0 20 40

CHATTANOOGA 6-22-42 8 M S 432A985 R.1

* *

JOHN LUCAS'S HEIRS
GIR 5089

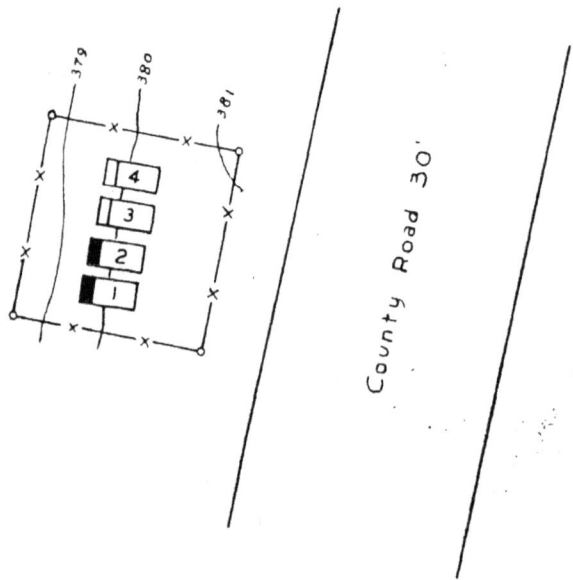

379   380   381

4
3
2
1

County Road 30'

N

DATA

4 graves
Private
Land map 139
Right bank Tenn. River, mi.93
Humphreys Co. Tenn.
P.T.S. 8 MS 432 A 808 - 36

LEGEND

▮ Graves with monuments and names

▯ Graves marked but unnamed

▭ Graves unmarked and unnamed

⌐ ⌐ Questionable graves

CEMETERIES	
LUCAS CEMETERY	NO. 36
KENTUCKY RESERVOIR TENNESSEE VALLEY AUTHORITY MAPS AND SURVEYS DIVISION SCALE OF FEET	
CHATTANOOGA 9-18-41 B ES 7 50AI-36 R.0	

* *

C.W. TURNER AND A.V. ANDERSON
GIR-5098

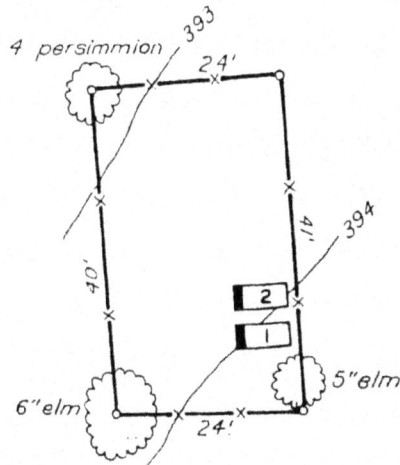

4 persimmion 393
24'
41' 394
2
1
5"elm
6"elm 24'

N

DATA

2 graves
Private
Land map 139, GIR-5104
Right bank Tennessee River mi. 92.5
Humphreys County, Tennessee
P.T.S.8MS432A652

LEGEND

Graves with monuments and names

Graves marked but unnamed

Graves unmarked and unnamed

Questionable graves

CEMETERIES	
TURNER #1 CEMETERY	NO. 38

KENTUCKY RESERVOIR
TENNESSEE VALLEY AUTHORITY
MAPS AND SURVEYS DIVISION

SCALE OF FEET

CHATTANOOGA   9-23-41   8 ES 7 50AI-38

* *

HENRY TURNER'S HEIRS
GIR-5095

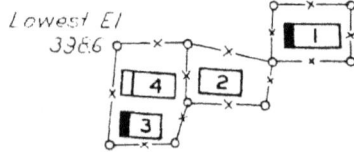

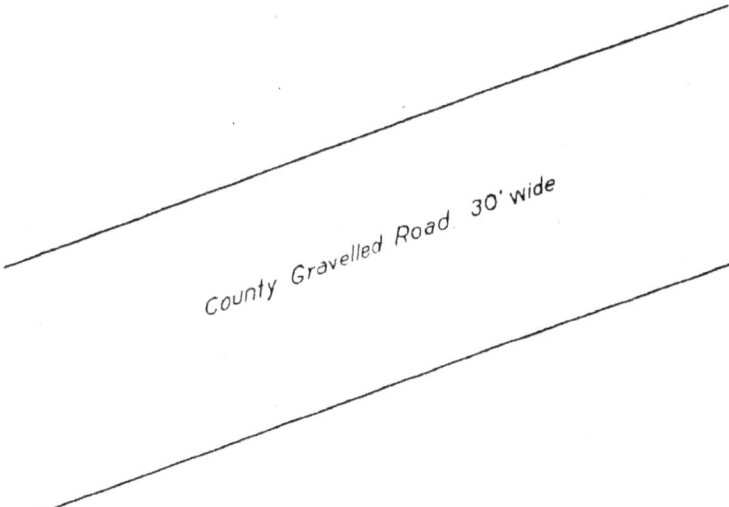

Lowest El.
398.6

4 2

1

3

County Gravelled Road 30' wide

N

DATA

4 graves
Private
Land map 139, GIR-5096
Right bank Tennessee River mi.92
Humphreys County, Tennessee
P.T.S. 8MS432A653-39

LEGEND

Graves with monuments and names

Graves marked but unnamed

Graves unmarked and unnamed

Questionable graves

CEMETERIES

TURNER # 2
CEMETERY

NO.
39

KENTUCKY RESERVOIR
TENNESSEE VALLEY AUTHORITY
MAPS AND SURVEYS DIVISION

SCALE OF FEET

CHATTANOOGA 9-22-41 8 ES 7 50AI-39 R.O.

* *

JOHN McCOWAN
GIR - 5131

6"cedar   3"elm

6"cedar

6"cedar

TVA stake

10"elm   6"elm

8"hackberry

8"elm   5"elm   10"elm   6"elm   44

10"elm   8"elm   30   8"elm

2   10"elm   31   12"elm

3   1   10"h.locust   ⊙12"elm stump

8"persimmon   7"twin   3"elm   6"elm
elm

12"elm

10"elm   29   12"h.locust

10"elm   12"elm   6"elm   8"elm

4   24   10"elm   10"elm   6"elm   40   41

5   6"cedar   39   42

123   25   8"elm   32   14"cedar

6   122   26   6"elm   133   4"w.cherry

7   21   8"elm   28   34   8"elm   43

8   20   27   35

19   4"red wood

18   36

17   10"cedar   37   8"hackberry   8"elm   12"oak

9   16   8"mulberry   38   6"oak   T.V.A.stake

10   15

11   14

13

12

JOHN McCOWAN
GIR - 5131

N

DATA

44 graves
Land Map 140
Right bank Tenn. River, mi. 94.5
Humphreys Co., Tenn.
P.T.S. 8MS 432 A808 - 42

LEGEND

▨ Graves with monuments and names

▯ Graves marked but unnamed

▭ Graves unmarked and unnamed

⬚ Questionable graves

CEMETERIES

NAPIER
CEMETERY

NO.
42

KENTUCKY RESERVOIR
TENNESSEE VALLEY AUTHORITY
MAPS AND SURVEYS DIVISION

SCALE OF FEET

CHATTANOOGA 4-28-42 8 MS 432 A973

* *

WILL LUCAS
GIR. 5124

6" Pathway

6" Hickory Stump

Stake

6" Elm

6

5

4

7" White Oak

MRS. JENNIE
NICHOLS

3

2

6" White Oak

1

6" White Oak

4" Sweet Gum

6" White Oak
Blazed

Stake

40'

6" Dogwood

N

DATA

6 Graves
Private
Land Map 140.
Right bank Tennessee River, mi 85.5
Humphreys County, Tennessee
P.T.S. 6MS 432 A808-43

LEGEND

▮▭ Graves with monuments and names

▯ Graves marked but unnamed

▭ Graves unmarked and unnamed

⊡ Questionable graves

CEMETERIES	
WILL LUCAS CEMETERY	NO. 43
KENTUCKY RESERVOIR TENNESSEE VALLEY AUTHORITY MAPS AND SURVEYS DIVISION	

SCALE OF FEET

CHATTANOOGA 9-22-41 8 ES 7 50AI-43 R.O.

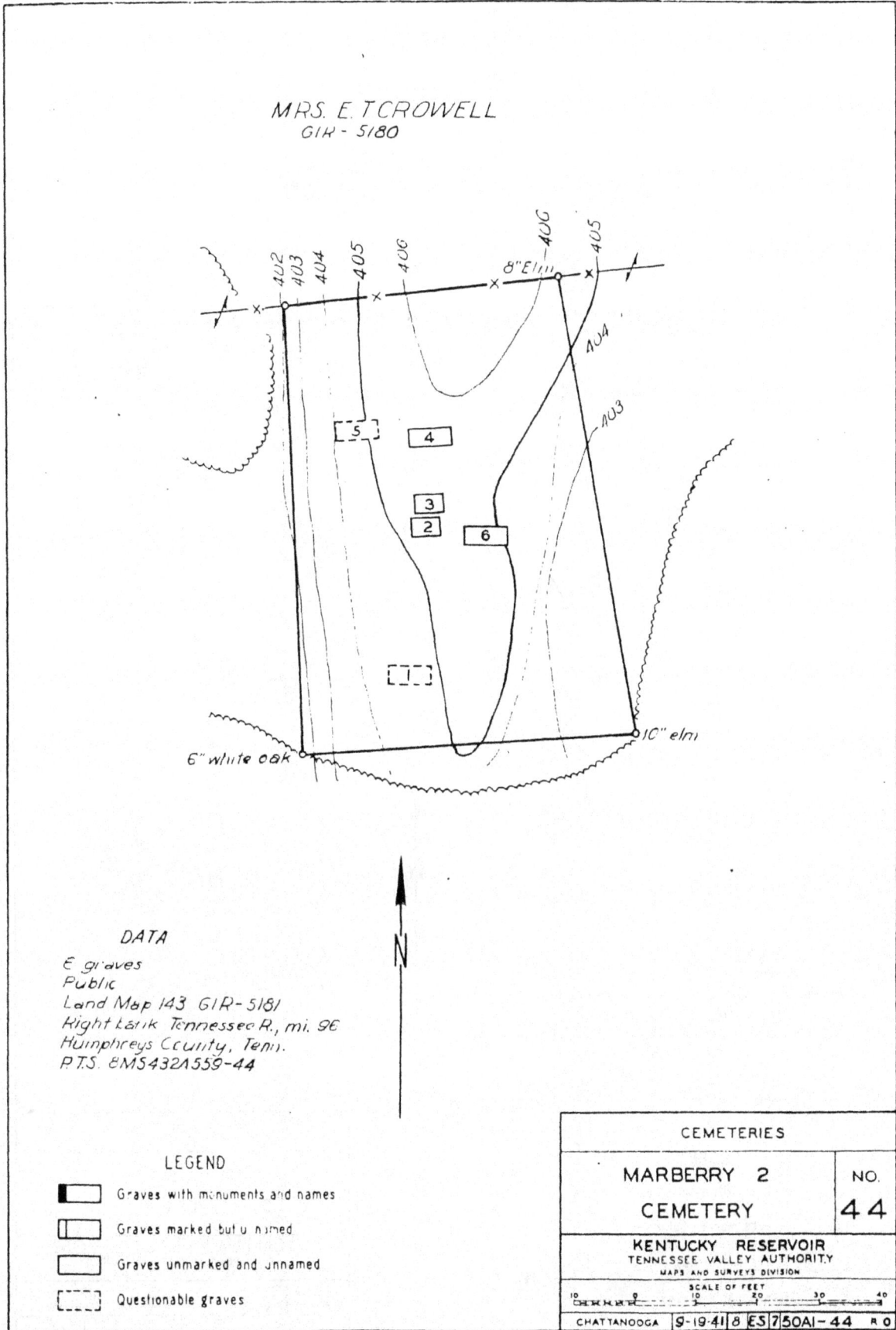

MRS. E.T CROWELL
GIR - 5180

DATA

E graves
Public
Land Map 143 GIR-5181
Right Bank Tennessee R., mi. 96
Humphreys County, Tenn.
P.T.S. 8MS432A559-44

N

LEGEND

Graves with monuments and names

Graves marked but unnamed

Graves unmarked and unnamed

Questionable graves

CEMETERIES

MARBERRY 2   NO.

CEMETERY   44

KENTUCKY RESERVOIR
TENNESSEE VALLEY AUTHORITY
MAPS AND SURVEYS DIVISION

SCALE OF FEET

CHATTANOOGA 9-19-41 8 ES 7 50AI-44 R 0

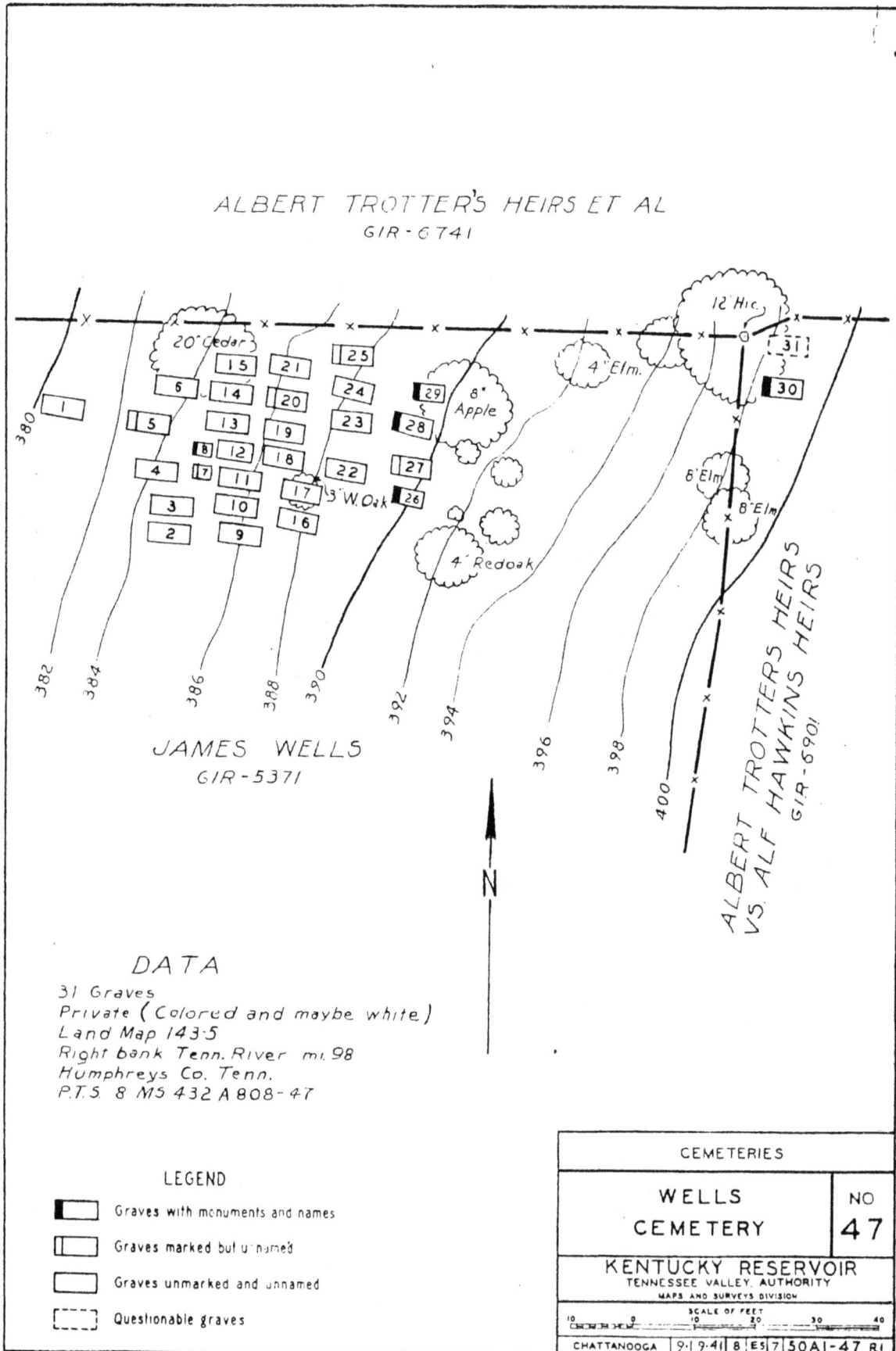

ALBERT TROTTER'S HEIRS ET AL
GIR-6741

JAMES WELLS
GIR-5371

N

DATA

31 Graves
Private (Colored and maybe white)
Land Map 143-5
Right bank Tenn. River mi. 98
Humphreys Co. Tenn.
P.T.S. 8 MS 432 A 808-47

LEGEND

Graves with monuments and names
Graves marked but unnamed
Graves unmarked and unnamed
Questionable graves

CEMETERIES	
WELLS CEMETERY	NO 47
KENTUCKY RESERVOIR TENNESSEE VALLEY AUTHORITY MAPS AND SURVEYS DIVISION	
SCALE OF FEET	
CHATTANOOGA 9-19-41 8 ES 7 50A1-47 R1	

* *

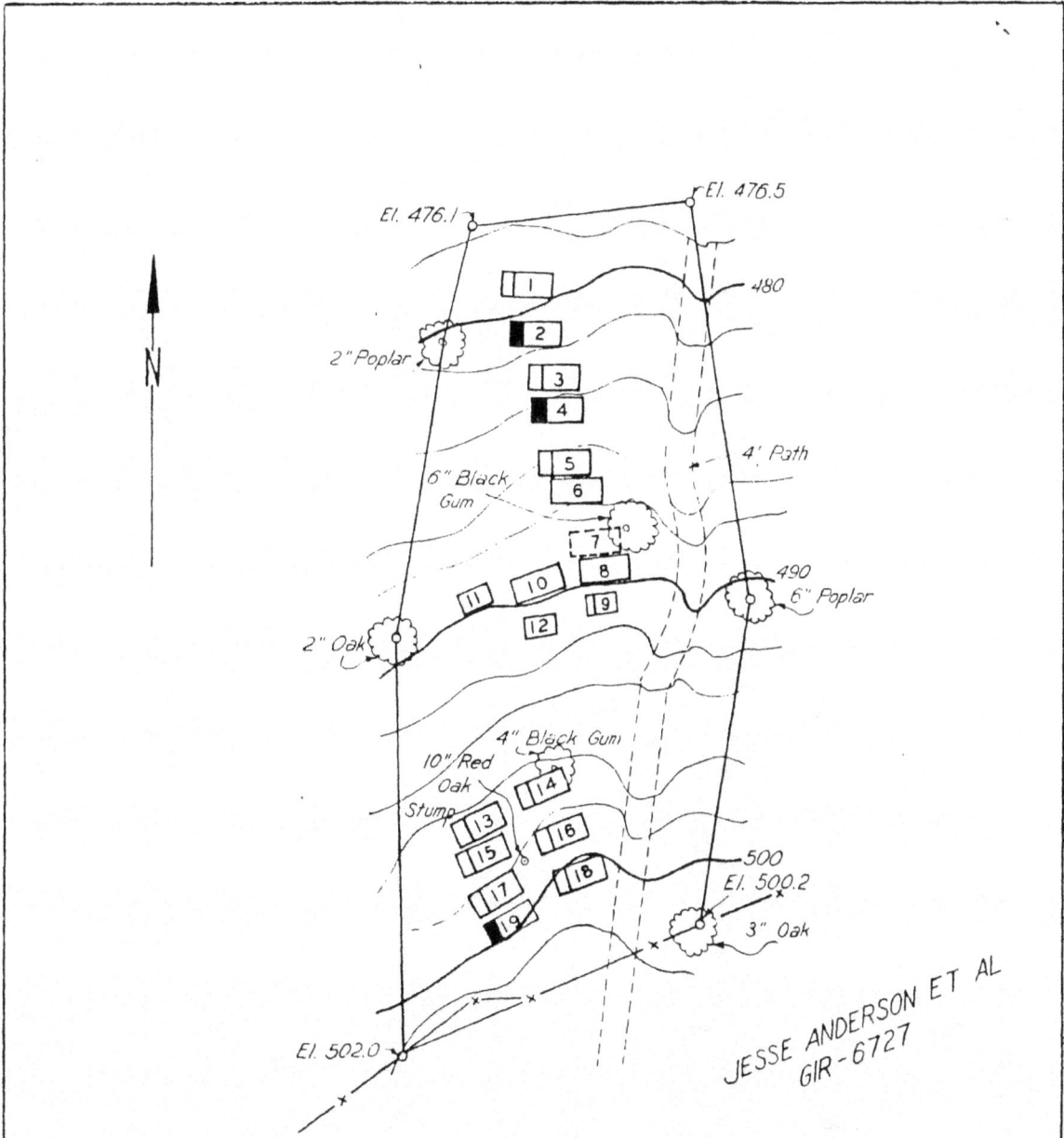

DATA

19 Graves
Private (colored)
Land Map 143-5
R. Bank Tenn. R., Mi. 98
Humphreys County, Tenn.
P.T.S. 8 MS 432 A 808-48

LEGEND

Graves with monuments and names

Graves marked but unnamed

Graves unmarked and unnamed

Questionable graves

CEMETERIES
NELS ANDERSON CEMETERY

NO 48

KENTUCKY RESERVOIR
TENNESSEE VALLEY AUTHORITY
MAPS AND SURVEYS DIVISION

SCALE OF FEET

CHATTANOOGA 9-23-41 8 ES 7 50 AI-48

* *

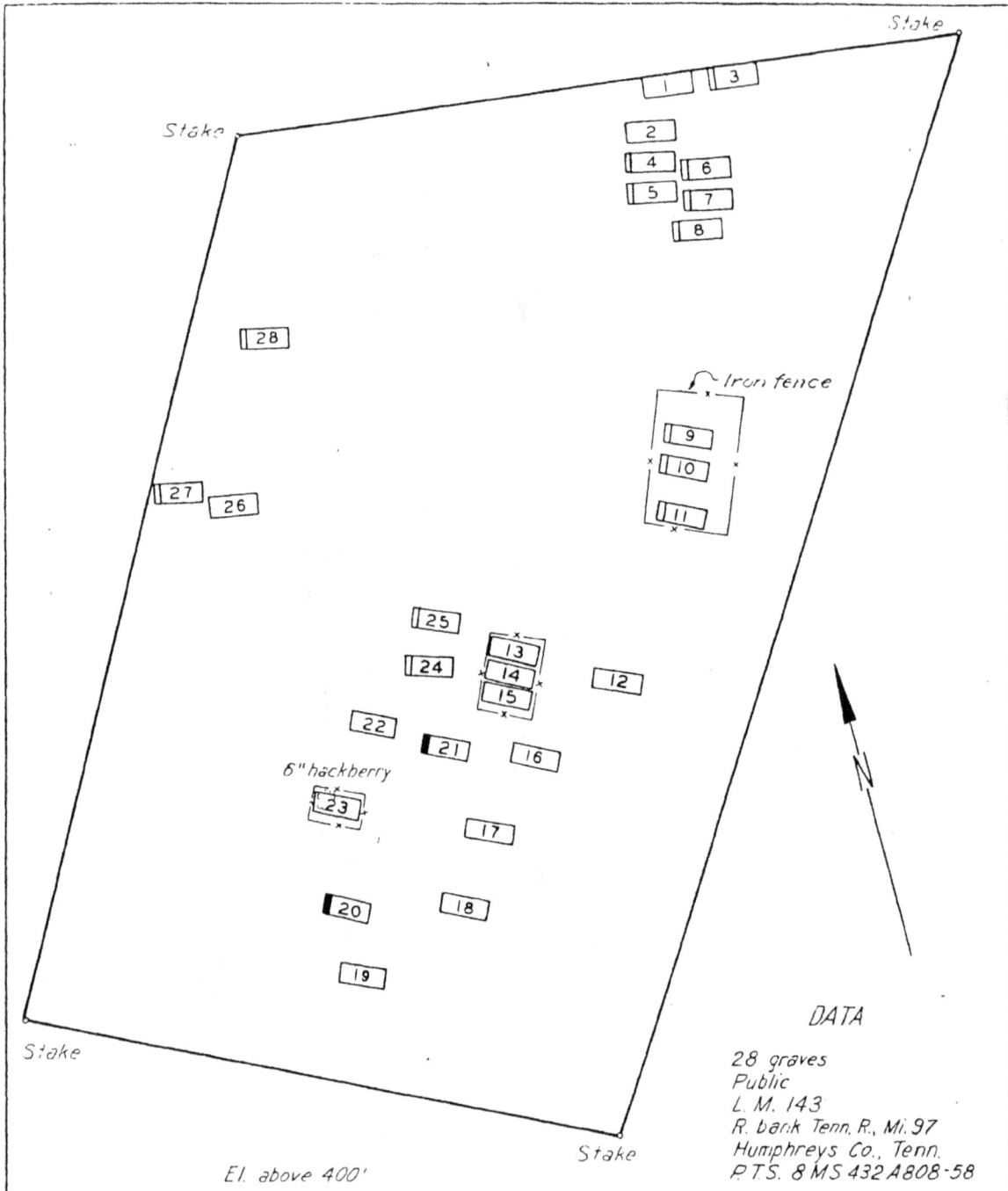

Stake

Stake

1   3

2

4   6

5   7

8

28

Iron fence

9

10

11

25

13

24   14   12

15

22

21   16

6" hackberry

23

17

20   18

19

N

DATA

28 graves
Public
L.M. 143
R. bank Tenn. R., Mi. 97
Humphreys Co., Tenn.
P.T.S. 8 MS 432 A 808-58

Stake

El. above 400'

LEGEND

■ Graves with monuments and names

▯ Graves marked but unnamed

▢ Graves unmarked and unnamed

⬚ Questionable graves

CEMETERIES

JOHNSONVILLE
CEMETERY

NO.
58

KENTUCKY RESERVOIR
TENNESSEE VALLEY AUTHORITY
MAPS AND SURVEYS DIVISION

SCALE OF FEET
10   0   10   20   30   40

CHATTANOOGA   8-24-42   8 MS 432 A 1009   R.0

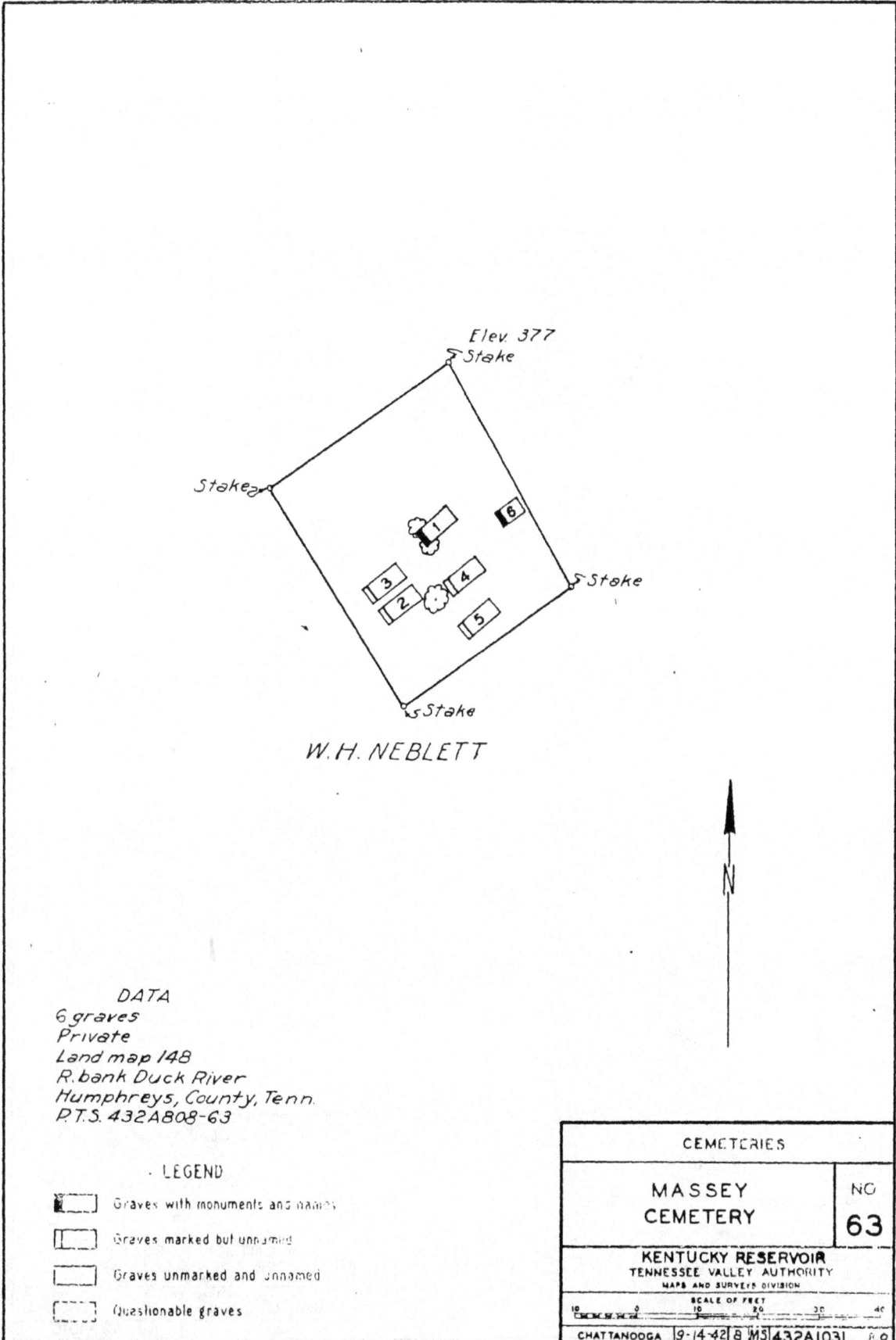

* *

Elev. 377
Stake

Stake

6

1

Stake

3

2

4

5

Stake

W.H. NEBLETT

N

DATA
6 graves
Private
Land map 148
R. bank Duck River
Humphreys, County, Tenn.
P.T.S. 432A808-63

LEGEND

Graves with monuments and names

Graves marked but unnamed

Graves unmarked and unnamed

Questionable graves

CEMETERIES	
MASSEY CEMETERY	NO 63

KENTUCKY RESERVOIR
TENNESSEE VALLEY AUTHORITY
MAPS AND SURVEYS DIVISION

SCALE OF FEET
10   0   10   20   30   40

CHATTANOOGA | 9-14-42 | 8 M5 | 432A1031 | R.0

* *

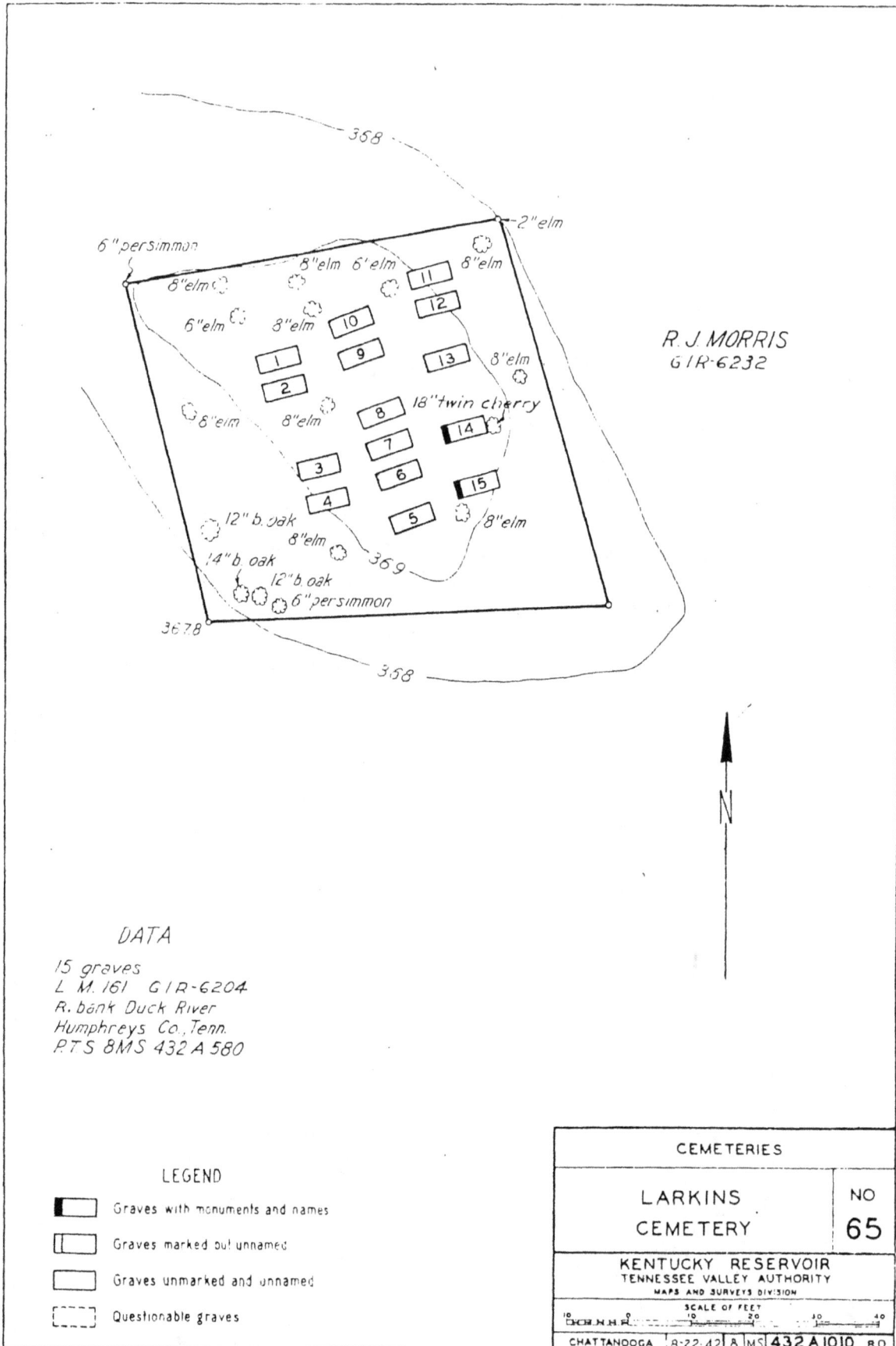

R. J. MORRIS
GIR-6232

DATA

15 graves
L M. 161 GIR-6204
R. bank Duck River
Humphreys Co., Tenn.
P.T.S 8MS 432 A 580

LEGEND

▮▯	Graves with monuments and names
▯▯	Graves marked but unnamed
▯	Graves unmarked and unnamed
⌐⌐	Questionable graves

CEMETERIES	
LARKINS CEMETERY	NO 65

KENTUCKY RESERVOIR
TENNESSEE VALLEY AUTHORITY
MAPS AND SURVEYS DIVISION

SCALE OF FEET

| CHATTANOOGA | 8-22-42 | 8 | MS | 432 A 1010 | RD |

* *

DATA

125 GRAVES

PUBLIC

LAND MAP 79, GIR-2968

RIGHT BANK TENNESSEE RIVER MI.71

STEWART COUNTY, TENNESSEE

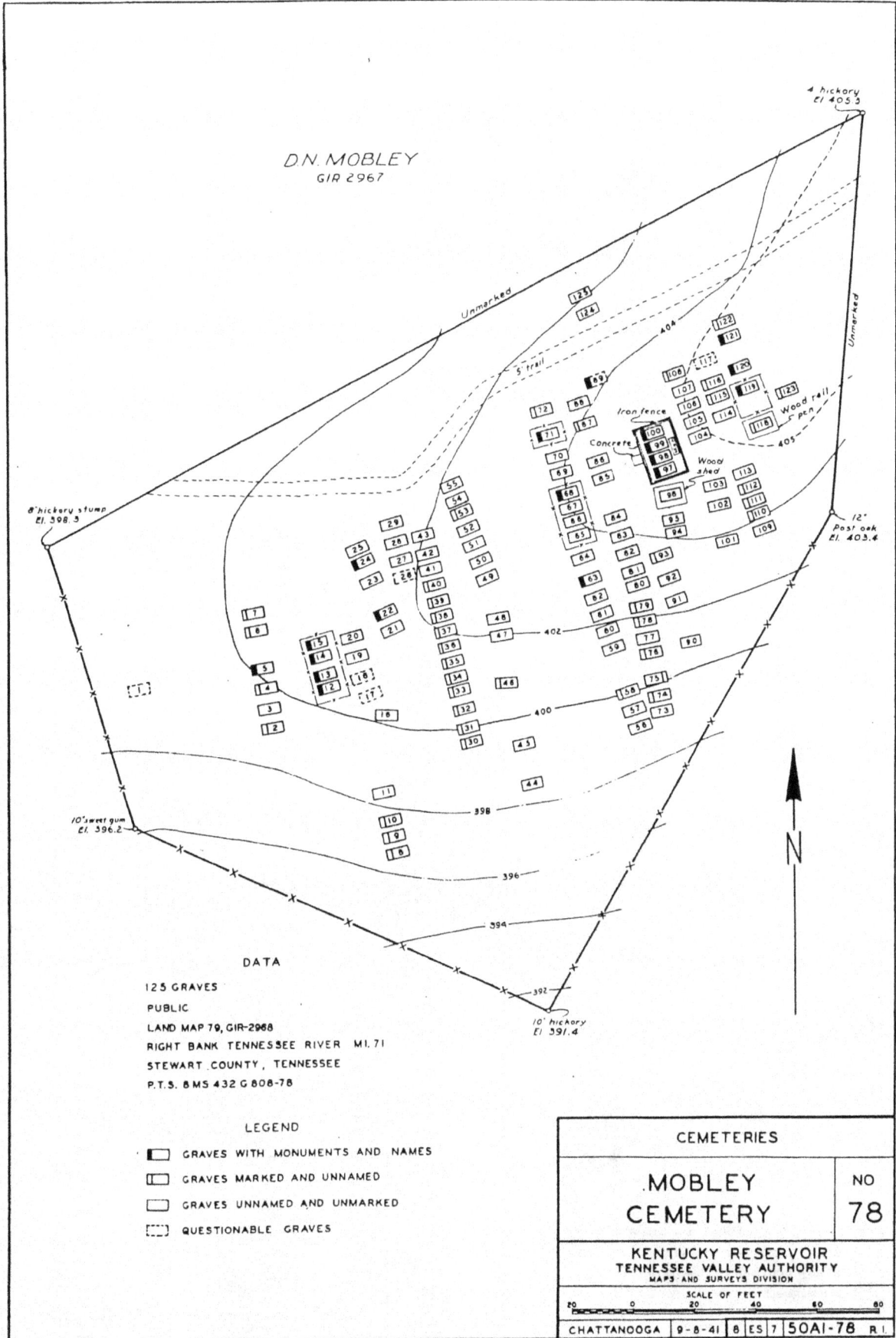

P.T.S. 8 MS 432 G 808-78

LEGEND

■☐ GRAVES WITH MONUMENTS AND NAMES

☐ GRAVES MARKED AND UNNAMED

☐ GRAVES UNNAMED AND UNMARKED

[☐] QUESTIONABLE GRAVES

CEMETERIES

.MOBLEY
CEMETERY

NO
78

KENTUCKY RESERVOIR
TENNESSEE VALLEY AUTHORITY
MAPS AND SURVEYS DIVISION

SCALE OF FEET

CHATTANOOGA 9-8-41 8 ES 7 50AI-78 R.I.

* *

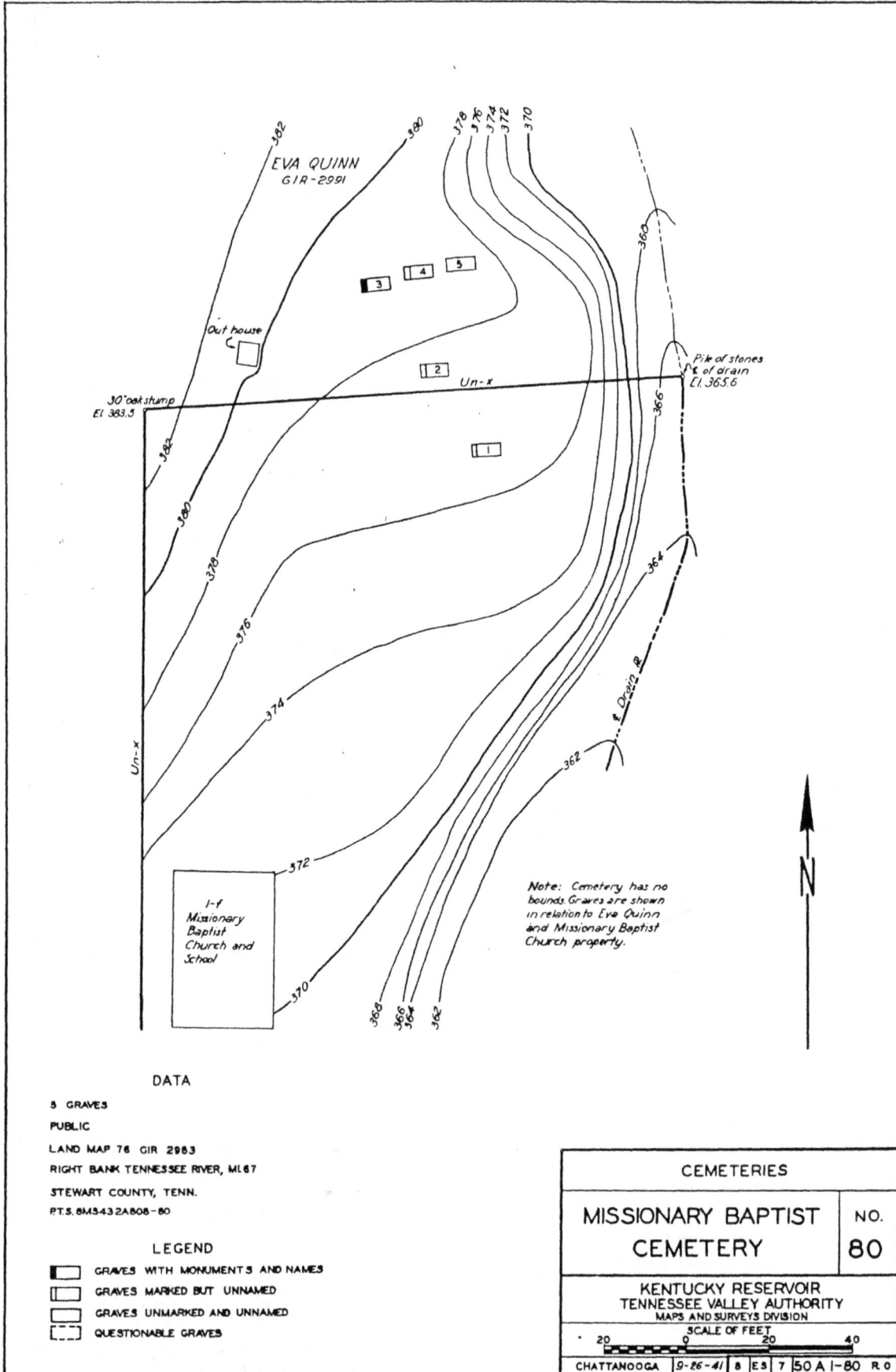

EVA QUINN
GIR-2991

Out house

30" oak stump
El. 383.5

Un-x

Pile of stones
C of drain
El. 365.6

Un-x

Un-x

E. Drain R.

I-f
Missionary
Baptist
Church and
School

Note: Cemetery has no
bounds. Graves are shown
in relation to Eva Quinn
and Missionary Baptist
Church property.

N

DATA

5 GRAVES

PUBLIC

LAND MAP 76 GIR 2983

RIGHT BANK TENNESSEE RIVER, ML 67

STEWART COUNTY, TENN.

P.T.S. 8MS43 2A808-80

LEGEND

GRAVES WITH MONUMENTS AND NAMES
GRAVES MARKED BUT UNNAMED
GRAVES UNMARKED AND UNNAMED
QUESTIONABLE GRAVES

CEMETERIES	
MISSIONARY BAPTIST CEMETERY	NO. 80
KENTUCKY RESERVOIR TENNESSEE VALLEY AUTHORITY MAPS AND SURVEYS DIVISION	

SCALE OF FEET

20   0   20   40

CHATTANOOGA 9-26-41 8 E3 7 50 A 1-80 R 0

* *

LEGEND

GRAVES WITH MONUMENTS AND NAMES
GRAVES MARKED BUT UNNAMED
GRAVES UNMARKED AND UNNAMED
QUESTIONABLE GRAVES

DATA

183 GRAVES
PUBLIC
LAND MAP 64, GIR-2879F
RIGHT BANK TENNESSEE RIVER MI. 60
RIGHT BANK PANTHER CREEK
STEWART COUNTY, TENNESSEE
PTS 8ES7-8302K

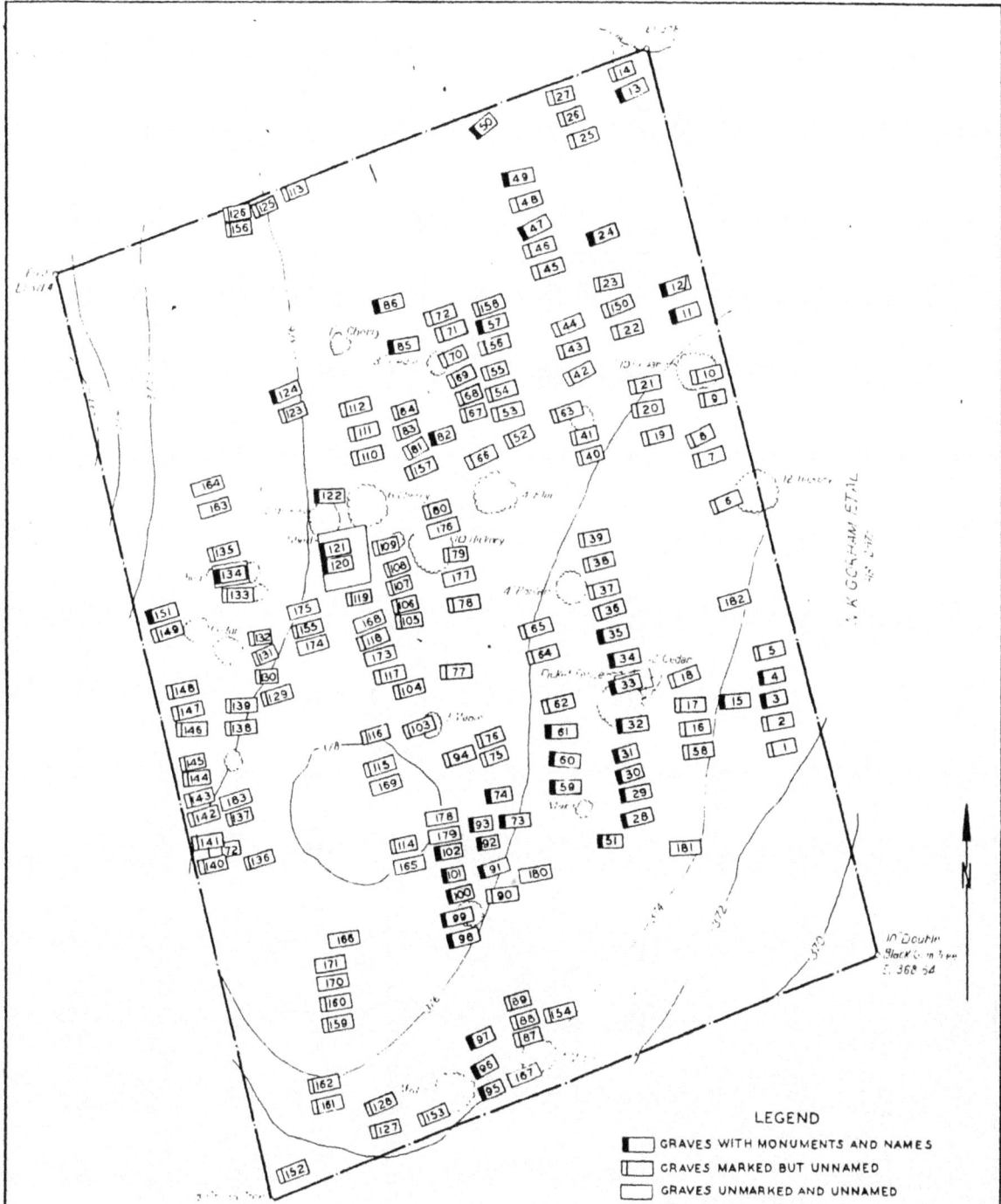

CEMETERIES

BOYD
CEMETERY

NO
100

KENTUCKY RESERVOIR
TENNESSEE VALLEY AUTHORITY
MAPS AND SURVEYS DIVISION

SCALE OF FEET
20   0   20   40

CHATTANOOGA | 1-28-41 | 8 MS 432-A-833 R.1

* *

MRS. MAE BUSH CHERRY
GIR - 3108

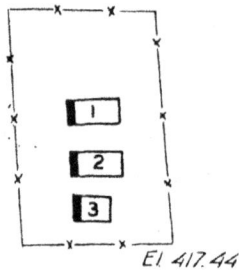

1
2
3

El. 417.44

N

DATA

3 Graves
Private
Land Map 119
Right bank Tenn. R., Mi. 76
Houston County, Tenn.
PTS. 8MS 432A692

LEGEND

Graves with monuments and names

Graves marked but unnamed

Graves unmarked and unnamed

Questionable graves

CEMETERIES	
CHERRY CEMETERY	NO. 134
KENTUCKY RESERVOIR TENNESSEE VALLEY AUTHORITY MAPS AND SURVEYS DIVISION	
SCALE OF FEET	
CHATTANOOGA 4-13-42 8 MS 432A942 R 0	

* *

F.C.

F.C.

[14

[13

[12

[11

[5   [10

[14

[3   [9

[8

[7

[6

Note:
     These bounds
do not check the
original survey.
Fence is now the
accepted bounds

[1 [2

F.C.

El. 390.00

N

F.C.

MRS. N.T. BUSH
GIR 3114

DATA
14 Graves
Private
Land Map 119
Right bank Tennessee River mi 77
Houston County, Tennessee
P.T.S. 8MS 432A808-135

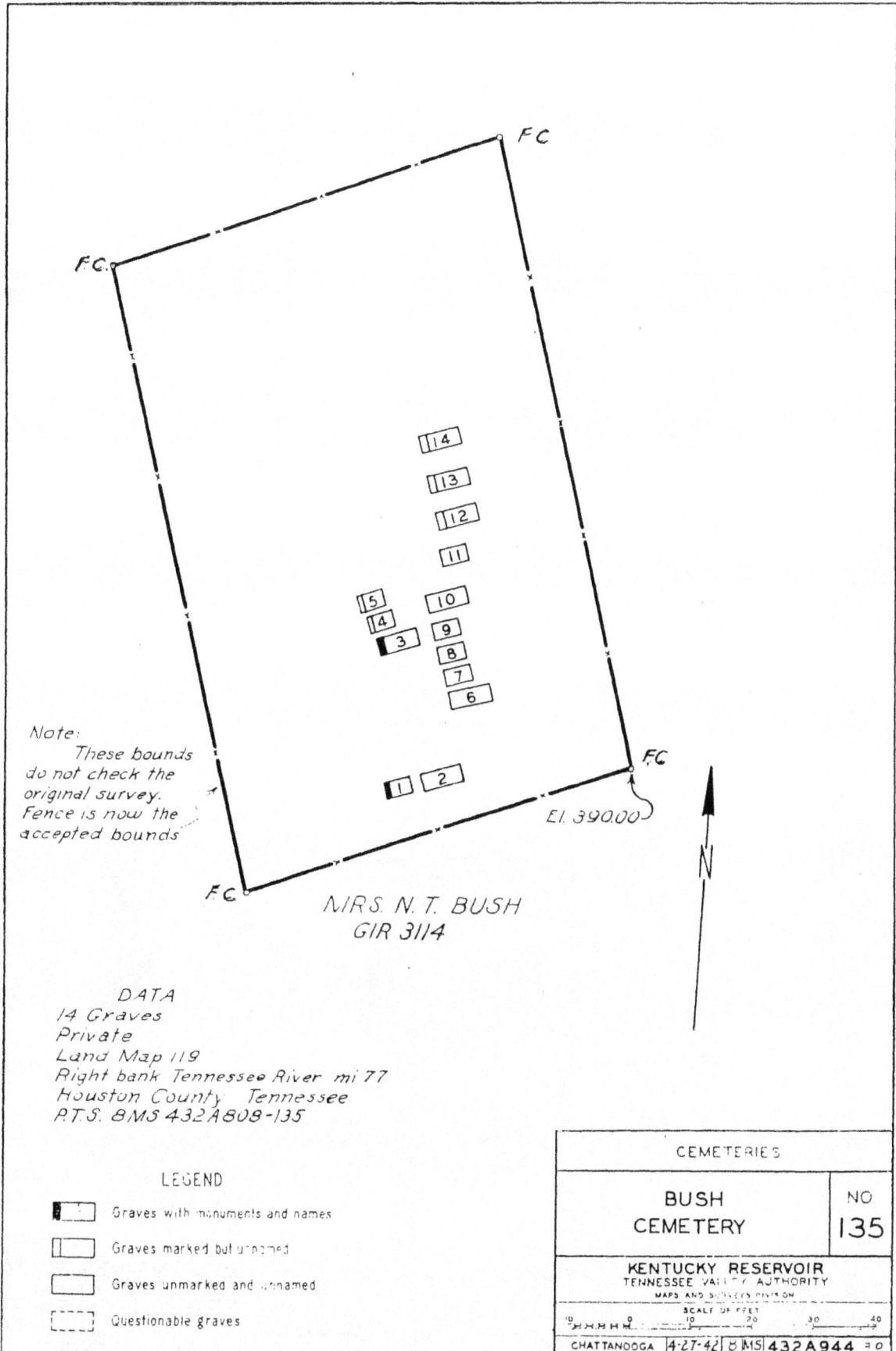

LEGEND

▮▭ Graves with monuments and names

▭ Graves marked but unnamed

▭ Graves unmarked and unnamed

⌐ ⌐ Questionable graves

CEMETERIES	
BUSH CEMETERY	NO 135

KENTUCKY RESERVOIR
TENNESSEE VALLEY AUTHORITY
MAPS AND SURVEYS DIVISION

SCALE OF FEET
0   10   20   30   40

CHATTANOOGA 4-27-42 8 MS 432A944

* *

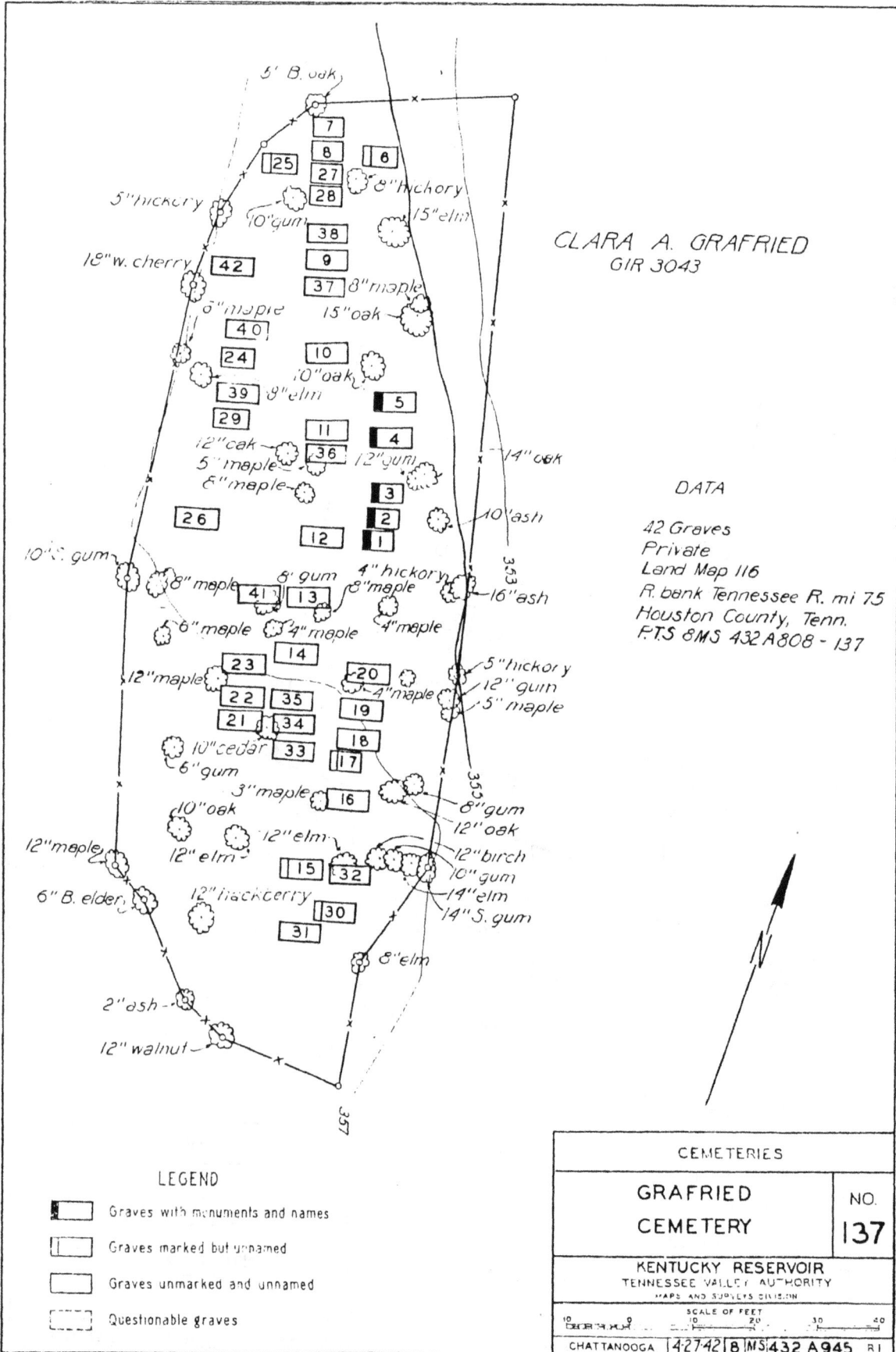

CLARA A. GRAFRIED
GIR 3043

DATA

42 Graves
Private
Land Map 116
R. bank Tennessee R. mi 75
Houston County, Tenn.
F.TS 8MS 432 A808 - 137

LEGEND

Graves with monuments and names

Graves marked but unnamed

Graves unmarked and unnamed

Questionable graves

CEMETERIES	
GRAFRIED CEMETERY	NO. 137

KENTUCKY RESERVOIR
TENNESSEE VALLEY AUTHORITY
MAPS AND SURVEYS DIVISION

SCALE OF FEET

CHATTANOOGA 4-27-42 8 MS 432 A945 R1

* *

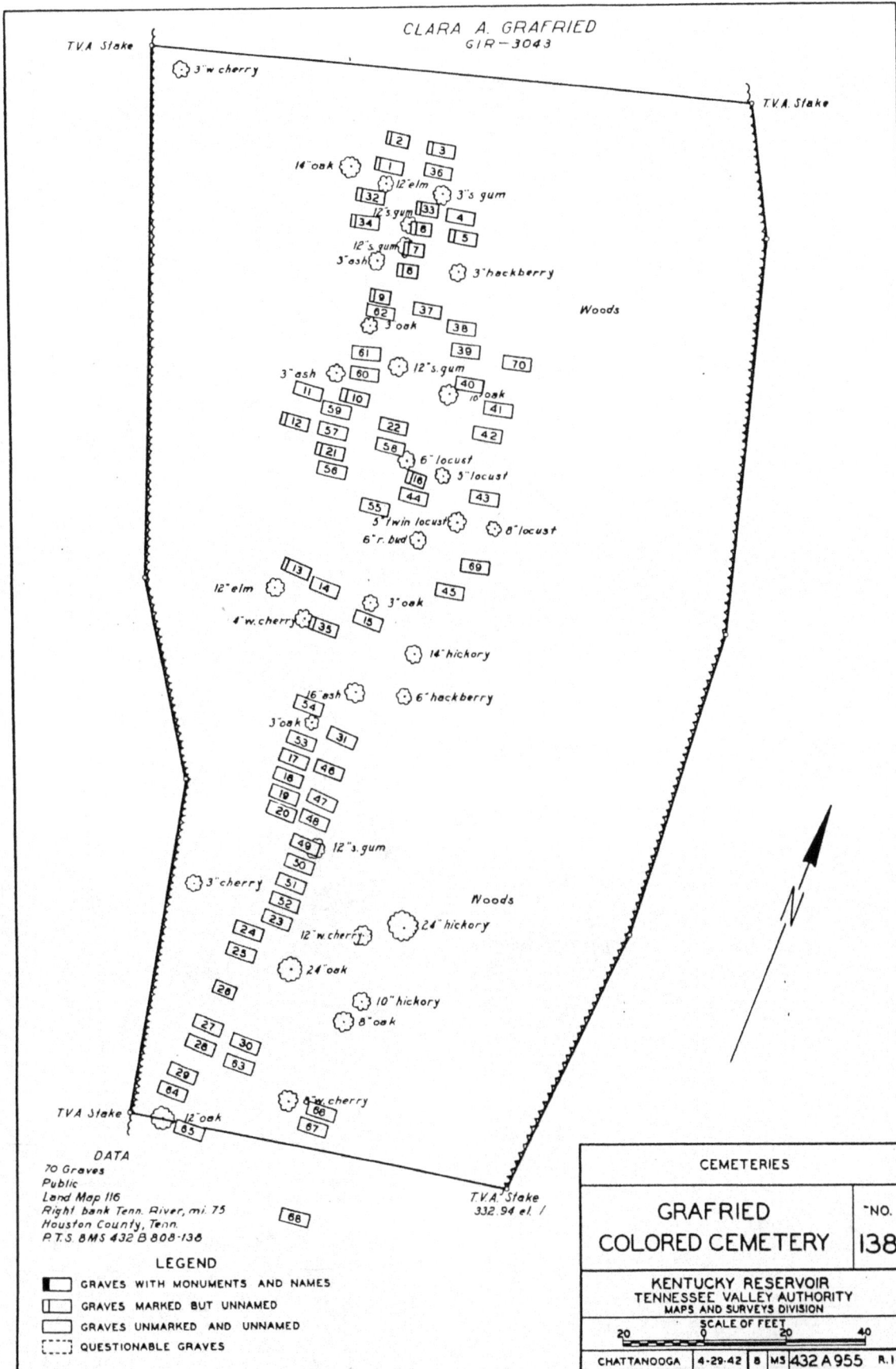

GRAFRIED COLORED CEMETERY No. 138

* *

F.C. Lowest Cor. El. 356.9

5"Ash

6"Elm

6"Elm

6"Elm

DATA

47 Graves
Public
Land Map 119
Right bank Tennessee River mi. 77
Houston County, Tennessee
P.T.S. SMS432B808-139

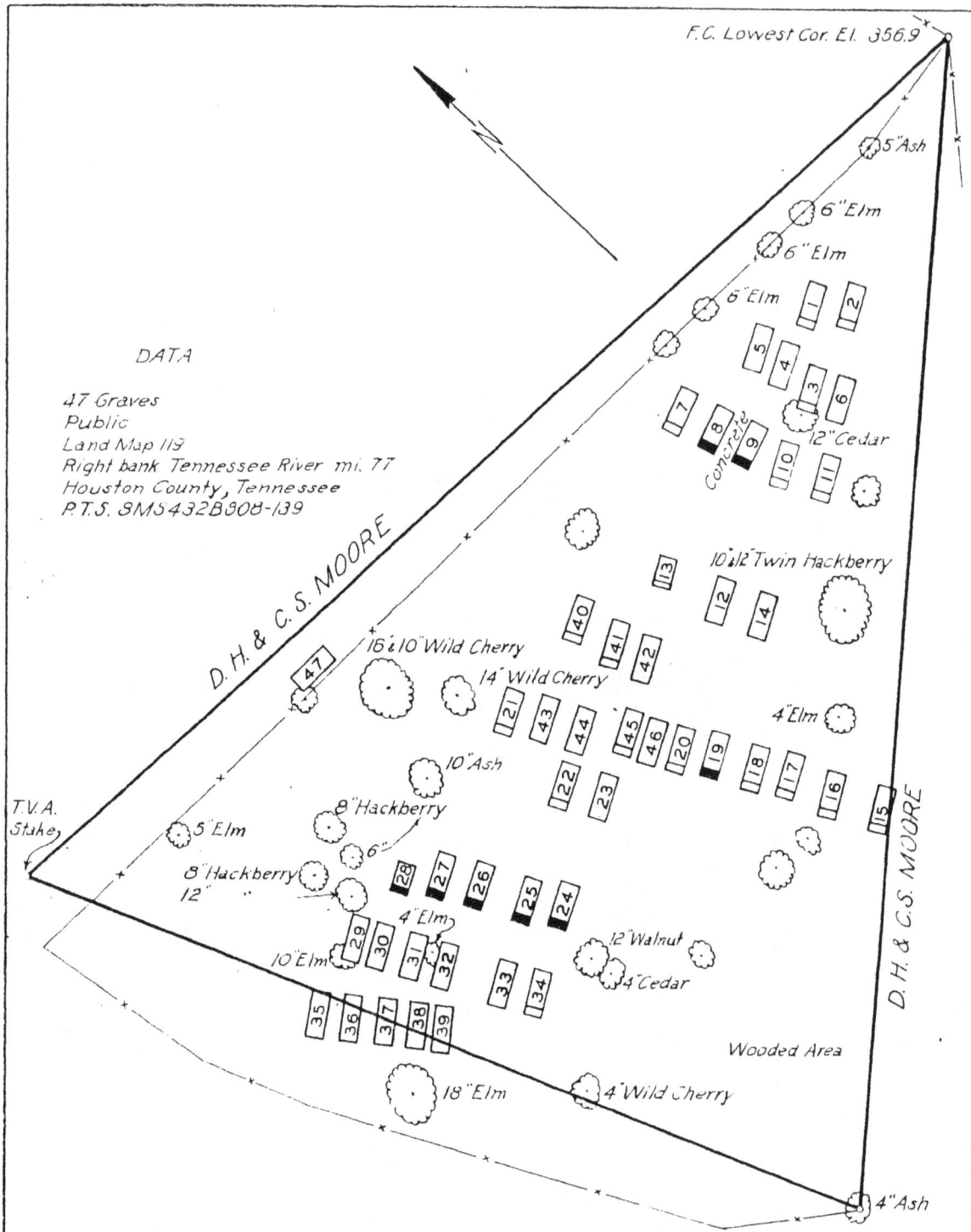

D.H. & C.S. MOORE

12"Cedar

Concrete

10 & 12" Twin Hackberry

16 & 10" Wild Cherry

14" Wild Cherry

4"Elm

T.V.A. Stake

10"Ash

8"Hackberry

5"Elm

6"

8"Hackberry
12"

4"Elm

12"Walnut

4"Cedar

10"Elm

18"Elm

4"Wild Cherry

Wooded Area

D.H. & C.S. MOORE

4"Ash

LEGEND

▆ Graves with monuments and names

▯ Graves marked but unnamed

▯ Graves unmarked and unnamed

⌐⌐ Questionable graves

CEMETERIES

CATHAY CEMETERY

NO. 139

KENTUCKY RESERVOIR
TENNESSEE VALLEY AUTHORITY
MAPS AND SURVEYS DIVISION
SCALE OF FEET

CHATTANOOGA | 4-25-42 | 8 | MS | 432A946

A F WEAVER
GIR 3407

A.F. WEAVER
GIR 3407

5" Black Oak
8" Black Oak
8" Locust
5" Black Oak
5" Red Oak
4" Locust
14" White Oak
8" Red Oak
12" White Oak
8" Chestnut
3" Hickory
8" Black Gum
El 381.8

DATA

26 GRAVES

PRIVATE

LAND MAP 122

RIGHT BANK TENNESSEE RIVER MI 80

HOUSTON COUNTY, TENNESSEE

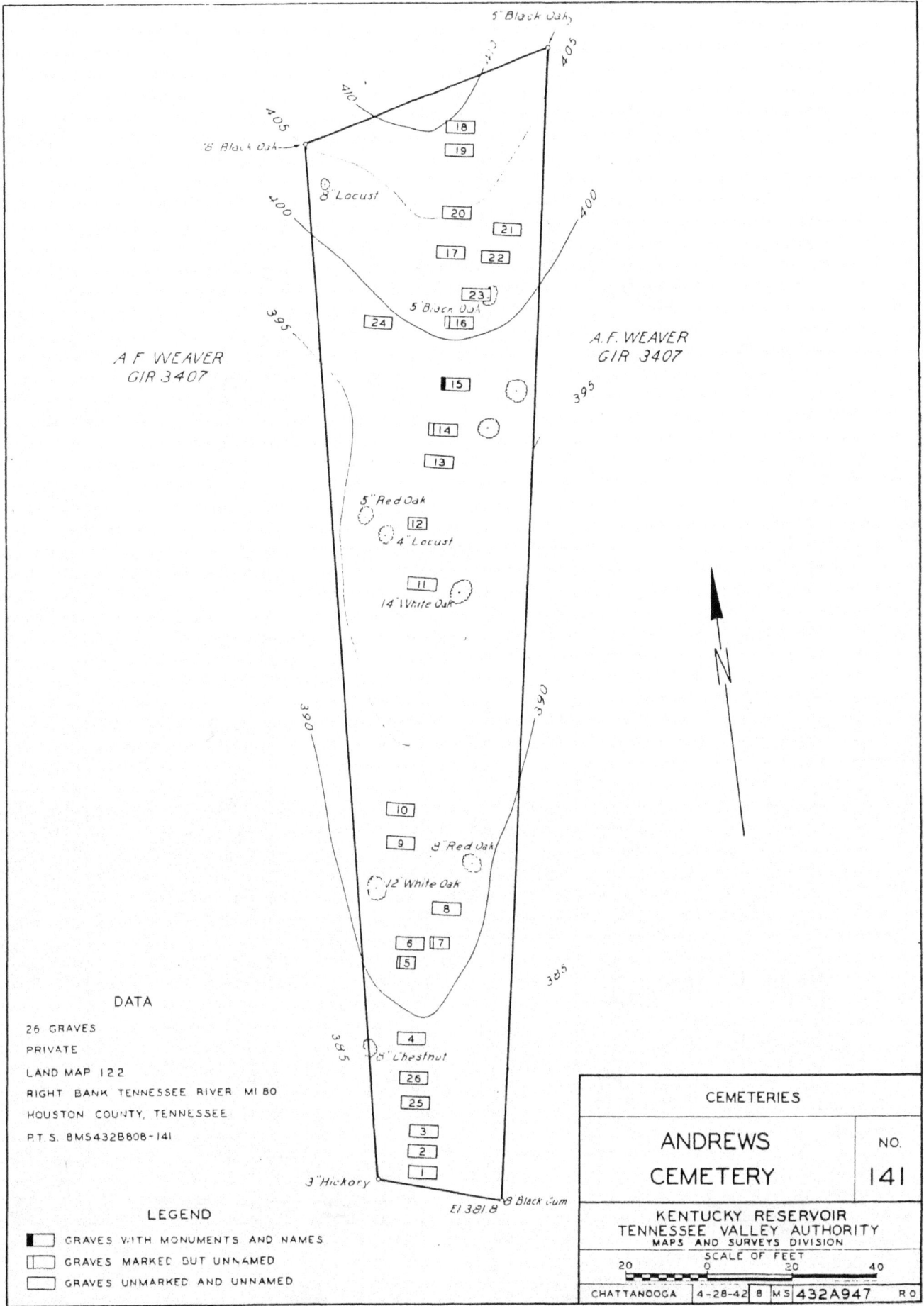

P.T.S. 8MS432B808-141

LEGEND

GRAVES WITH MONUMENTS AND NAMES

GRAVES MARKED BUT UNNAMED

GRAVES UNMARKED AND UNNAMED

CEMETERIES

ANDREWS CEMETERY

NO. 141

KENTUCKY RESERVOIR
TENNESSEE VALLEY AUTHORITY
MAPS AND SURVEYS DIVISION

SCALE OF FEET
20   0   20   40

CHATTANOOGA   4-28-42   8   MS   432A947   R.O

* *

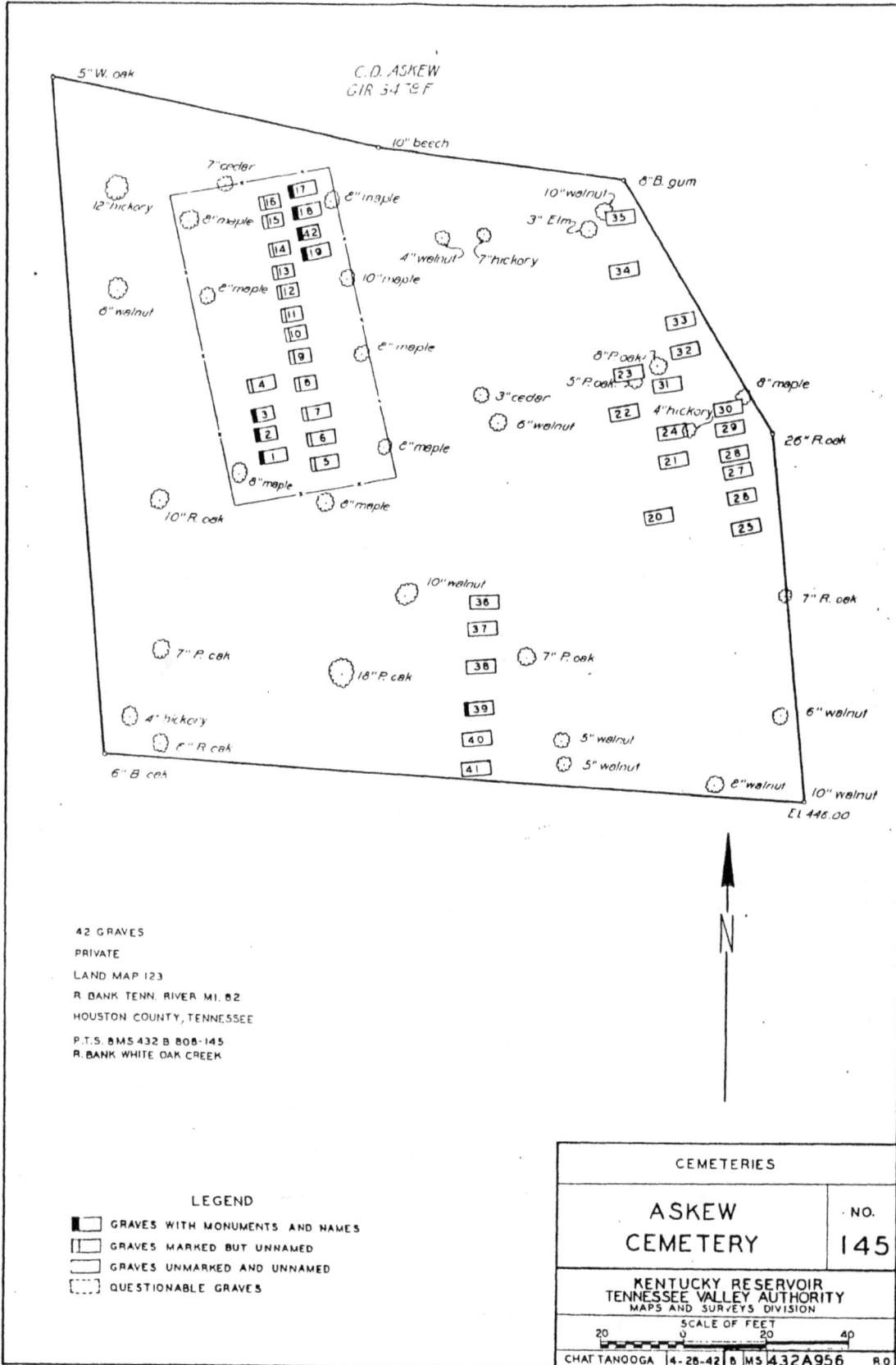

C.D. ASKEW
GIR 3-4 &F

42 GRAVES

PRIVATE

LAND MAP 123

R. BANK TENN. RIVER MI. 82

HOUSTON COUNTY, TENNESSEE

P.T.S. 8MS 432 B 808-145
R. BANK WHITE OAK CREEK

N

LEGEND

■□	GRAVES WITH MONUMENTS AND NAMES
□	GRAVES MARKED BUT UNNAMED
▭	GRAVES UNMARKED AND UNNAMED
⬚	QUESTIONABLE GRAVES

CEMETERIES	
ASKEW CEMETERY	NO. 145
KENTUCKY RESERVOIR TENNESSEE VALLEY AUTHORITY MAPS AND SURVEYS DIVISION	

SCALE OF FEET
20 0 20 40

CHATTANOOGA 4-28-42 8 MS 432A956 RO

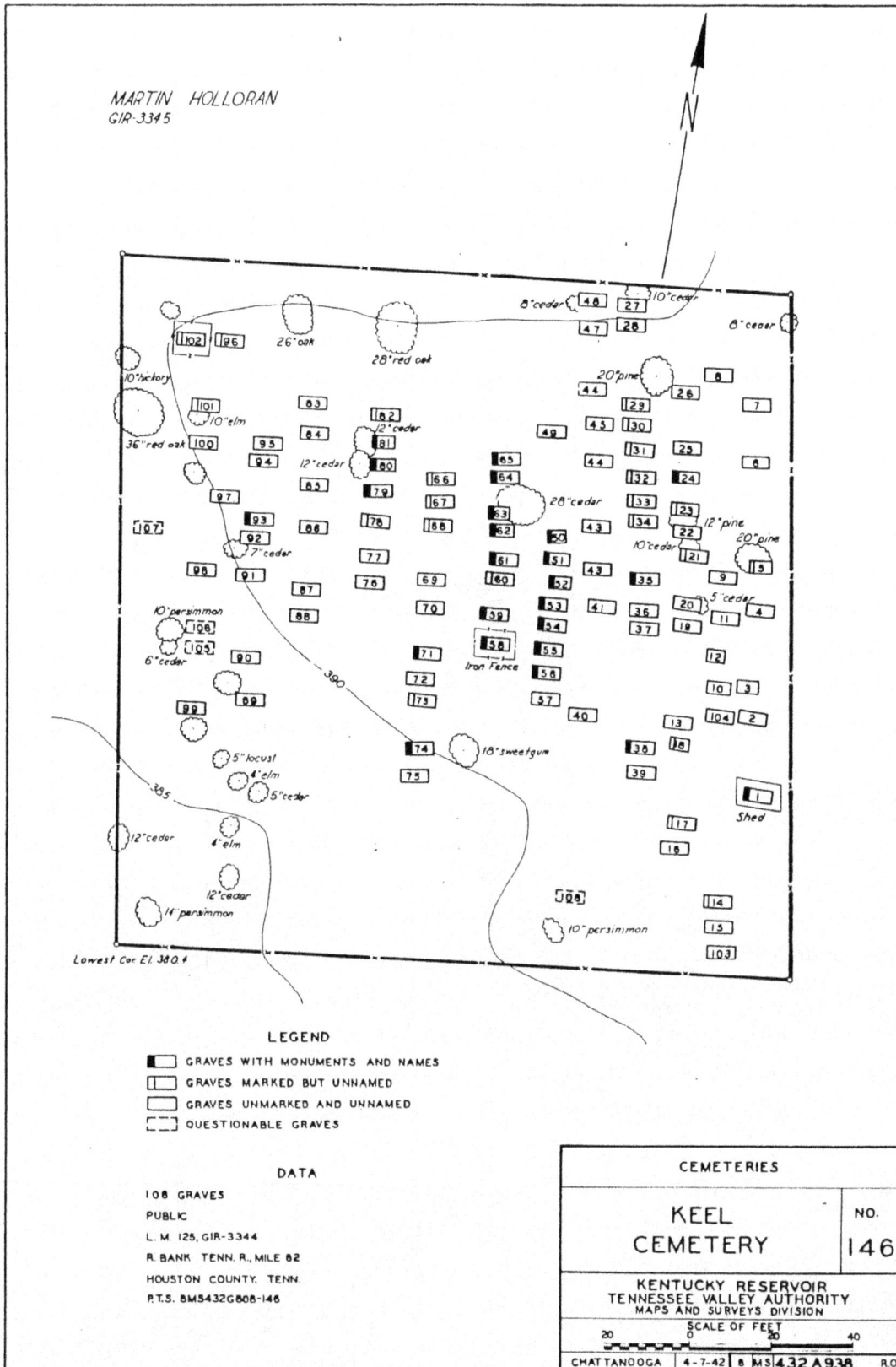

MARTIN HOLLORAN
GIR-3345

LEGEND

▮▮ GRAVES WITH MONUMENTS AND NAMES
□ GRAVES MARKED BUT UNNAMED
▭ GRAVES UNMARKED AND UNNAMED
⌐⌐ QUESTIONABLE GRAVES

DATA

108 GRAVES
PUBLIC
L. M. 125, GIR-3344
R. BANK TENN. R., MILE 82
HOUSTON COUNTY, TENN.
P.T.S. 8M5432G808-146

CEMETERIES	
KEEL CEMETERY	NO. 146

KENTUCKY RESERVOIR
TENNESSEE VALLEY AUTHORITY
MAPS AND SURVEYS DIVISION

SCALE OF FEET
20 0 20 40

CHATTANOOGA 4-7-42 8 MS 432 A 938 R.O

* *

JB SNOW ET UX, BETTIE

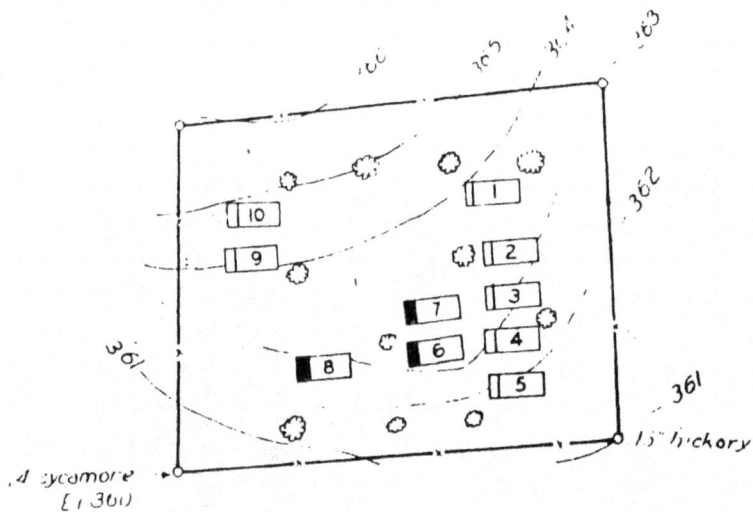

DATA

10 graves

Private

Land map No.69

Left bank Cypress Cr

Left bank Tenn R m 63

PTS No 8CS10 8246 C

Henry Co Tenn

Cr 230M

LEGEND

CEMETERIES

SNOW
CEMETERY

NO
352

KENTUCKY RESERVOIR

432A 840

* *

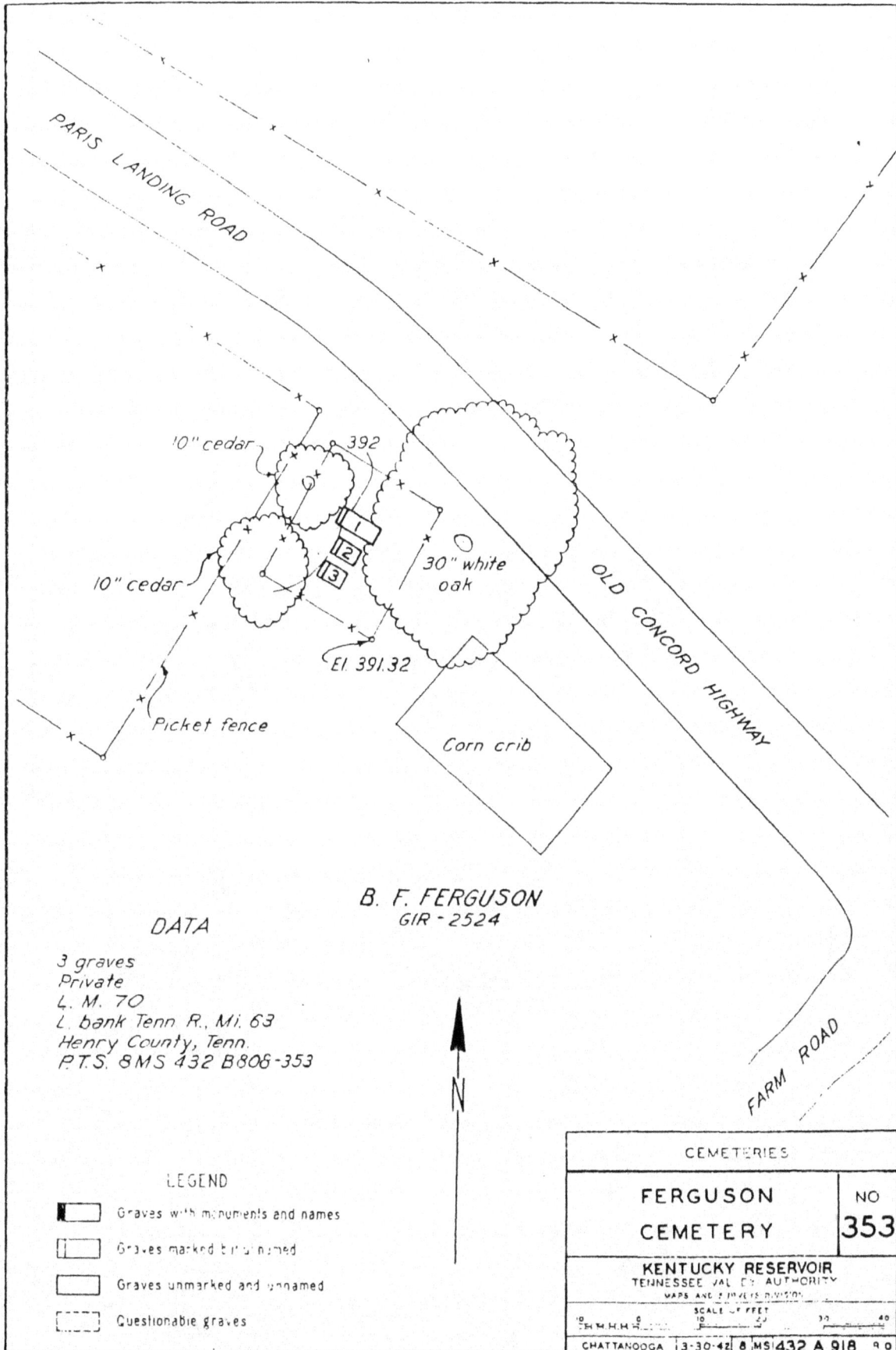

PARIS LANDING ROAD

OLD CONCORD HIGHWAY

FARM ROAD

10" cedar

392

10" cedar

1
2
3

30" white oak

El. 391.32

Picket fence

Corn crib

B. F. FERGUSON
GIR - 2524

DATA

3 graves
Private
L. M. 70
L. bank Tenn R., Mi. 63
Henry County, Tenn.
P.T.S. 8 MS 432 B 808-353

N

LEGEND

Graves with monuments and names

Graves marked but unnamed

Graves unmarked and unnamed

Questionable graves

CEMETERIES

FERGUSON
CEMETERY

NO
353

KENTUCKY RESERVOIR
TENNESSEE VALLEY AUTHORITY
MAPS AND SURVEYS DIVISION

SCALE OF FEET

CHATTANOOGA | 3-30-42 | 8 MS 432 A 918 | 9 0

* *

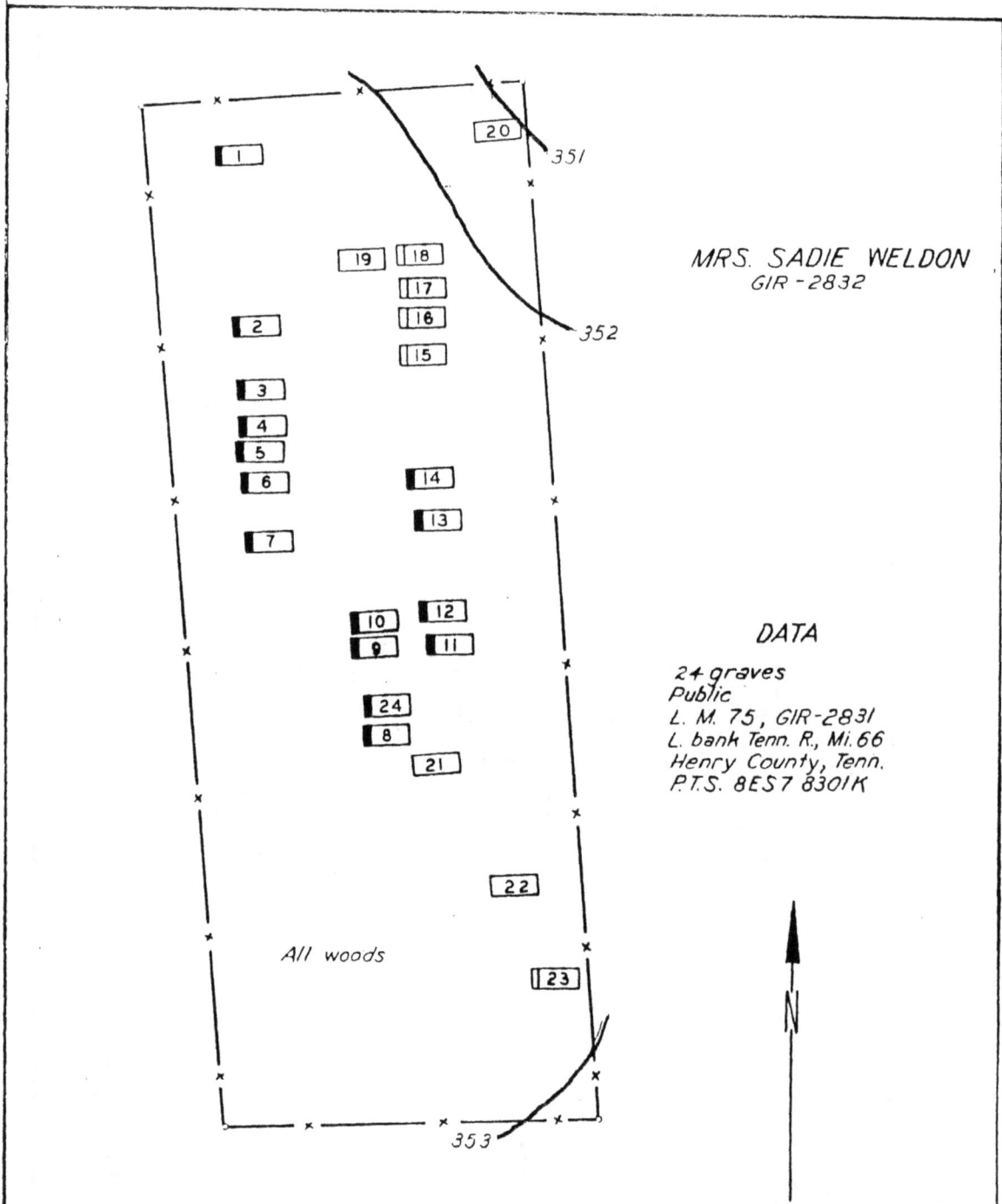

MRS. SADIE WELDON
GIR - 2832

351

352

All woods

353

DATA

24 graves
Public
L. M. 75, GIR-2831
L. bank Tenn. R., Mi.66
Henry County, Tenn.
P.T.S. 8ES7 8301K

N

LEGEND

Graves with monuments and names

Graves marked but unnamed

Graves unmarked and unnamed

Questionable graves

CEMETERIES	
WELDON CEMETERY	NO. **354**

KENTUCKY RESERVOIR
TENNESSEE VALLEY AUTHORITY
MAPS AND SURVEYS DIVISION

SCALE OF FEET

CHATTANOOGA | 4-3-42 | 8 | MS | 432 A 919

* *

C. B. THOMPSON ET UX STELLA
GIR - 2839

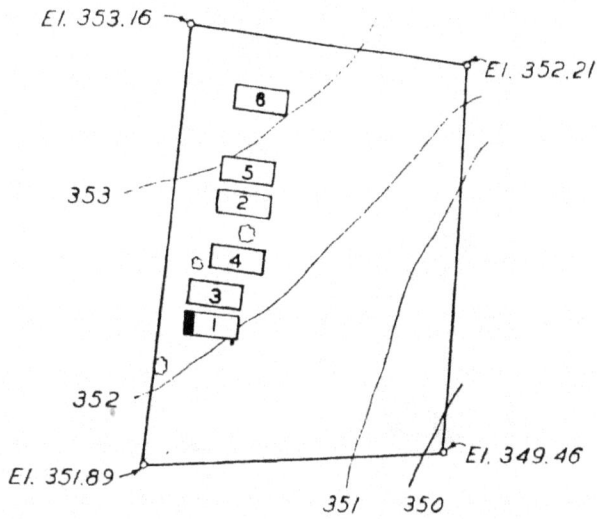

El. 353.16

El. 352.21

6

353

5

2

4

3

1

352

El. 351.89

El. 349.46

351 350

N

DATA

1 graves
Private
L. M. 75, GIR - 2838
L Bank Tenn. R., Mi. 67
Henry County, Tenn.
P.T.S. 8 ES 10 - E300K

Note: Stakes set at 4 corners
by T.V.A. Corners shown
by C. B. Thompson Agreed

LEGEND

� Graves with monuments and names

☐ Graves marked but unnamed

☐ Graves unmarked and unnamed

[☐] Questionable graves

CEMETERIES	
BRADFORD NO. 2 CEMETERY	NO 356
KENTUCKY RESERVOIR TENNESSEE VALLEY AUTHORITY MAPS AND SURVEYS DIVISION	

SCALE OF FEET
10   20   30   40

CHATTANOOGA | 2-3-42 | 8 | MS | 432 A 889 R 1

* *

M. H. CAMPBELL
GIR – 2847

El. 997

Note: Stakes set at 4 corners
by T.V.A. Lines not m'kd.
Agreed

N

DATA
1 grave
Private
L.M. 71
L. Bank Tenn. R., Mi. 65
Henry County, Tenn.
P.T.S. 8 ES 10 -8300 K

LEGEND

▭ Graves with monuments and names

▭ Graves marked but unnamed

▭ Graves unmarked and unnamed

▭ Questionable graves

CEMETERIES	
DODSON CEMETERY	NO. 357
KENTUCKY RESERVOIR TENNESSEE VALLEY AUTHORITY MAPS AND SURVEYS DIVISION	
SCALE OF FEET	
CHATTANOOGA 2-3-42 8 MS 432 A 893 RO	

* *

MRS MARY OWENS et al
GIR 3175F

s white oak

T fence int.

Stake set by TVA at
E1448BL fence corner

LAURA MIDYETT GIR-2894

WHITE SECTION

COLORED SECTION

8" post oak

Stake set by TVA

Stake set by TVA

N

DATA

38 WHITE, 54 COLORED GRAVES

PUBLIC

L.M. 74

LEFT BK. TENN RI, MI.88

HENRY CO., TENNESSEE

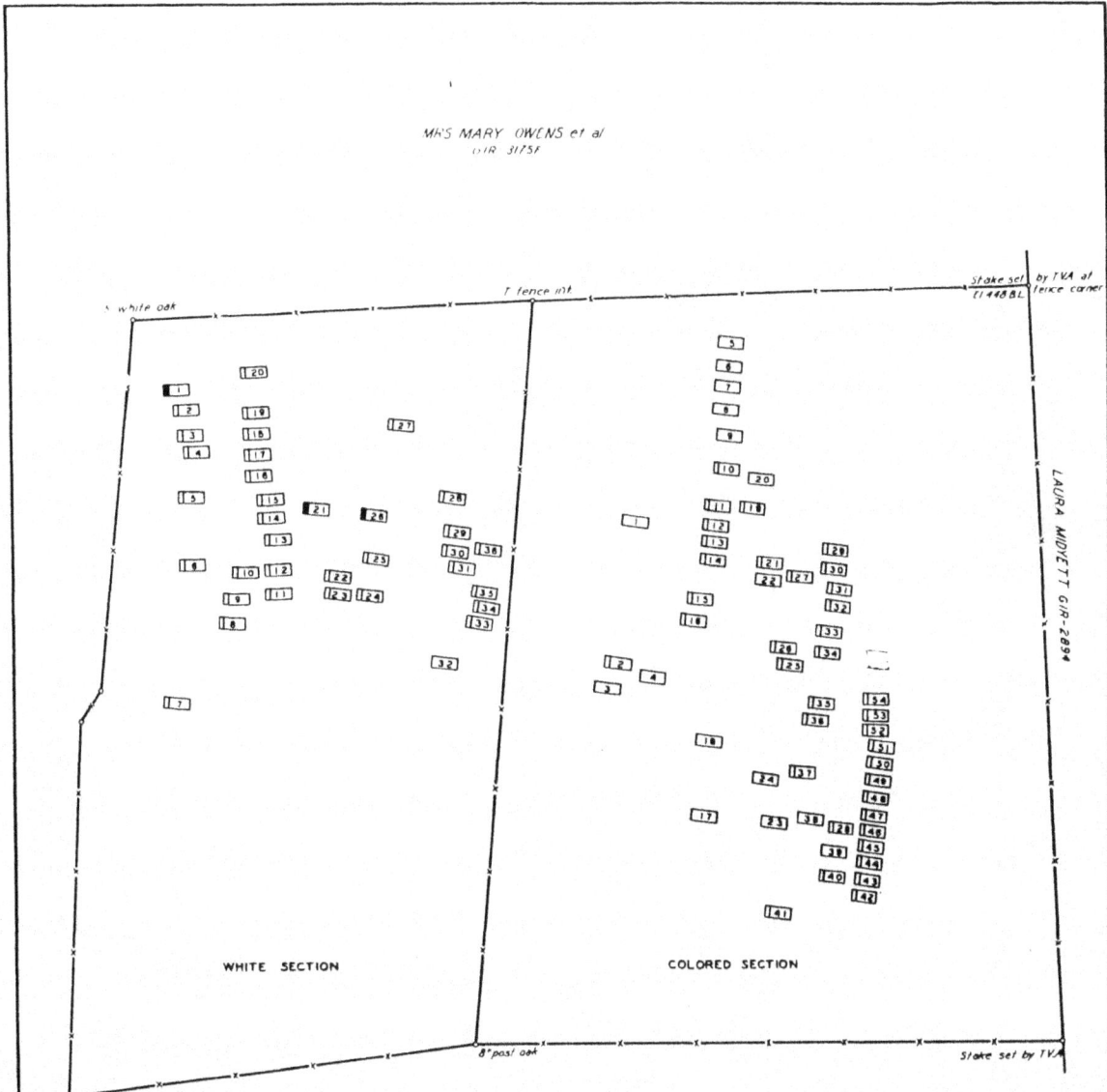

P.T.S. 8MS 10 8300K

LEGEND

�▊ GRAVES WITH MONUMENTS

▭ GRAVES MARKED BUT UNNAMED

▭ GRAVES UNNAMED AND UNMARKED

▭ QUESTIONABLE GRAVES

CEMETERIES	
BRADFORD#3 CEMETERY	NO. 364
KENTUCKY RESERVOIR TENNESSEE VALLEY AUTHORITY MAPS AND SURVEYS DIVISION	
SCALE OF FEET 20 0 20 40 80 80	
CHATTANOOGA 2-6-42 8 MS 432A894	R.O

* *

A. H. PRESNELL
6IR - 2899

El. 426

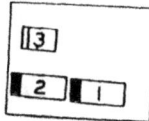

In clump of small trees.

DATA

3 graves
Private
L. M. 74
L. bank Tenn. R., Mi. 66
Henry County, Tenn.
P.T.S. 8ES10 8298K

N

LEGEND

◼ Graves with monuments and names

▭ Graves marked but unnamed

▭ Graves unmarked and unnamed

⬚ Questionable graves

CEMETERIES	
TAYLOR	NO.
CEMETERY	365

KENTUCKY RESERVOIR
TENNESSEE VALLEY AUTHORITY
MAPS AND SURVEYS DIVISION

SCALE OF FEET

CHATTANOOGA | 4-3-42 | 8 | MS | 432 A 921 | RO

* *

J.B. RICE CIR 3181F

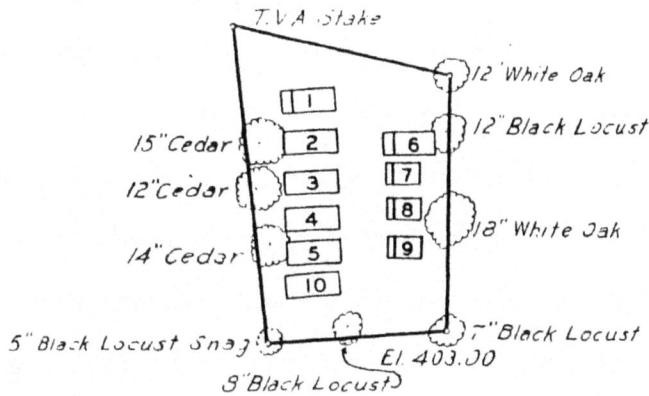

T.V.A. Stake

12"White Oak

12"Black Locust

15"Cedar

12"Cedar

14"Cedar

| 1 |
| 2 |
| 3 |
| 4 |
| 5 |
| 10 |

| 6 |
| 7 |
| 8 |
| 9 |

18" White Oak

5"Black Locust Snag

7"Black Locust

El. 403.00

8"Black Locust

Note: All corners were agreed.

N

DATA

10 Graves
Private
Land Map 74
Left bank Tennessee River mi 67
Henry County, Tennessee
P.T.S. 6MS 432.A 308-370

LEGEND

Graves with monuments and names

Graves marked but unnamed

Graves unmarked and unnamed

Questionable graves

CEMETERIES	
RICE CEMETERY	NO 370
KENTUCKY RESERVOIR TENNESSEE VALLEY AUTHORITY MAPS AND SURVEYS DIVISION	
SCALE OF FEET	
CHATTANOOGA 4-23-42 3 MS 432A957	

* *

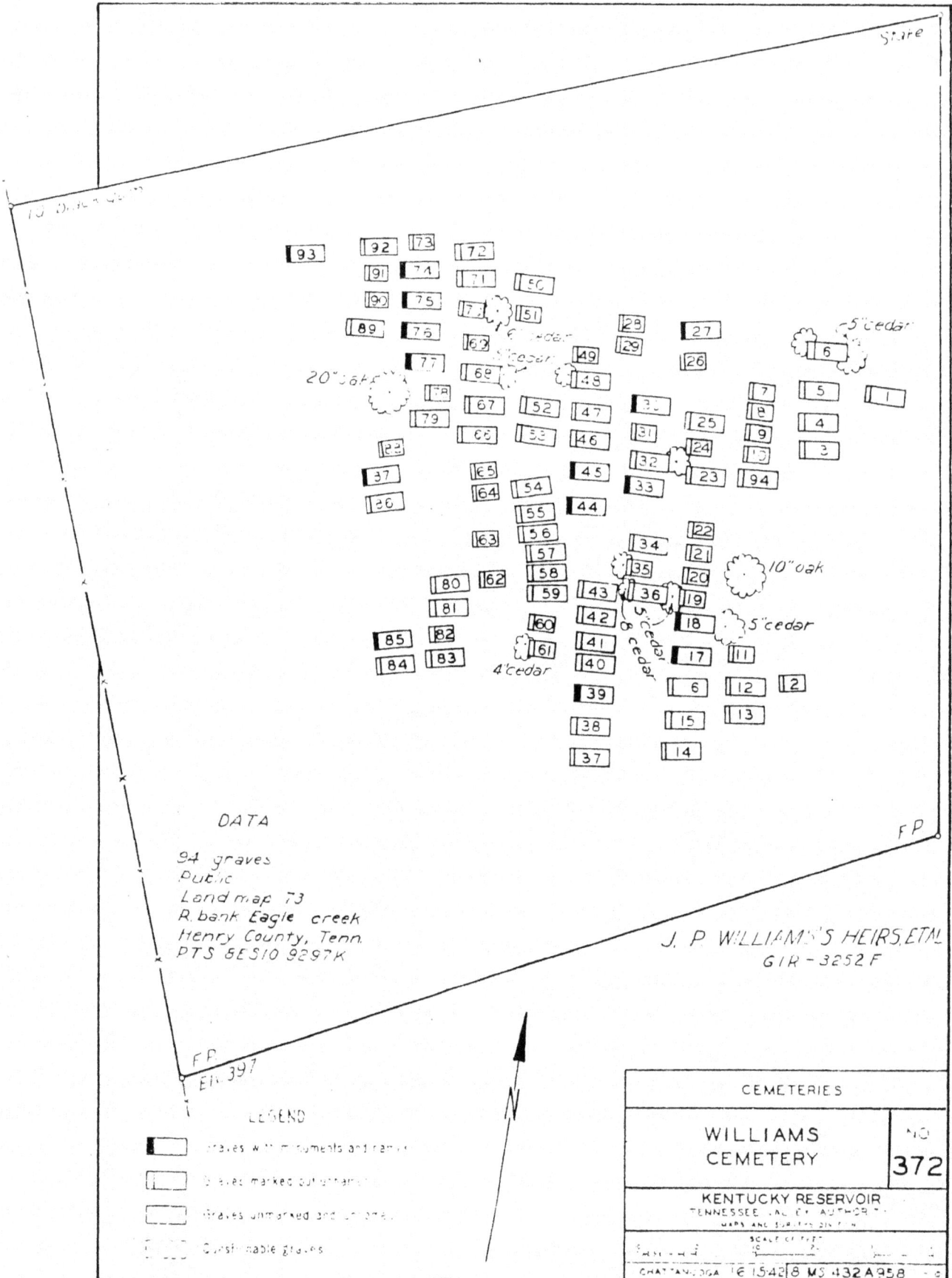

DATA

94 graves
Public
Land map 73
R. bank Eagle creek
Henry County, Tenn.
PTS 5ES10 9297K

J. P. WILLIAMS'S HEIRS, ETAL
GIR-3252F

F P

F P
EL. 397

LEGEND

Graves with monuments and names

Graves marked but no names

Graves unmarked and no names

Questionable graves

CEMETERIES	
WILLIAMS CEMETERY	NO 372
KENTUCKY RESERVOIR TENNESSEE VALLEY AUTHORITY MAPS AND SURVEYS DIVISION	
CHATTANOOGA 16 15-42 8 MS 432 A 958	

* *

G. L. WRIGHT'S HEIRS
GIR 3222

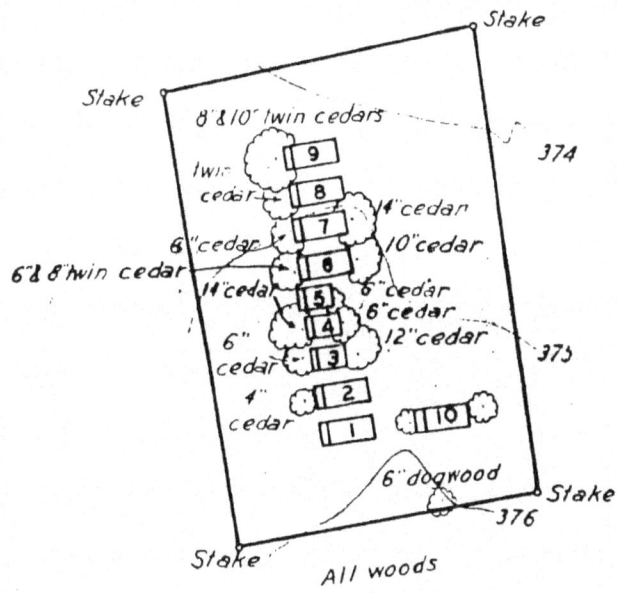

Stake

8"&10" twin cedars

Stake

twin cedar

9

8

14" cedar

7

6" cedar

10" cedar

374

6"&8" twin cedar

6

14" cedar

5

6" cedar

6" cedar

4

6" cedar

12" cedar

3

375

6" cedar

4" cedar

2

1

10

6" dogwood

Stake

376

Stake

All woods

DATA
10 graves
Private
Land Map 77 GIR 3231 F
Left bank Big Sandy River
Henry County, Tenn.
P.T.S. 8ES10-8297K

G. L. WRIGHT'S HEIRS
GIR 3222

N

LEGEND

Graves with monuments and names

Graves marked but unnamed

Graves unmarked and unnamed

Questionable graves

CEMETERIES	
LEMOND CEMETERY	NO 374
KENTUCKY RESERVOIR TENNESSEE VALLEY AUTHORITY MAPS AND SURVEYS DIVISION	
SCALE OF FEET	
CHATTANOOGA 6-16-42 8 MS 432A959 R O	

* *

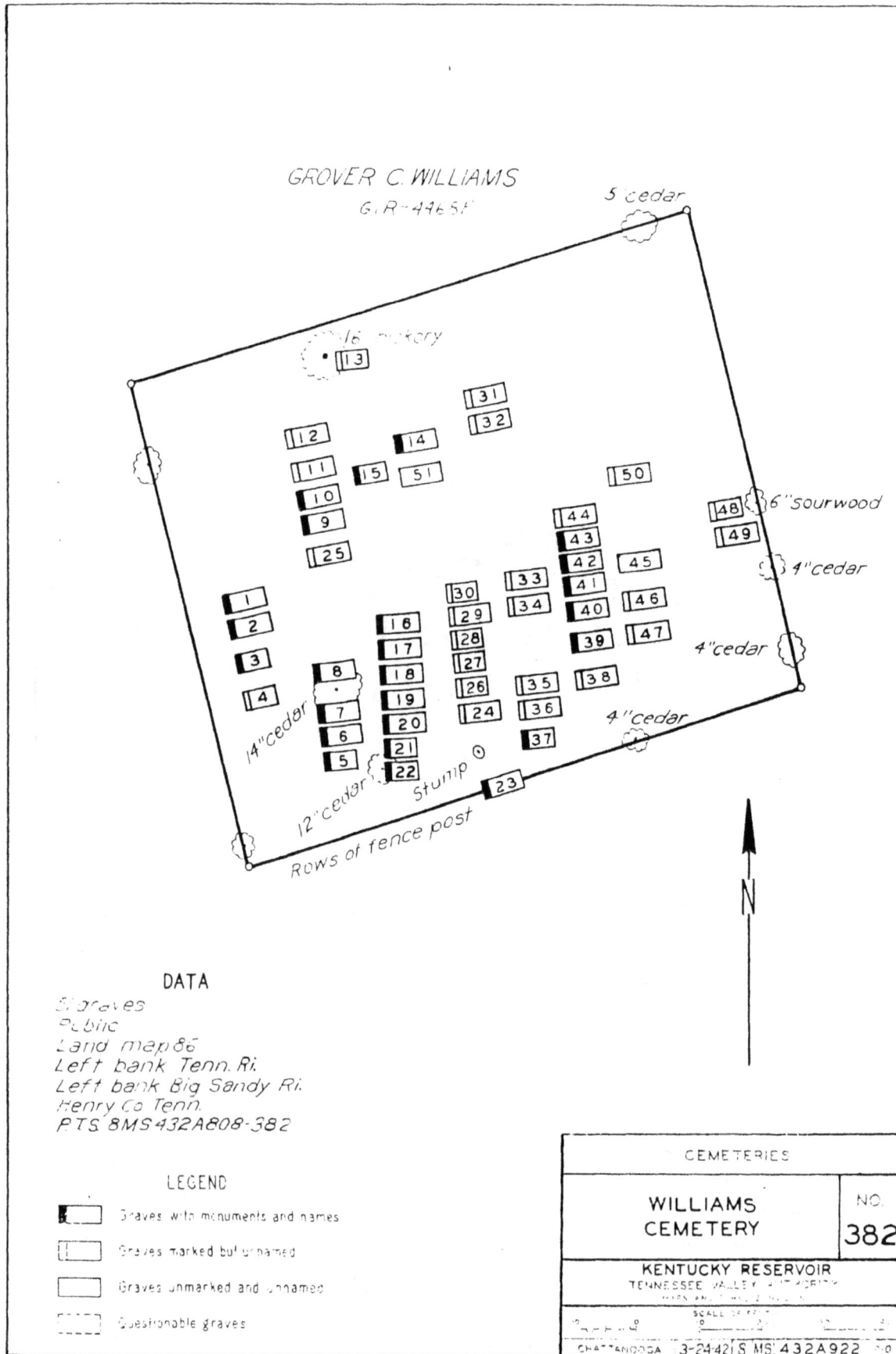

GROVER C. WILLIAMS
G.R-4465F

DATA

5 graves
Public
Land map 86
Left bank Tenn. Ri.
Left bank Big Sandy Ri.
Henry Co. Tenn.
P.T.S 8MS 432A808-382

LEGEND

Graves with monuments and names

Graves marked but unnamed

Graves unmarked and unnamed

Questionable graves

CEMETERIES	
WILLIAMS CEMETERY	NO. 382
KENTUCKY RESERVOIR	

TENNESSEE VALLEY AUTHORITY

SCALE OF FEET

CHATTANOOGA   3-24-42 S MS 432A922

* *

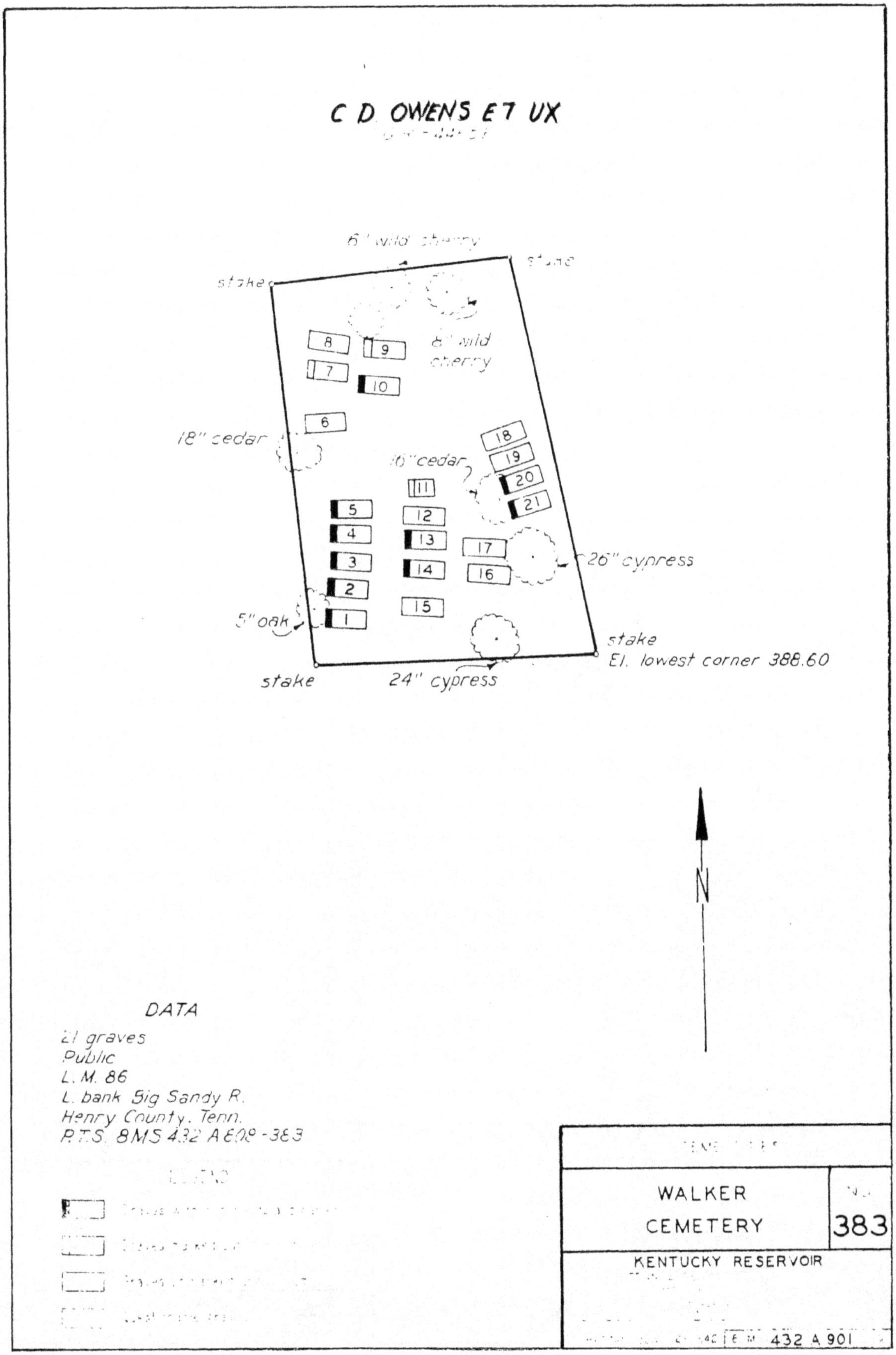

C D OWENS ET UX

DATA

21 graves
Public
L.M. 86
L. bank Big Sandy R.
Henry County, Tenn.
P.T.S. 8 MS 432 A E00 -383

WALKER CEMETERY

383

KENTUCKY RESERVOIR

E M 432 A 901

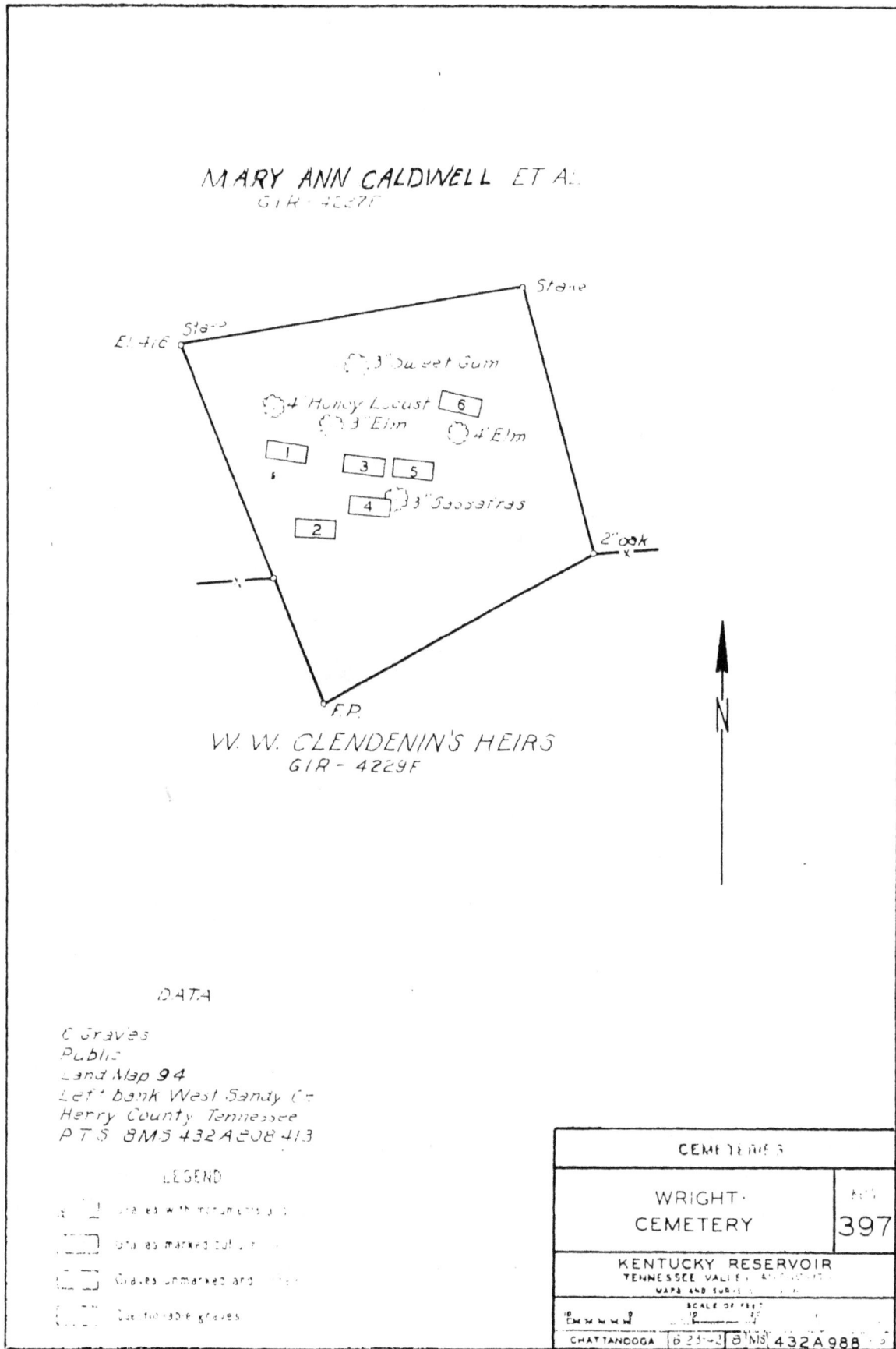

* *

MARY ANN CALDWELL ET AL
GIR - 4227F

Stone

El 416   Stone

3" Sweet Gum

4" Honey Locust   6

3" Elm   4" Elm

1

3   5

4   3" Sassafras

2

Brook
x

F.P.

W. W. CLENDENIN'S HEIRS
GIR - 4229F

N

DATA

6 Graves
Public
Land Map 94
Left bank West Sandy Cr
Henry County Tennessee
PTS 8MS 432A 208 413

LEGEND

Graves with monuments and
Graves marked but
Graves unmarked and
Destroyed graves

CEMETERIES

WRIGHT
CEMETERY

397

KENTUCKY RESERVOIR
TENNESSEE VALLEY AUTHORITY
MAPS AND SURVEYS

SCALE OF FEET

CHATTANOOGA   6 23   432A 988

* *

OZANE & ATCHIE MOODY

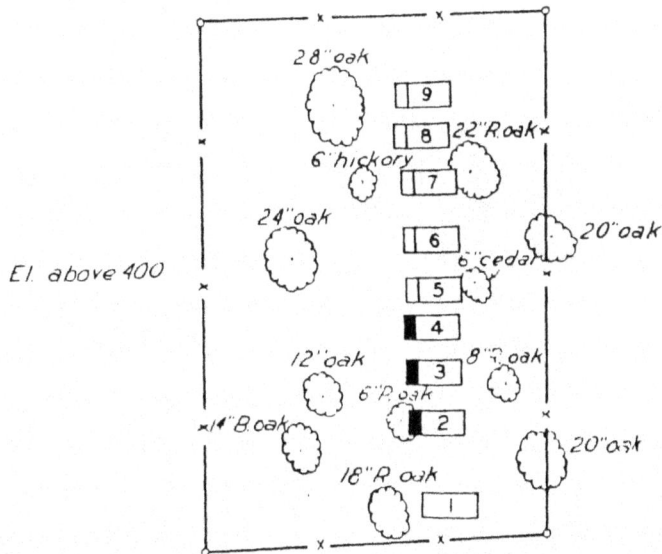

28"oak

9

8   22"R.oak×

6"hickory   7

24"oak   6

El. above 400   6"cedar   20"oak

5

4

12"oak   3   8"R.oak

6"R.oak

×14"B.oak   2

20"osk

18"R.oak   1

OZANE & ATCHIE MOODY

N

DATA
9 graves
Private
Land Map 93, marginal
Left bank Sandy Creek
Henry County, Tenn.
P.T.S. 8.MS432A808-413

LEGEND

▮▭ Graves with monuments and names
▯ Graves marked but unnamed
▭ Graves unmarked and unnamed
⌐ ⌐ Questionable graves

CEMETERIES		
RILEY CEMETERY	NO 413	
KENTUCKY RESERVOIR TENNESSEE VALLEY AUTHORITY MAPS AND SURVEYS DIVISION		
SCALE OF FEET		
CHATTANOOGA	6 9-42	8 MS 432A977

* *

El. 390

1

2

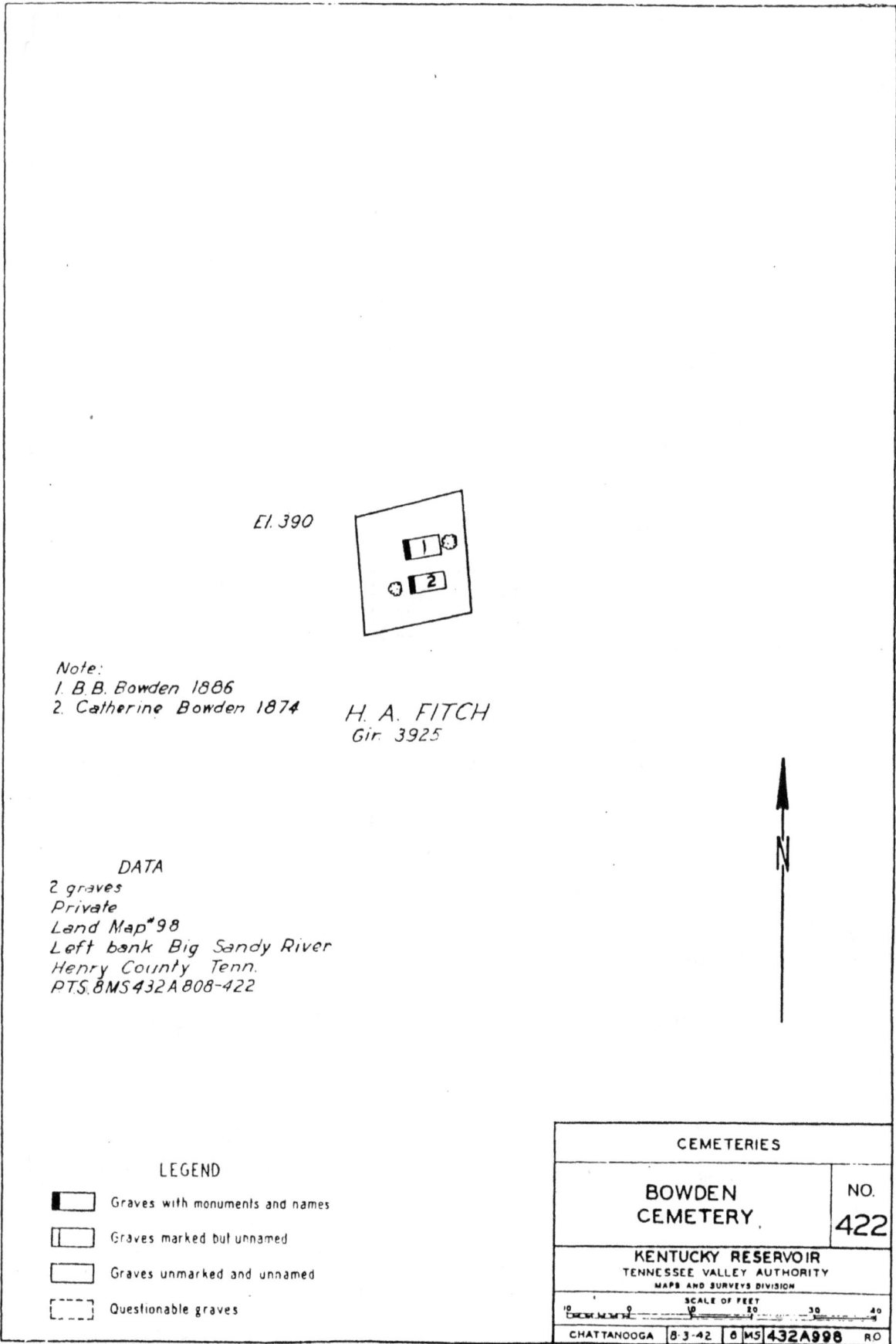

Note:
1. B.B. Bowden 1886
2. Catherine Bowden 1874

H. A. FITCH
Gir. 3925

DATA
2 graves
Private
Land Map #98
Left bank Big Sandy River
Henry County Tenn.
P.T.S. 8MS 432A 808-422

N

LEGEND

▬ Graves with monuments and names

▭ Graves marked but unnamed

▭ Graves unmarked and unnamed

┈ Questionable graves

CEMETERIES	
BOWDEN CEMETERY	NO. 422
KENTUCKY RESERVOIR TENNESSEE VALLEY AUTHORITY MAPS AND SURVEYS DIVISION	
SCALE OF FEET	
CHATTANOOGA 8-3-42 6 MS 432A998 R.O.	

* *

W. D. McSWAIN

Mon 15'sg.

El 390±

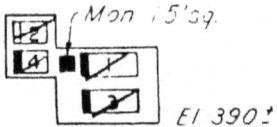

Note: The boundry lines of cem.
is edge of concrete slab
covering graves.

C. A. WIMBERLEY ET UX
GIR - 4050

N

DATA

4 graves
Private
L M. 95
L bank Big Sandy R
at Cane Creek
Henry County, Tenn
PTS SMS 432 A 808-423

CEMETERIES

BUCY
CEMETERY

NO
423

KENTUCKY RESERVOIR
TENNESSEE

CHATTANOOGA   3-31-42   8 MS 432 A 923

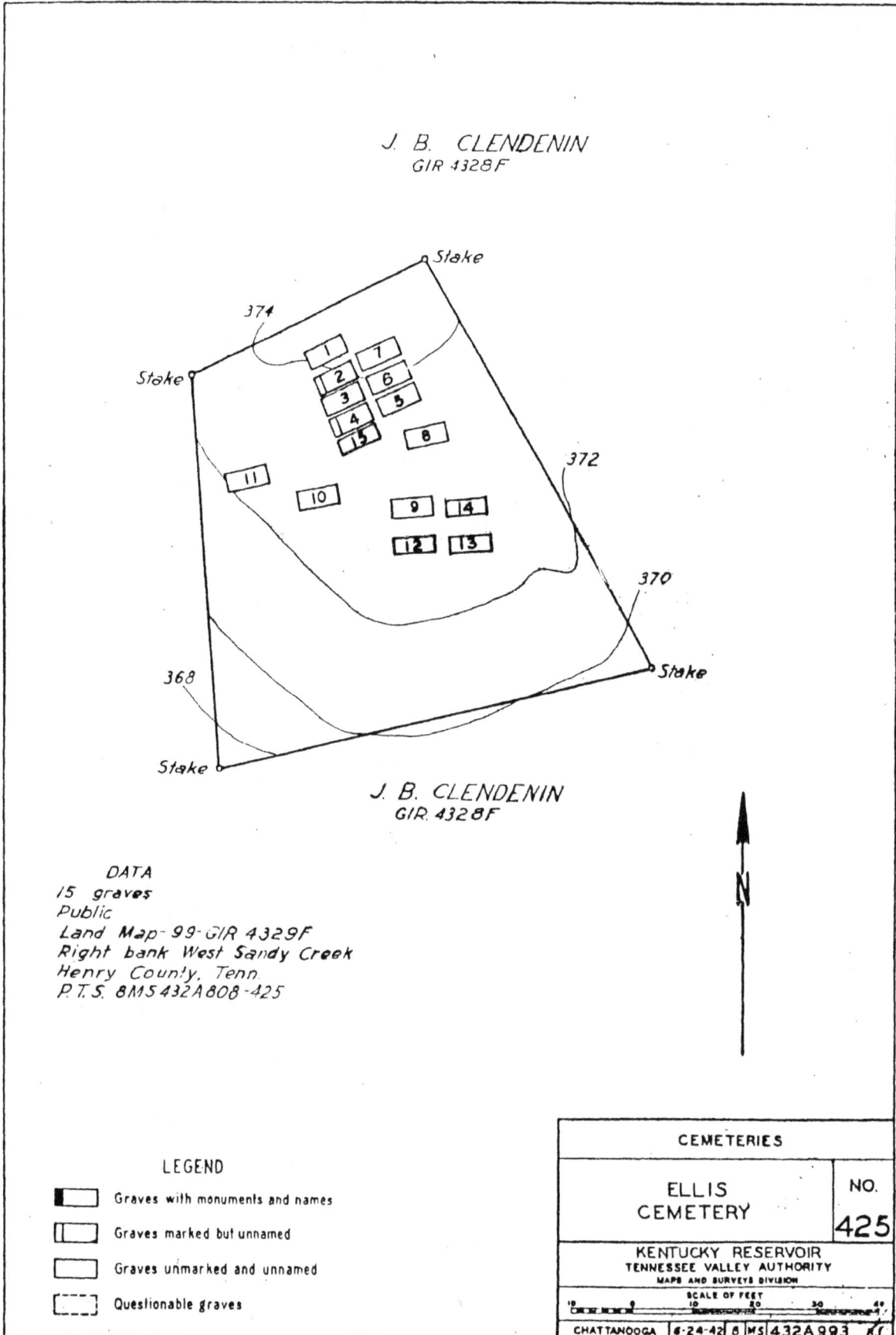

* *

J. B. CLENDENIN
GIR 4328F

Stake

374

Stake

1 7
2 6
3
4 5
15 8

11
10
9 14
12 13

372

370

Stake

368

Stake

J. B. CLENDENIN
GIR 4328F

N

DATA
15 graves
Public
Land Map-99-GIR 4329F
Right bank West Sandy Creek
Henry County, Tenn.
P.T.S. 8MS432A808-425

LEGEND

▮▯ Graves with monuments and names

▯▯ Graves marked but unnamed

▯ Graves unmarked and unnamed

⌐ ¬ Questionable graves

CEMETERIES	
ELLIS CEMETERY	NO. 425

KENTUCKY RESERVOIR
TENNESSEE VALLEY AUTHORITY
MAPS AND SURVEYS DIVISION
SCALE OF FEET

CHATTANOOGA 6-24-42 8 MS 432A993

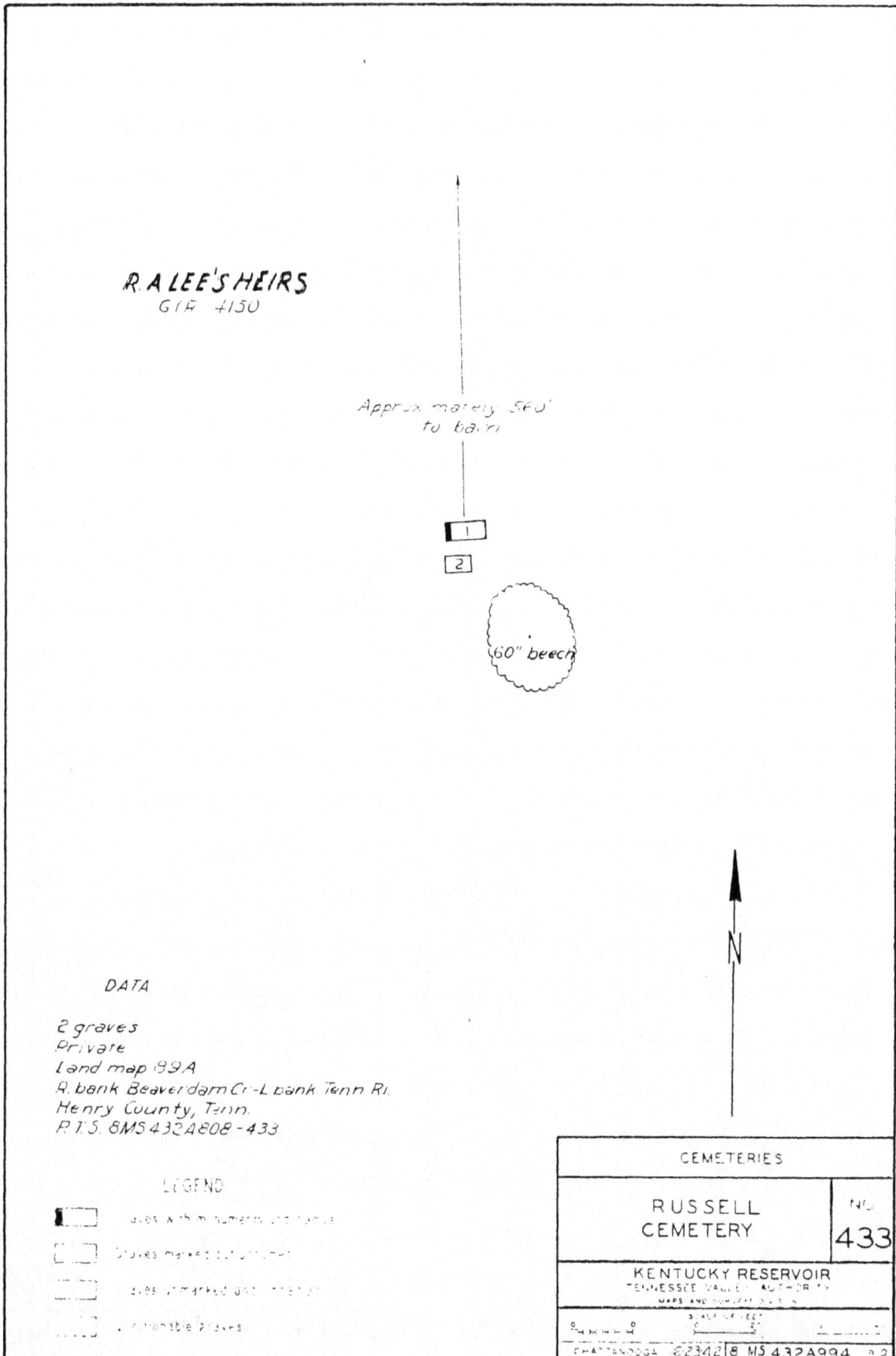

* *

R.A LEE'S HEIRS
GfR 4150

Approximately 560'
to barn

1

2

60" beech

N

DATA

2 graves
Private
Land map 99A
R. bank Beaverdam Cr-L bank Tenn Ri.
Henry County, Tenn.
P.T.S. 8MS 432A808 - 433

LEGEND

⬛ graves with monuments and names

▢ Graves marked but unnamed

▢ graves unmarked but located

⠿ Probable graves

CEMETERIES		
RUSSELL CEMETERY	NO.	433
KENTUCKY RESERVOIR TENNESSEE VALLEY AUTHORITY MAPS AND SURVEYS DIVISION		
CHATTANOOGA	C-2342	8 MS 432A994

* *

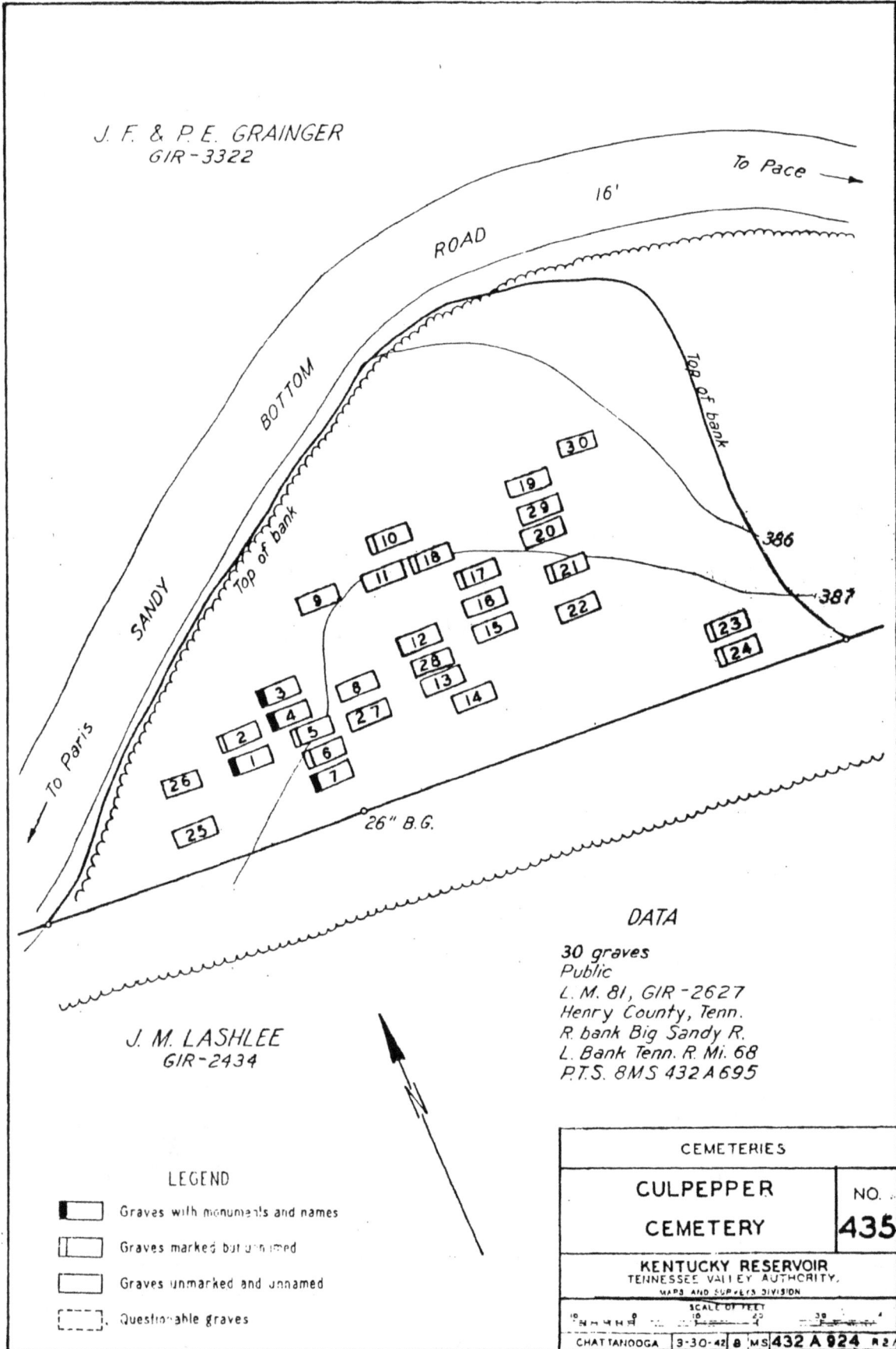

J. F. & P. E. GRAINGER
GIR-3322

To Pace →

16'

ROAD

BOTTOM

Top of bank

SANDY

Top of bank

To Paris

386

387

30

19

29

20

10

18

11

17

9

16

121

15

22

12

123

28

124

3

13

8

4

14

2

5

27

26

1

6

7

25

26" B.G.

J. M. LASHLEE
GIR-2434

N

DATA

30 graves
Public
L. M. 81, GIR-2627
Henry County, Tenn.
R. bank Big Sandy R.
L. Bank Tenn. R. Mi. 68
P.T.S. 8MS 432 A695

LEGEND

▮ Graves with monuments and names

▯ Graves marked but unnamed

▢ Graves unmarked and unnamed

⌐ ⌐ Questionable graves

CEMETERIES

CULPEPPER

CEMETERY

NO.
435

KENTUCKY RESERVOIR
TENNESSEE VALLEY AUTHORITY,
MAPS AND SURVEYS DIVISION

SCALE OF FEET

CHATTANOOGA 3-30-42 8 MS 432 A 924 R2/

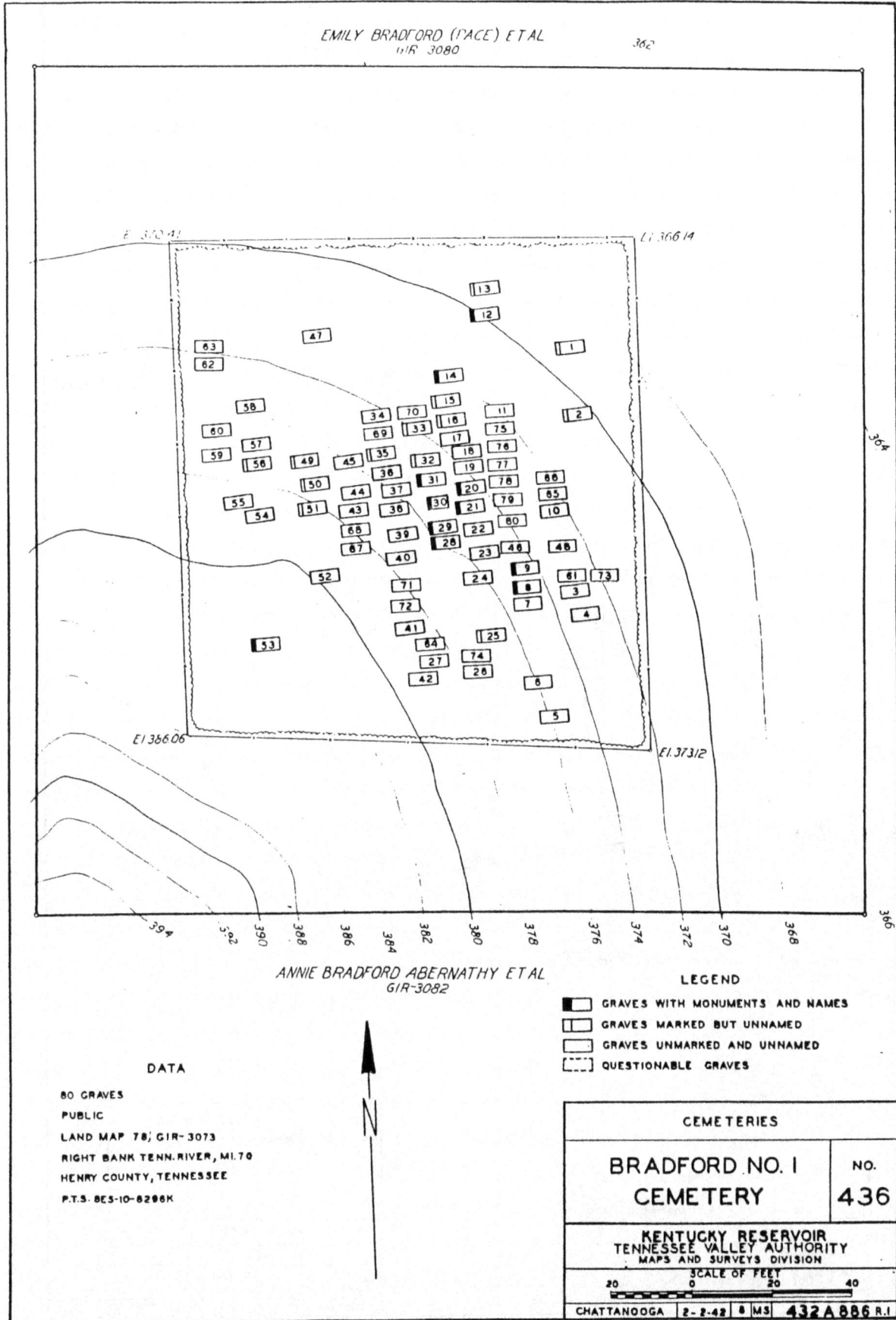

* *

EMILY BRADFORD (PACE) ET AL
GIR 3080

ANNIE BRADFORD ABERNATHY ET AL
GIR-3082

N

DATA

80 GRAVES

PUBLIC

LAND MAP 78; GIR-3073

RIGHT BANK TENN. RIVER, MI.70

HENRY COUNTY, TENNESSEE

P.T.S. 8E5-10-8298K

LEGEND

GRAVES WITH MONUMENTS AND NAMES

GRAVES MARKED BUT UNNAMED

GRAVES UNMARKED AND UNNAMED

QUESTIONABLE GRAVES

CEMETERIES

BRADFORD NO. 1 CEMETERY

NO. 436

KENTUCKY RESERVOIR
TENNESSEE VALLEY AUTHORITY
MAPS AND SURVEYS DIVISION

SCALE OF FEET

20   0   20   40

CHATTANOOGA | 2-2-42 | 8 MS | 432A886 R.I

Henry County, Tennessee

* *

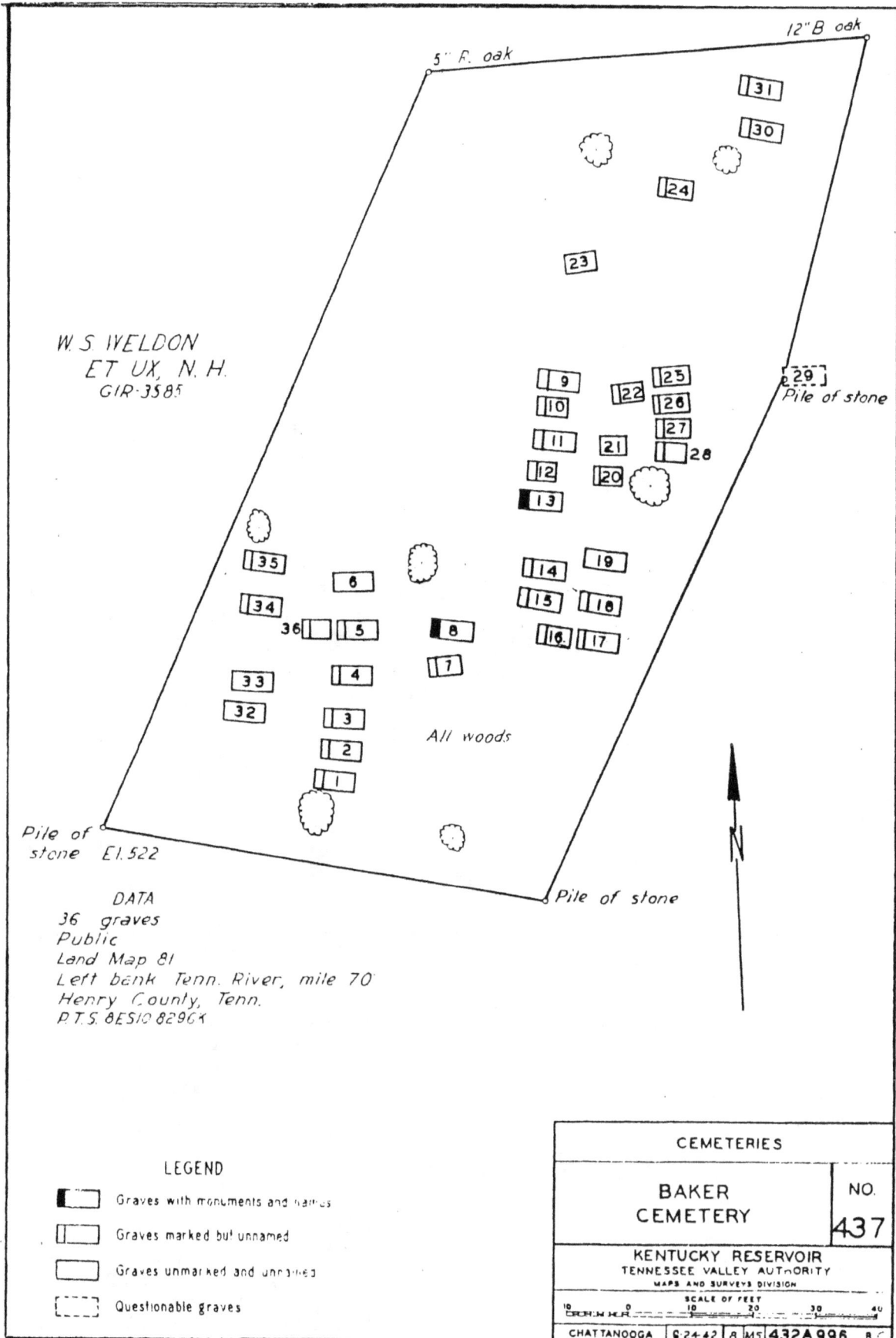

5" R. oak

12" B oak

31

30

24

23

W. S. WELDON
ET UX, N. H.
GIR-3585

9

10

22

25

26

29

Pile of stone

11

21

27

12

20

28

13

35

19

6

14

34

15

18

36

5

8

16

17

7

33

4

32

3

All woods

2

1

N

Pile of
stone   El.522

DATA
36 graves
Public
Land Map 81
Left bank Tenn. River, mile 70
Henry County, Tenn.
P.T.S. 8ES10 8296 x

Pile of stone

LEGEND

Graves with monuments and names

Graves marked but unnamed

Graves unmarked and unnamed

Questionable graves

CEMETERIES

BAKER
CEMETERY

NO.

437

KENTUCKY RESERVOIR
TENNESSEE VALLEY AUTHORITY
MAPS AND SURVEYS DIVISION

SCALE OF FEET
10   0   10   20   30   40

CHATTANOOGA   6-24-42   8   MS   432A996   R C

* *

MRS. R. F. KENDALL ET AL
GIR - 3857

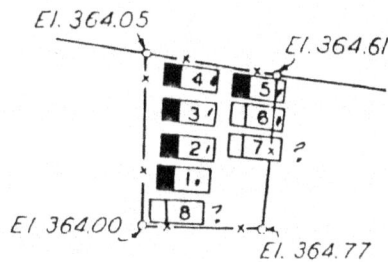

El. 364.05

El. 364.61

4 · 4 | 5 ·

3 · | 6 ·

2 · | 7 × | ?

1 ·

El. 364.00 | 8 | ?

El. 364.77

W. F. BOWLES ET AL
GIR - 3855

N

DATA
8 Graves
Private
L.M. 67, GIR - 3854
L. Bank Big Sandy R.
Henry County, Tenn.
P.T.S. 8 MS 432 A 783

LEGEND

▮▯ Graves with monuments and names

▯ Graves marked but unnamed

▭ Graves unmarked and unnamed

┌╌╌┐ Questionable graves

CEMETERIES

BOND
CEMETERY

NO
439

KENTUCKY RESERVOIR
TENNESSEE VALLEY AUTHORITY
MAPS AN SURVEYS DIVSION

SCALE OF FEET

CHATTANOOGA | 2-3-42 | 8 MS | 432 A 875

* *

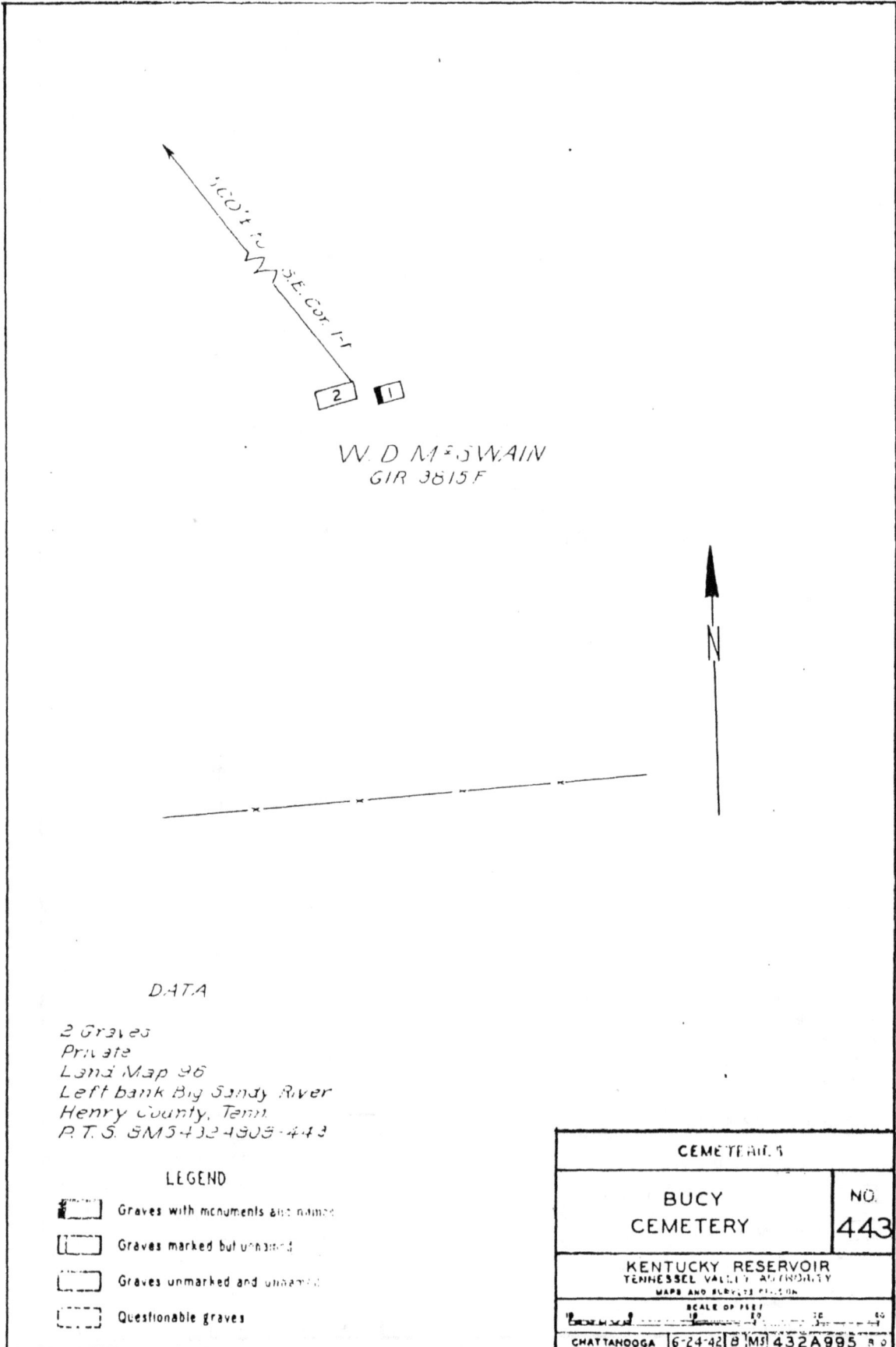

W. D. McSWAIN
GIR 3815F

DATA

2 Graves
Private
Land Map 96
Left bank Big Sandy River
Henry County, Tenn.
P.T.S. SMS-432-4905-443

LEGEND

▨ Graves with monuments and names
▥ Graves marked but unnamed
▢ Graves unmarked and unnamed
⬚ Questionable graves

CEMETERIES	
BUCY CEMETERY	NO. 443
KENTUCKY RESERVOIR TENNESSEE VALLEY AUTHORITY MAPS AND SURVEYS DIVISION	
SCALE OF FEET	
CHATTANOOGA 6-24-42 8 MS 432A995 R 0	

* *

UNITED BAPTIST CHURCH

LG ROBBINS

J H HUTCHISON

A DUNN ET AL

JOE HAMPTON'S HEIRS

MERTON GREY ET UX, DILLA

DATA

184 GRAVES

PUBLIC

L. M. NO. 82

L. BANK TENN. R. MI. 71

HENRY COUNTY, TENNESSEE

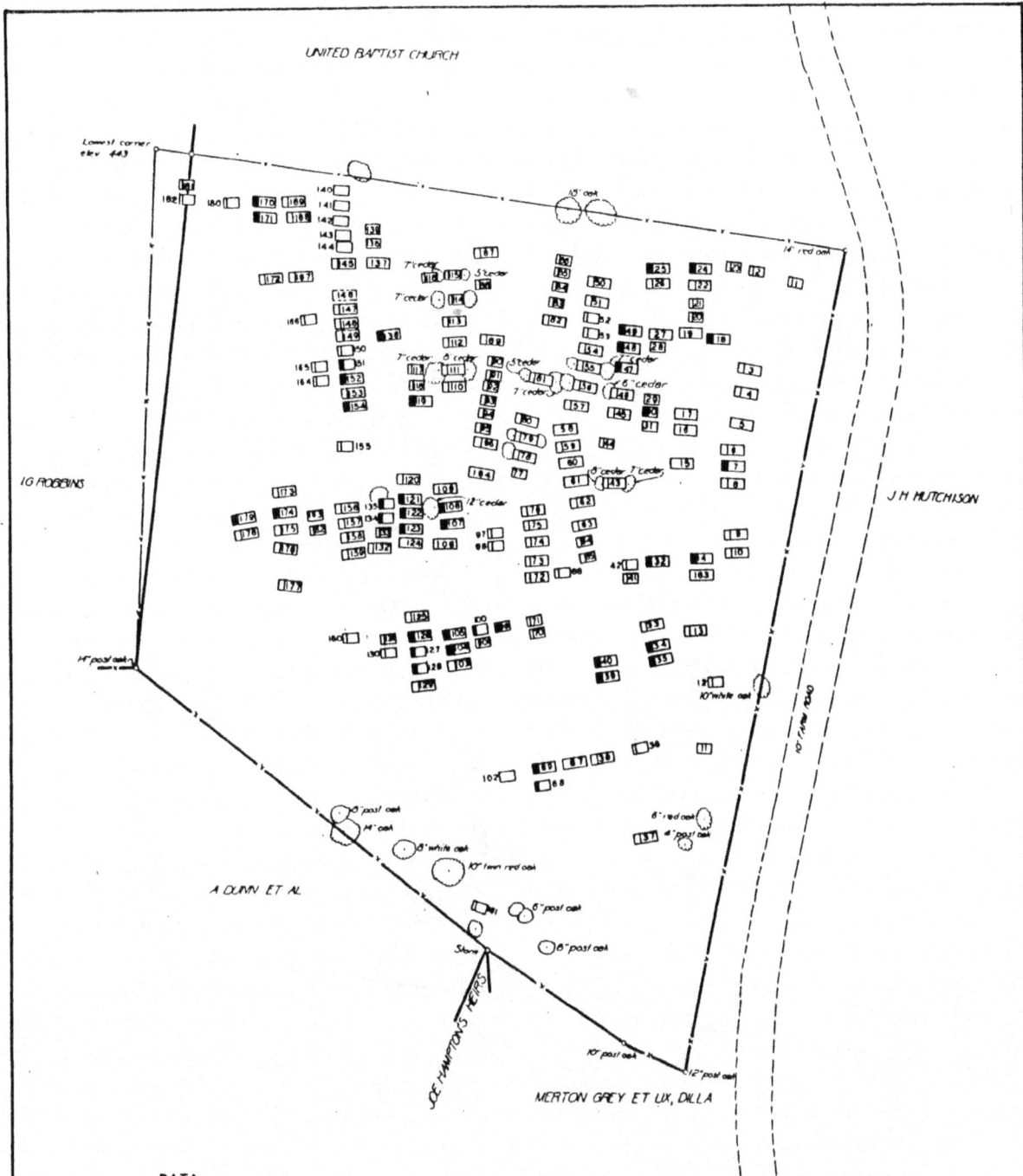

P.T.S. 8 MS 432 G 808 - 444

LEGEND

GRAVES WITH MONUMENTS AND NAMES

GRAVES MARKED BUT UNNAMED

GRAVES UNNAMED AND UNMARKED

QUESTIONABLE GRAVES

CEMETERIES	
MT. ZION CEMETERY	NO. 444
KENTUCKY RESERVOIR TENNESSEE VALLEY AUTHORITY MAPS AND SURVEYS DIVISION	
SCALE OF FEET	
CHATTANOOGA 4-8-42 8 MS 432 A 939 R.I	

Henry County, Tennessee

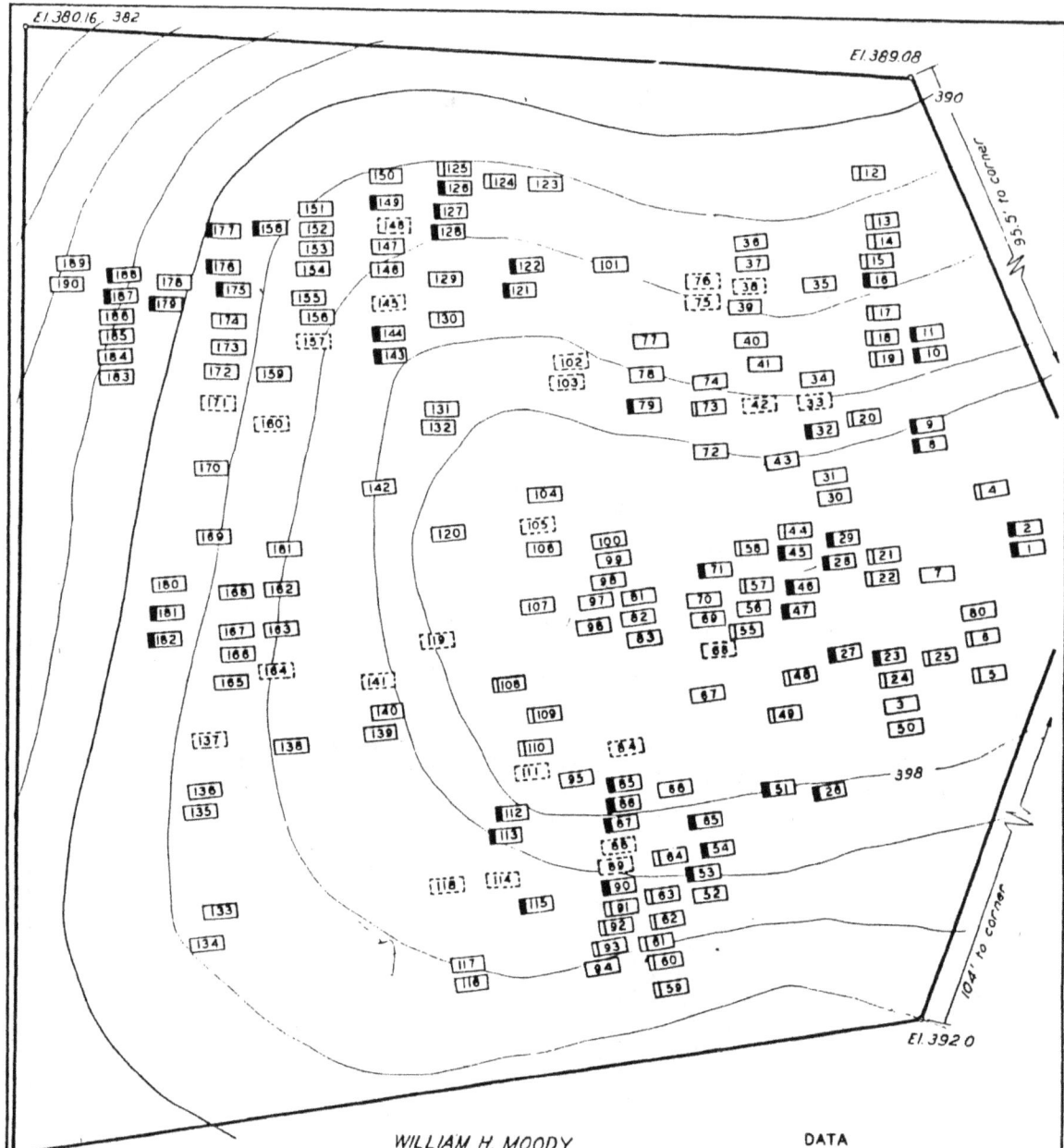

* *

WILLIAM H. MOODY
6IR-4093

Note. Woods line follows lines of cemetery.
Cemetery cleared except for scattered
cedars and pines.

DATA

190 GRAVES

PUBLIC

LAND MAP 103

R. BANK WEST SANDY CREEK

HENRY COUNTY, TENN.

P.T.S. 8MS 432 G 808-451

N

LEGEND

■ GRAVES WITH MONUMENTS AND NAMES

[ ] GRAVES MARKED BUT UNNAMED

☐ GRAVES UNMARKED AND UNNAMED

[⁻ ⁻] QUESTIONABLE GRAVES

CEMETERIES

MANLEYVILLE CHAPEL CEMETERY

NO 451

KENTUCKY RESERVOIR
TENNESSEE VALLEY AUTHORITY
MAPS AND SURVEYS DIVISION

SCALE OF FEET
20   20   40

CHATTANOOGA   2-14-42   8 MS   432 A 879   R.1

* *

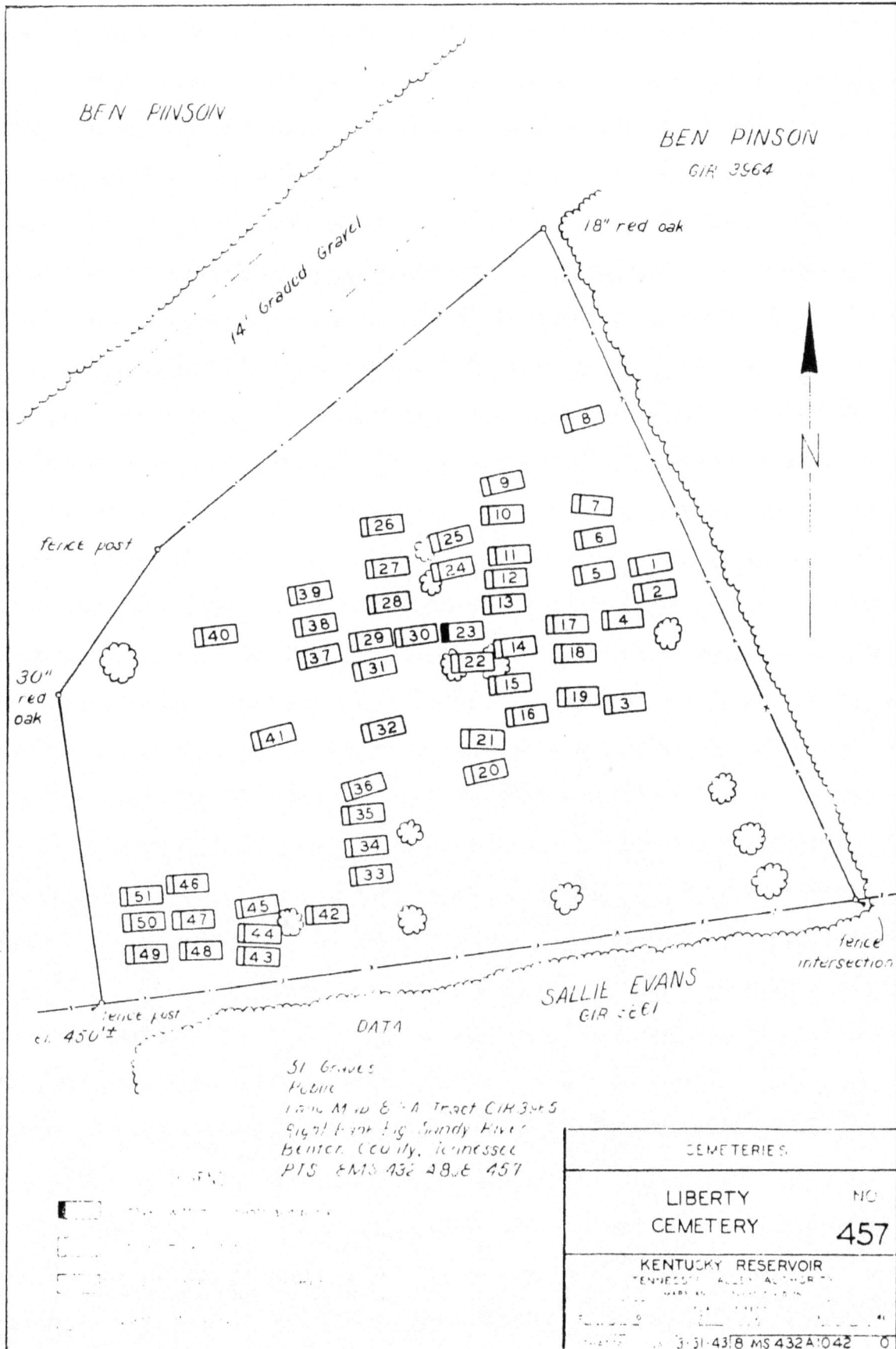

BEN PINSON

BEN PINSON
GIR 3964

18" red oak

14' Graded Gravel

fence post

30"
red
oak

N

DATA

51 Graves
Public
Land M N & H A Tract CIR 3465
Right Bank Big Sandy River
Benton County, Tennessee
PTS EM13 432 28 & 457

fence post
el 450'±

SALLIE EVANS
GIR 861

fence
intersection

CEMETERIES	
LIBERTY CEMETERY	NO 457
KENTUCKY RESERVOIR	

* *

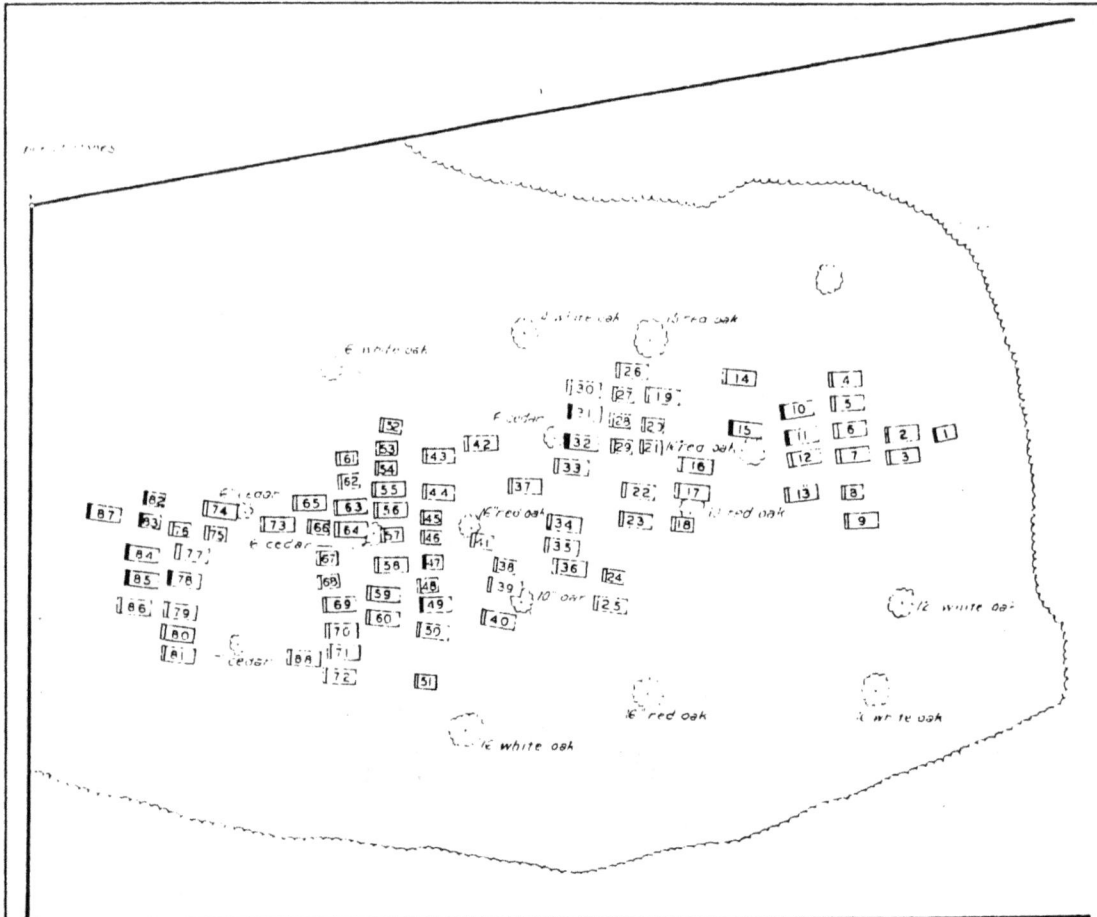

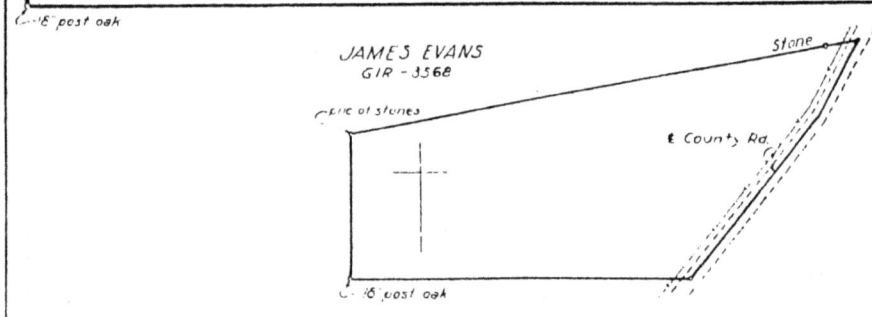

JAMES EVANS
GIR - 3568

E County Rd.

LOCATION SKETCH

0   100   200
SCALE OF FEET

N

DATA

88 GRAVES

PUBLIC

LAND MAP 87 GIR-3845

L BANK TENNESSEE RIVER

BENTON COUNTY, TENN

F T S BMS 432 K 781

LEGEND

[▭] GRAVES WITH MONUMENTS AND NAMES

[▯] GRAVES MARKED BUT UNNAMED

[▭] GRAVES UNMARKED AND UNNAMED

[▭] QUESTIONABLE GRAVES

CEMETERIES	
EVANS CEMETERY	NO 458
KENTUCKY RESERVOIR TENNESSEE VALLEY AUTHORITY MAPS AND SURVEYS DIVISION	

SCALE OF FEET
20   0   20   40

CHATTANOOGA | 6-10-42 | 8 |MS| 432 A 976 | RO

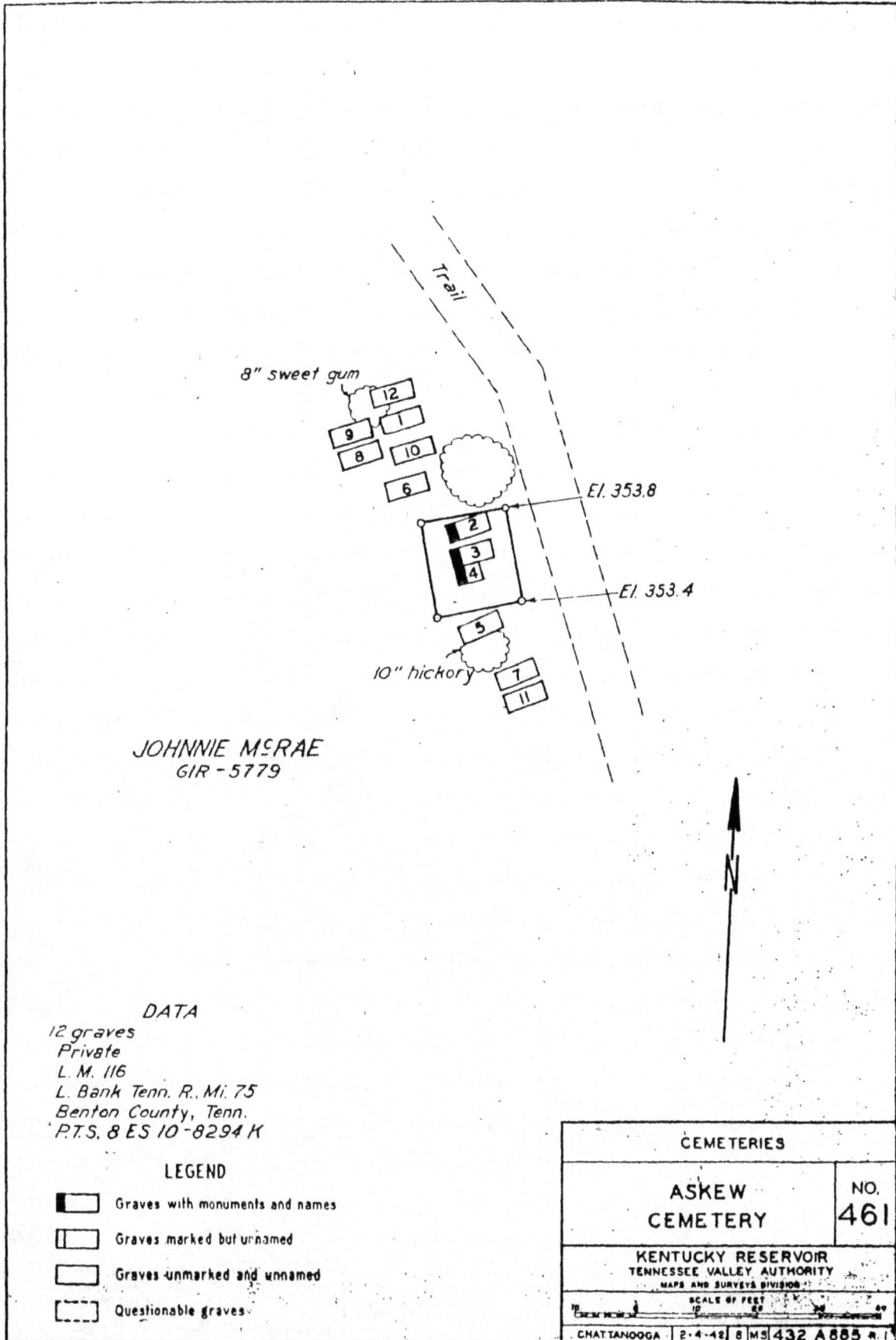

* *

Trail

8" sweet gum

12

9   1

8   10

6

El. 353.8

2

3

4

El. 353.4

5

10" hickory

7

11

JOHNNIE MᶜRAE
GIR - 5779

N

DATA
12 graves
Private
L. M. 116
L. Bank Tenn. R. Mi. 75
Benton County, Tenn.
P.T.S. 8 ES 10 - 8294 K

LEGEND

▮▭   Graves with monuments and names

▯▯   Graves marked but unnamed

▭   Graves unmarked and unnamed

⌐⌐   Questionable graves

CEMETERIES	
ASKEW CEMETERY	NO. 461
KENTUCKY RESERVOIR TENNESSEE VALLEY AUTHORITY MAPS AND SURVEYS DIVISION	
SCALE OF FEET	
CHATTANOOGA 2-4-42 8 MS 432 A 885 R.1	

* *

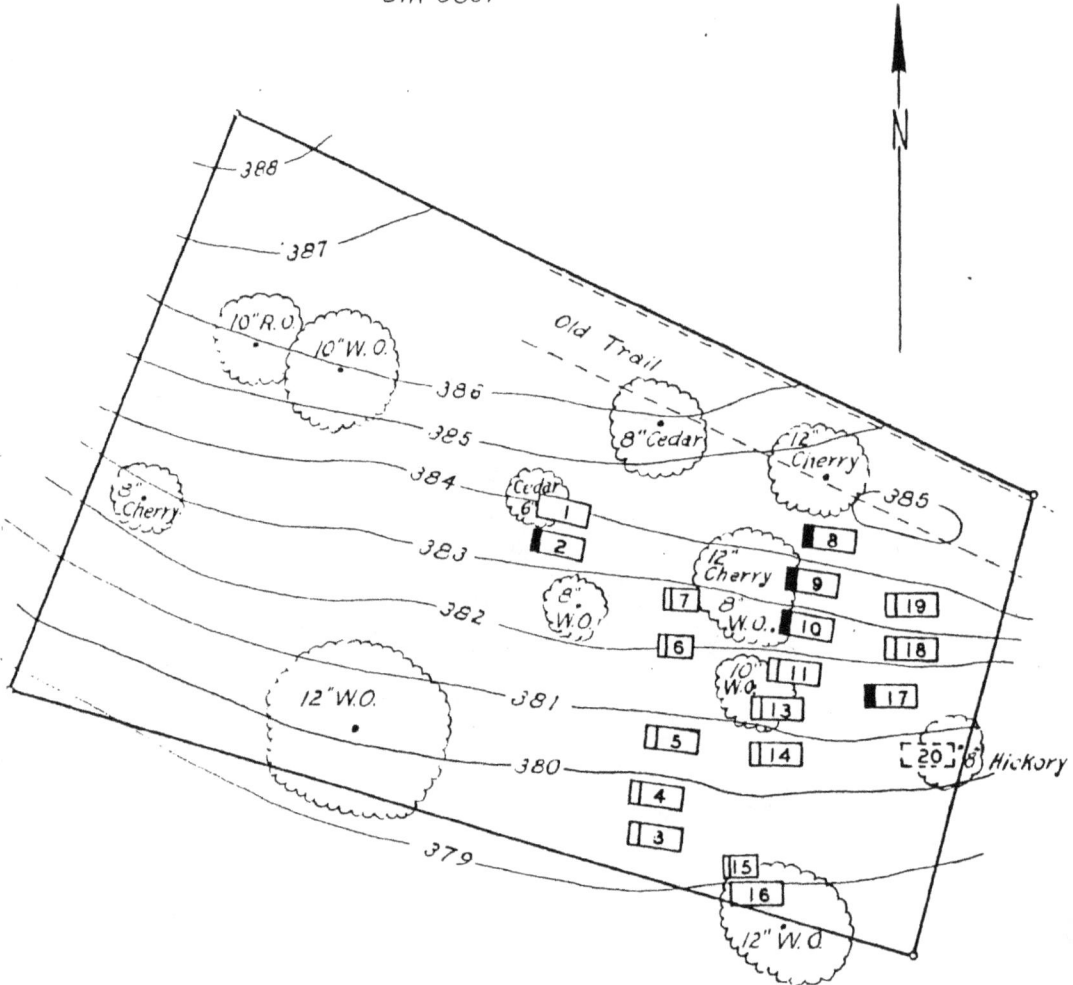

OLIVER E. LOCKMAN ET UX ANGIE
GIR 5307

N

388
387
10" R.O.
10" W.O.
386
Old Trail
385
8" Cedar
384 Cedar 12"
3" Cherry   6" 1   Cherry 385
383   2   8
382   12"   9
          Cherry   19
8"   7   8   10   18
W.O.   6   W.O.
381   10"   11
12" W.O.   W.O.   17
          13
380   5   14
          20 6" Hickory
379   4
          3
          15
          16
12" W.O.

DATA

19 Graves
Private
Land Map 115
Left bank Tennessee River Mi. 75
Benton County, Tennessee
P.T.S. 8ES1082.94K

Note: No Grave numbered 12

LEGEND

■□ Graves with monuments and names

[|□] Graves marked but unnamed

□ Graves unmarked and unnamed

[┈┈] Questionable graves

CEMETERIES	
RALLS CEMETERY	NO 464

KENTUCKY RESERVOIR
TENNESSEE VALLEY AUTHORITY
MAPS AND SURVEYS DIVISION

SCALE OF FEET

CHATTANOOGA 2-7-42 8MS432A-884 R.O.

* *

W. J. STOCKDALE
GIR-5792

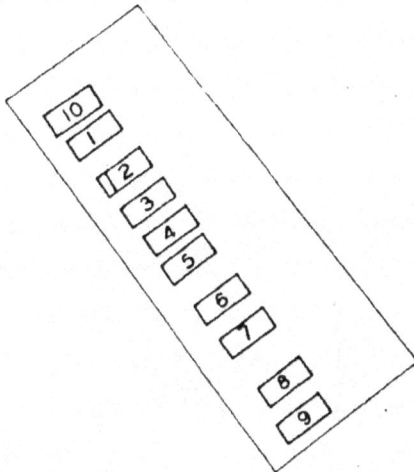

Elev. 358

N

DATA

10 Graves
Private
Land Map 115
Left bank Tennessee River, mi. 74
Benton County, Tennessee
P.T.S. 8 MS 432 A 808 - 465

LEGEND

▮▯ Graves with monuments and names

▯▯ Graves marked but unnamed

▭ Graves unmarked and unnamed

⌐⌐ Questionable graves

CEMETERIES	
NO NAME CEMETERY	NO. 465

KENTUCKY RESERVOIR
TENNESSEE VALLEY AUTHORITY
MAPS AND SURVEYS DIVISION

SCALE OF FEET
10 0   10   20   30   40

CHATTANOOGA | 8-24-42 | 8 | MS | 432 A 1013 | R. 1

* *

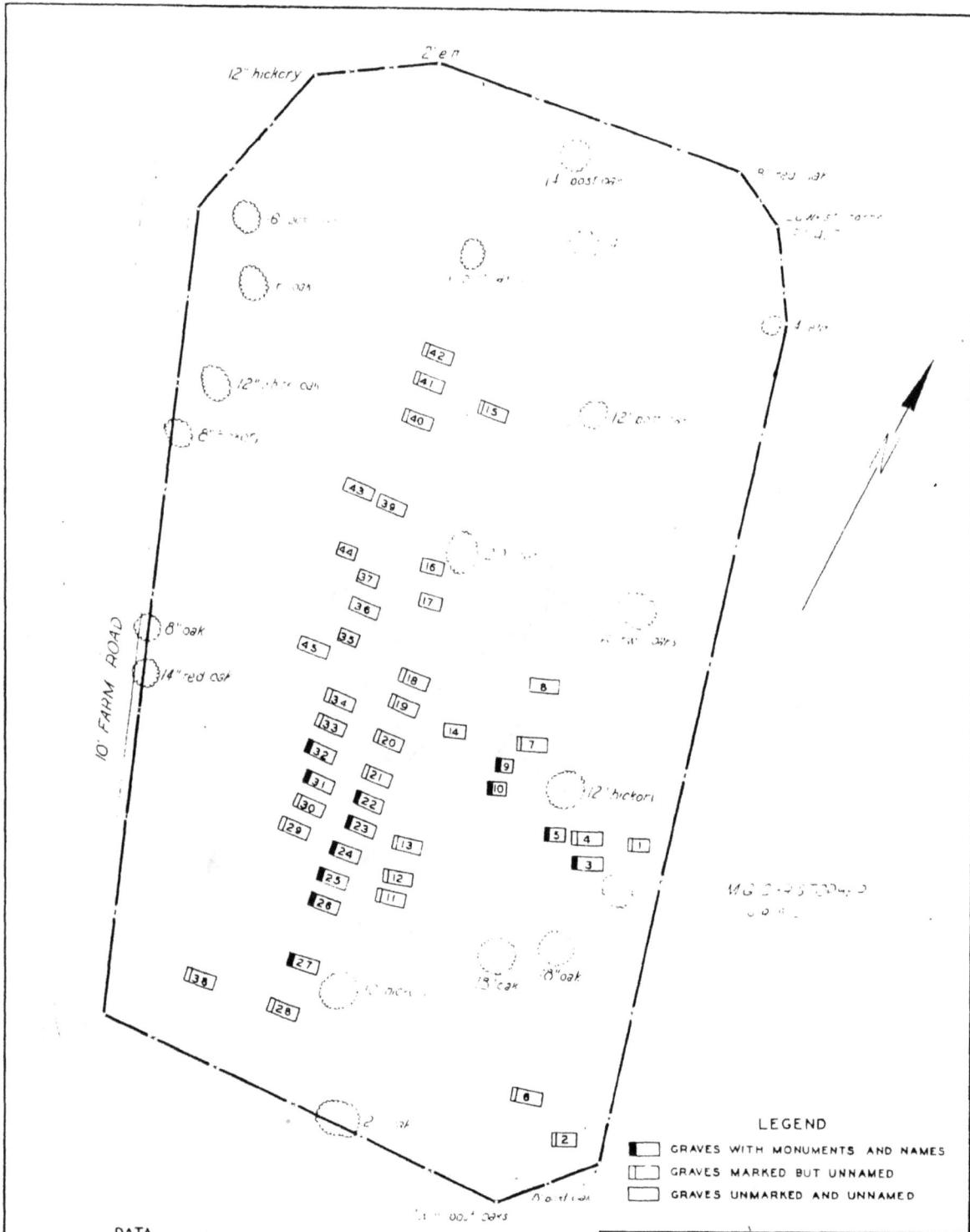

LEGEND

▮▯ GRAVES WITH MONUMENTS AND NAMES
▯ GRAVES MARKED BUT UNNAMED
▯ GRAVES UNMARKED AND UNNAMED

DATA

45 GRAVES
PUBLIC
L M. 126, GIR-5652
L BANK TENN RIVER, MI 80
BENTON COUNTY, TENN.
R T S. 8 MS 432 B 801-467

CEMETERIES

WYNN
CEMETERY

NO.
467

KENTUCKY RESERVOIR
TENNESSEE VALLEY AUTHORITY
MAPS AND SURVEYS DIVISION

SCALE OF FEET
20   0   20   40

CHATTANOOGA 4-4-42 8 MS 432 A 925 R-O

* *

Elev 395

ALLIE WILSON'S HEIRS ET AL
G.F 5713

DATA

59 GRAVES

PUBLIC

AND MAP 121 GIR 5714

BANK TENNESSEE R M 18C

BENTON COUNTY, TENN

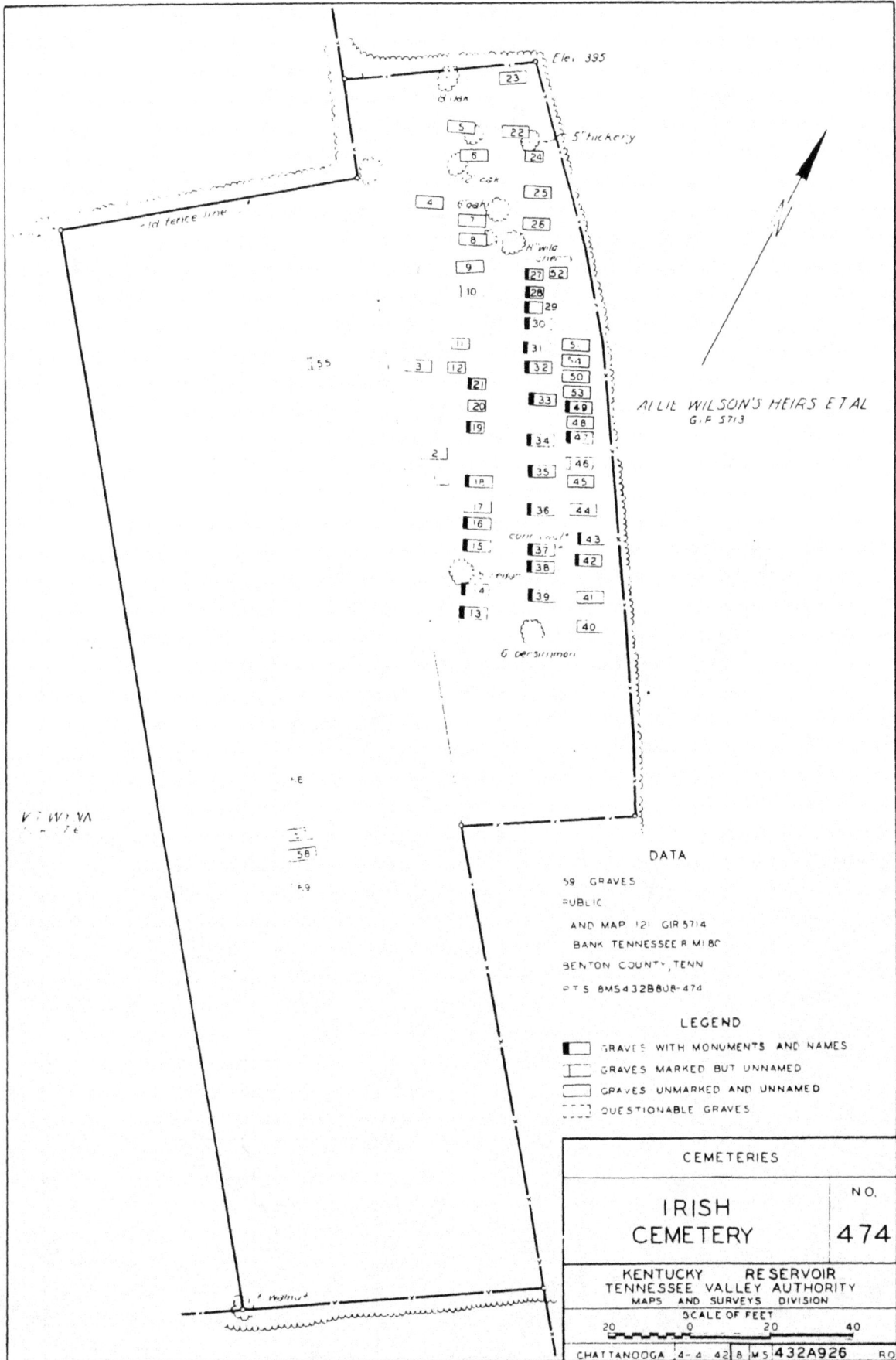

P T S 8MS 432BB08-474

LEGEND

	GRAVES WITH MONUMENTS AND NAMES
	GRAVES MARKED BUT UNNAMED
	GRAVES UNMARKED AND UNNAMED
	QUESTIONABLE GRAVES

CEMETERIES

IRISH
CEMETERY

NO.
474

KENTUCKY RESERVOIR
TENNESSEE VALLEY AUTHORITY
MAPS AND SURVEYS DIVISION

SCALE OF FEET
20   0   20   40

CHATTANOOGA 4-4 42 8 MS 432A926   BO

* *

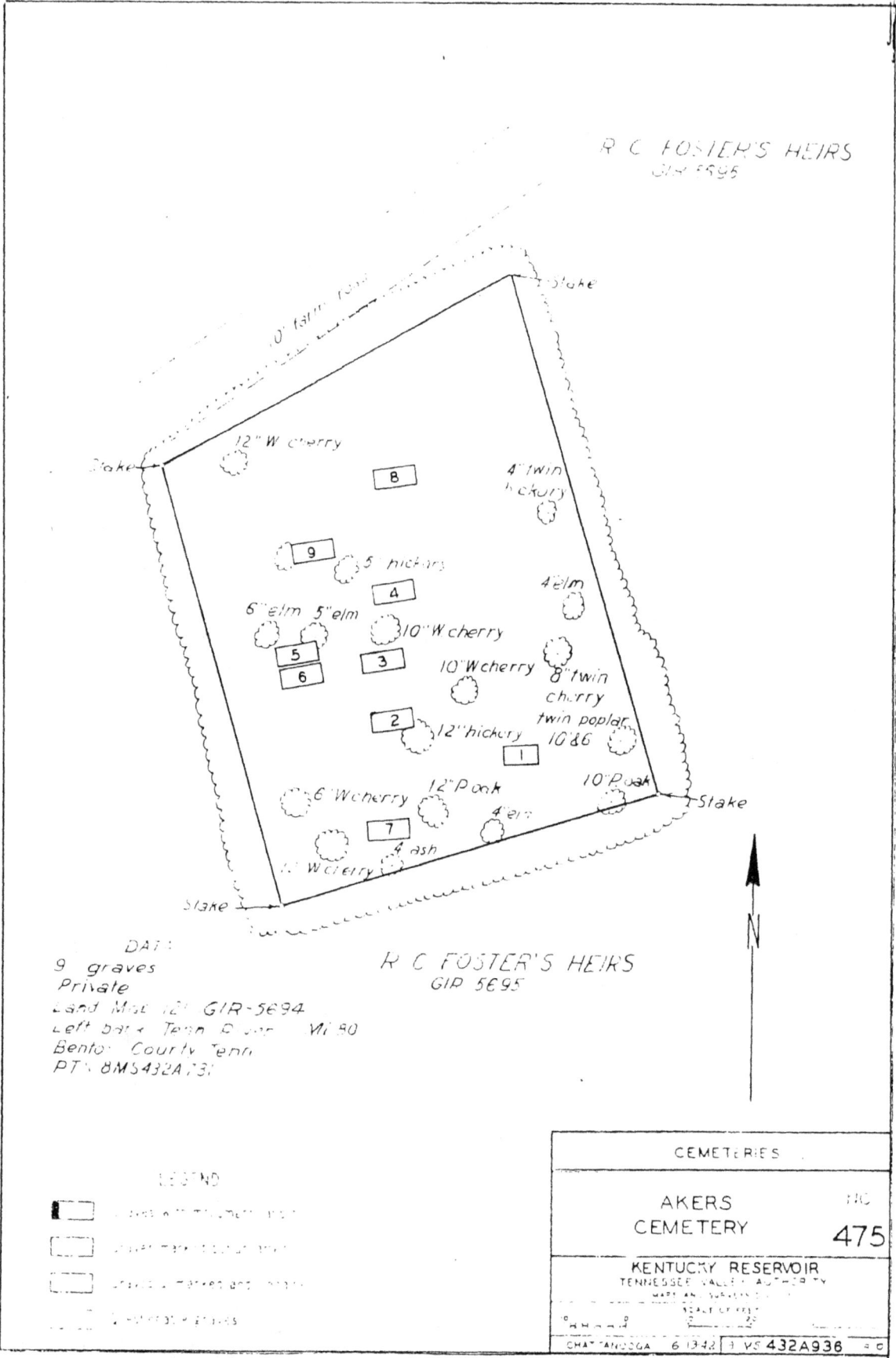

R C FOSTER'S HEIRS
GIR 5E95

12" W cherry

8

4" twin
hickory

9   5 hickory

4 elm

4

6" elm 5" elm

10" W cherry

5   3   10" W cherry   8" twin
6   cherry

twin poplar
10 & 6

2   12" hickory

1

6 W cherry   12" P oak   10" P oak
                                        Stake

7   4 elm
  4 ash
W cherry

DATA
9 graves
Private
Land Map No. GIR-5E94
Left bank Tenn River   Mi 80
Benton County Tenn
PT. BMS432A 73

N

R C FOSTER'S HEIRS
GIR 5E95

LEGEND

CEMETERIES

AKERS
CEMETERY

NO

475

KENTUCKY RESERVOIR
TENNESSEE VALLEY AUTHORITY
MAPS AND SURVEYS

CHATTANOOGA   6 1342   VS 432A936

* *

DATA

23 GRAVES

PUBLIC

L.M. 127

L. BANK TENN.R., MI.84

BENTON COUNTY. TENN.

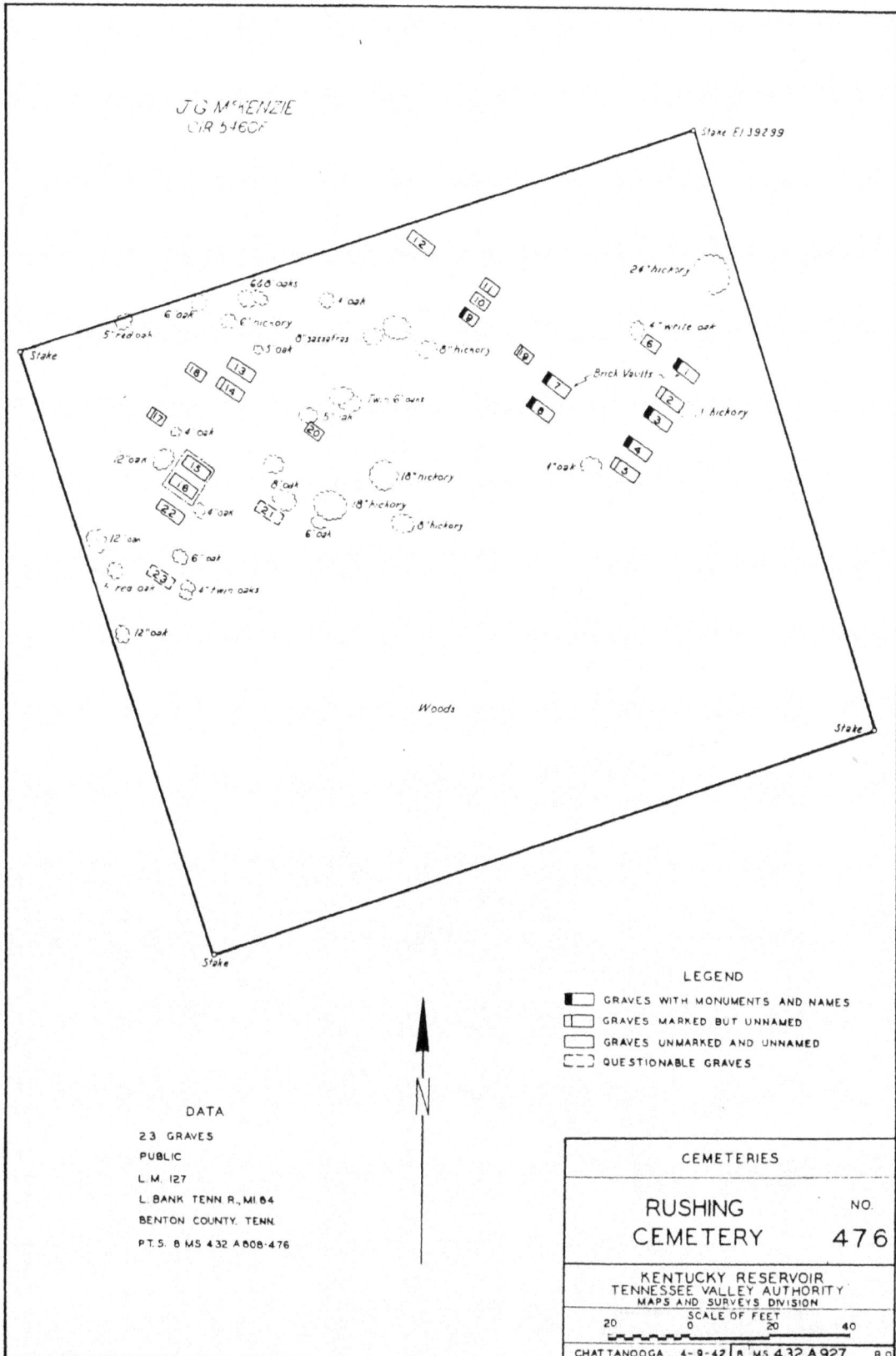

P.T.S. 8 MS 432 A808-476

LEGEND

GRAVES WITH MONUMENTS AND NAMES

GRAVES MARKED BUT UNNAMED

GRAVES UNMARKED AND UNNAMED

QUESTIONABLE GRAVES

CEMETERIES

RUSHING
CEMETERY

NO.
476

KENTUCKY RESERVOIR
TENNESSEE VALLEY AUTHORITY
MAPS AND SURVEYS DIVISION

SCALE OF FEET

20   0   20   40

CHATTANOOGA   4-9-42   8 MS 432 A 927   R 0

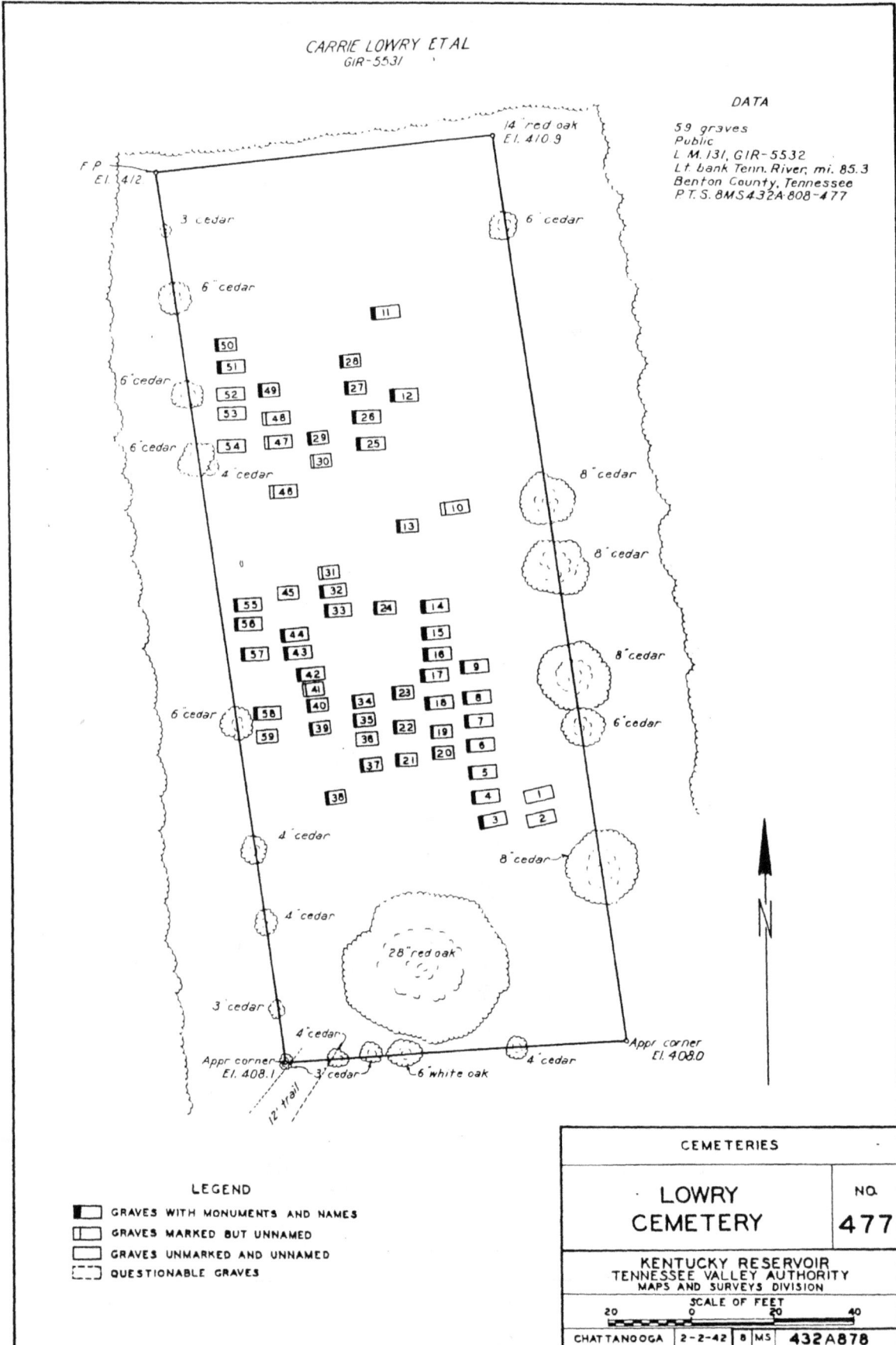

* *

CARRIE LOWRY ET AL
GIR-5531

DATA

59 graves
Public
L.M. 131, GIR-5532
Lt. bank Tenn. River, mi. 85.3
Benton County, Tennessee
P.T.S. 8MS432A·808-477

LEGEND

■ GRAVES WITH MONUMENTS AND NAMES
▯ GRAVES MARKED BUT UNNAMED
▢ GRAVES UNMARKED AND UNNAMED
⊏⊐ QUESTIONABLE GRAVES

CEMETERIES	
LOWRY **CEMETERY**	NO. **477**
KENTUCKY RESERVOIR TENNESSEE VALLEY AUTHORITY MAPS AND SURVEYS DIVISION	
SCALE OF FEET	
CHATTANOOGA 2-2-42 8 MS 432A878	

* *

FORREST CEMETERY

NO. 481

KENTUCKY RESERVOIR

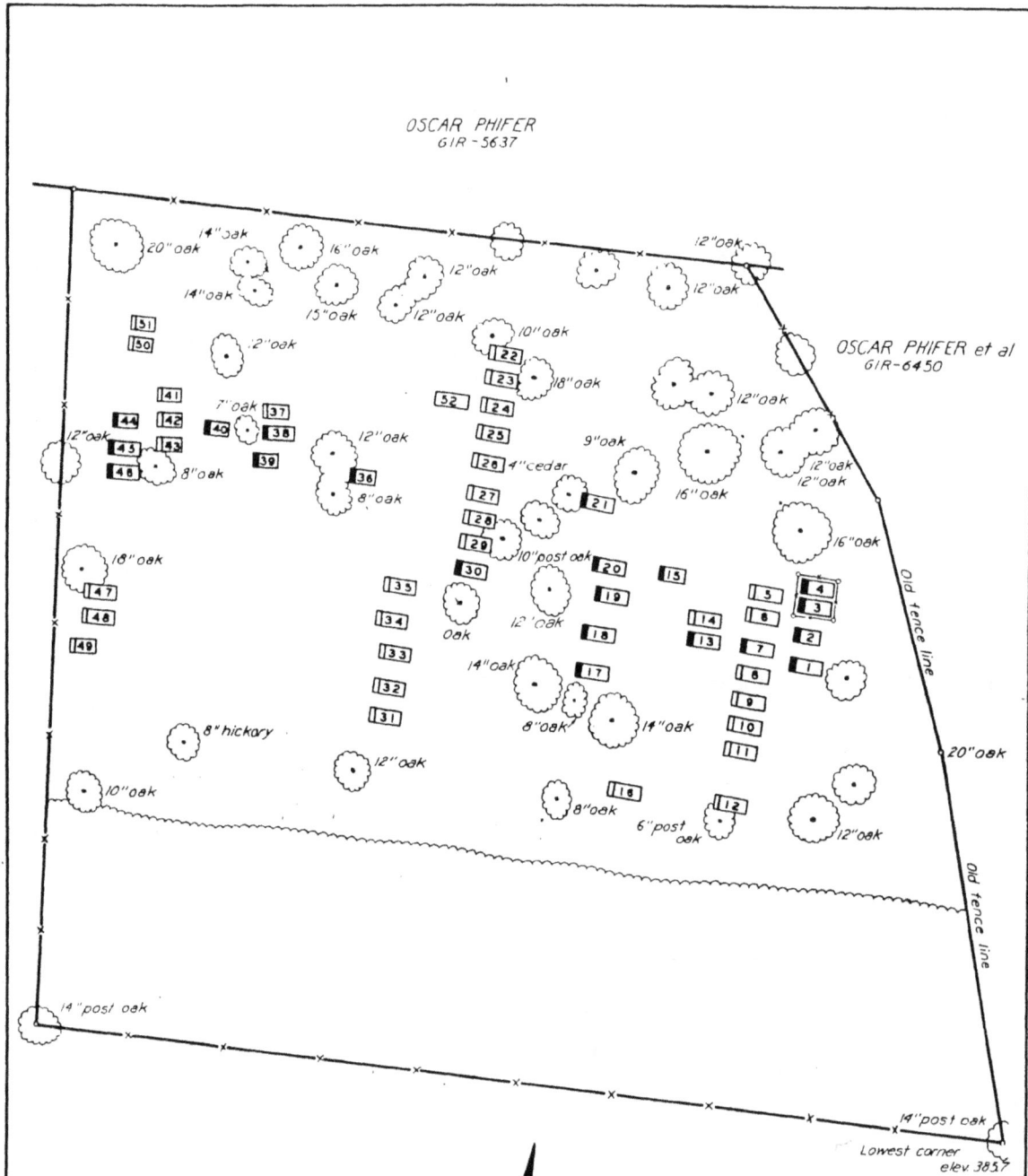

OSCAR PHIFER
GIR-5637

OSCAR PHIFER et al
GIR-6450

Old fence line

Old fence line

Lowest corner
elev. 385.7

DATA

52 GRAVES

PUBLIC

LAND MAP 132, GIR-6945

LEFT BANK TENN. RI., MLBB

BENTON CO., TENN.

P.T.S. 8M3 432 B 808-482

LEGEND

■ GRAVES WITH MONUMENTS AND NAMES

▯ GRAVES MARKED BUT UNNAMED

▭ GRAVES UNMARKED AND UNNAMED

▯ QUESTIONABLE GRAVES

CEMETERIES

PHIFER
CEMETERY

NO.
482

KENTUCKY RESERVOIR
TENNESSEE VALLEY AUTHORITY
MAPS AND SURVEYS DIVISION

SCALE OF FEET
20   0   20   40

CHATTANOOGA   2-14-42   8 MS   432A898   R.I

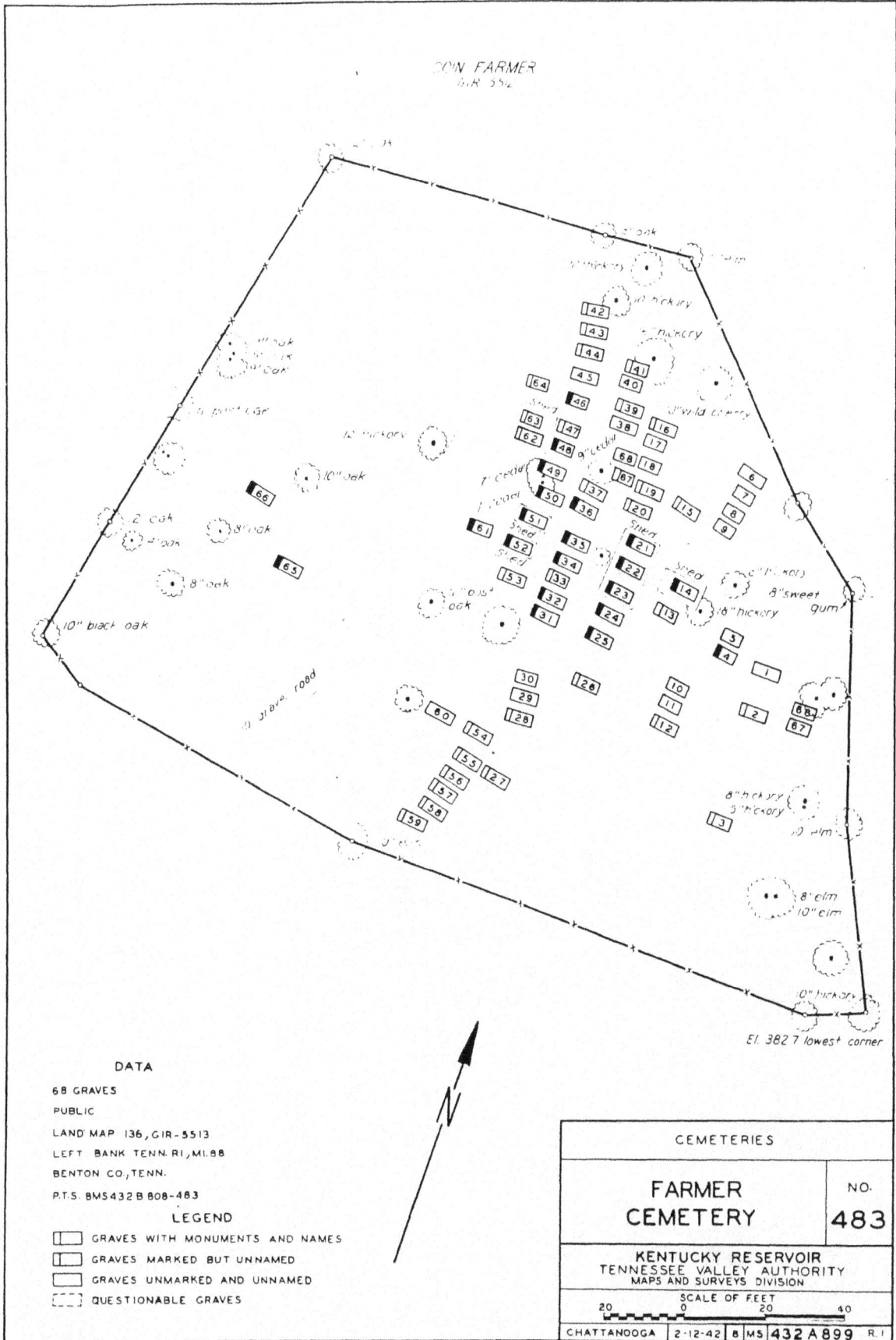

DATA

68 GRAVES

PUBLIC

LAND MAP 136, GIR-5513

LEFT BANK TENN. R1, MI. 88

BENTON CO., TENN.

P.T.S. BMS 432 B 808-483

LEGEND

GRAVES WITH MONUMENTS AND NAMES

GRAVES MARKED BUT UNNAMED

GRAVES UNMARKED AND UNNAMED

QUESTIONABLE GRAVES

CEMETERIES	
FARMER CEMETERY	NO. 483
KENTUCKY RESERVOIR TENNESSEE VALLEY AUTHORITY MAPS AND SURVEYS DIVISION	

SCALE OF FEET

20   0   20   40

CHATTANOOGA   2-12-42   B MS   432 A 899   R.1

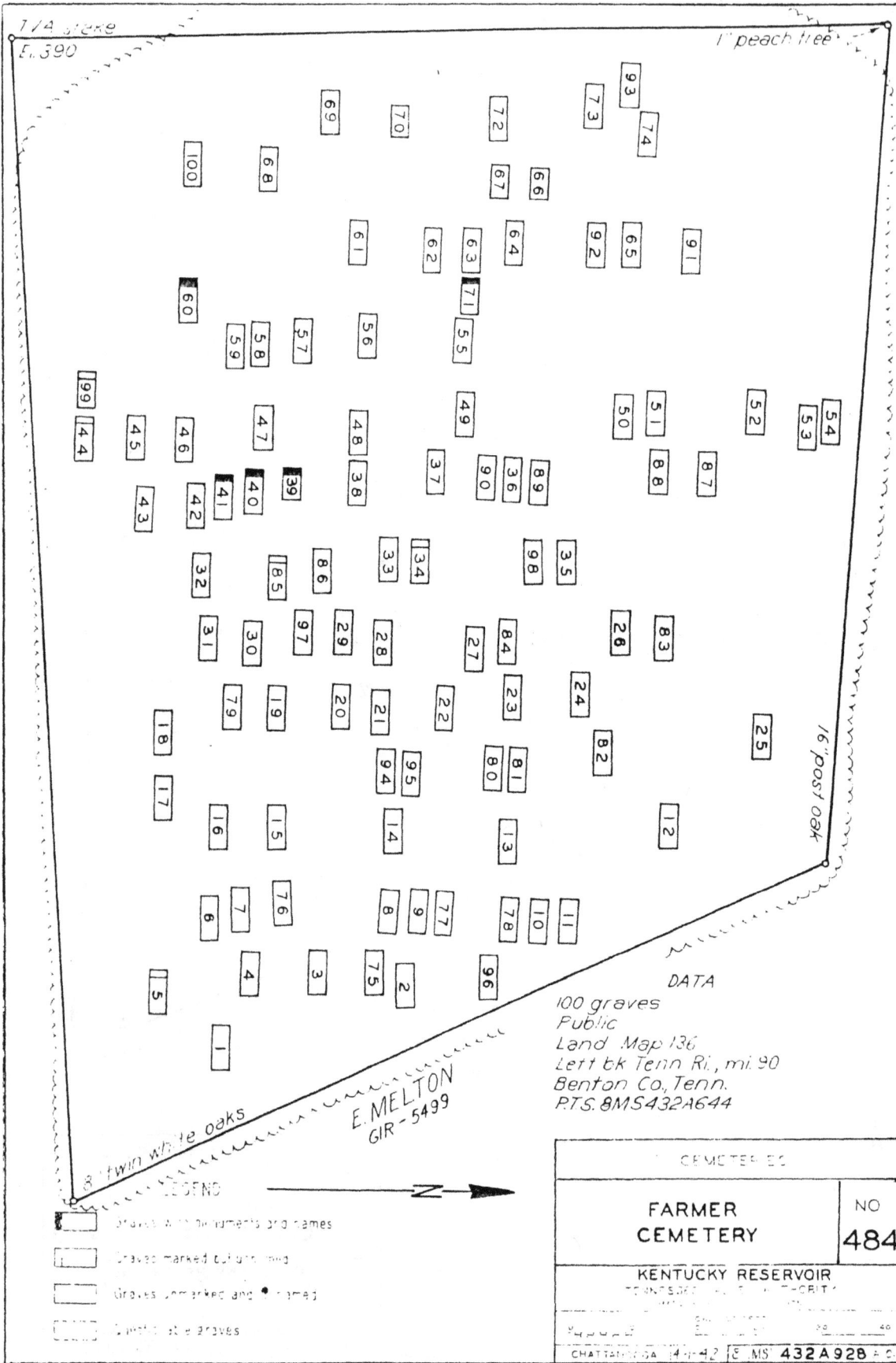

* *

1/4 stake
El.390

1" peach tree

16" post oak

E. MELTON
GIR-5499

8" twin white oaks

DATA
100 graves
Public
Land Map 136
Left bk Tenn Ri., mi. 90
Benton Co., Tenn.
P.T.S. 8MS432A644

LEGEND

Graves with monuments and names

Graves marked but unnamed

Graves unmarked and unnamed

Limits of the graves

N

CEMETERIES

FARMER
CEMETERY

NO
484

KENTUCKY RESERVOIR

CHATTANOOGA 4-1-42   8 MS 432A928

* *

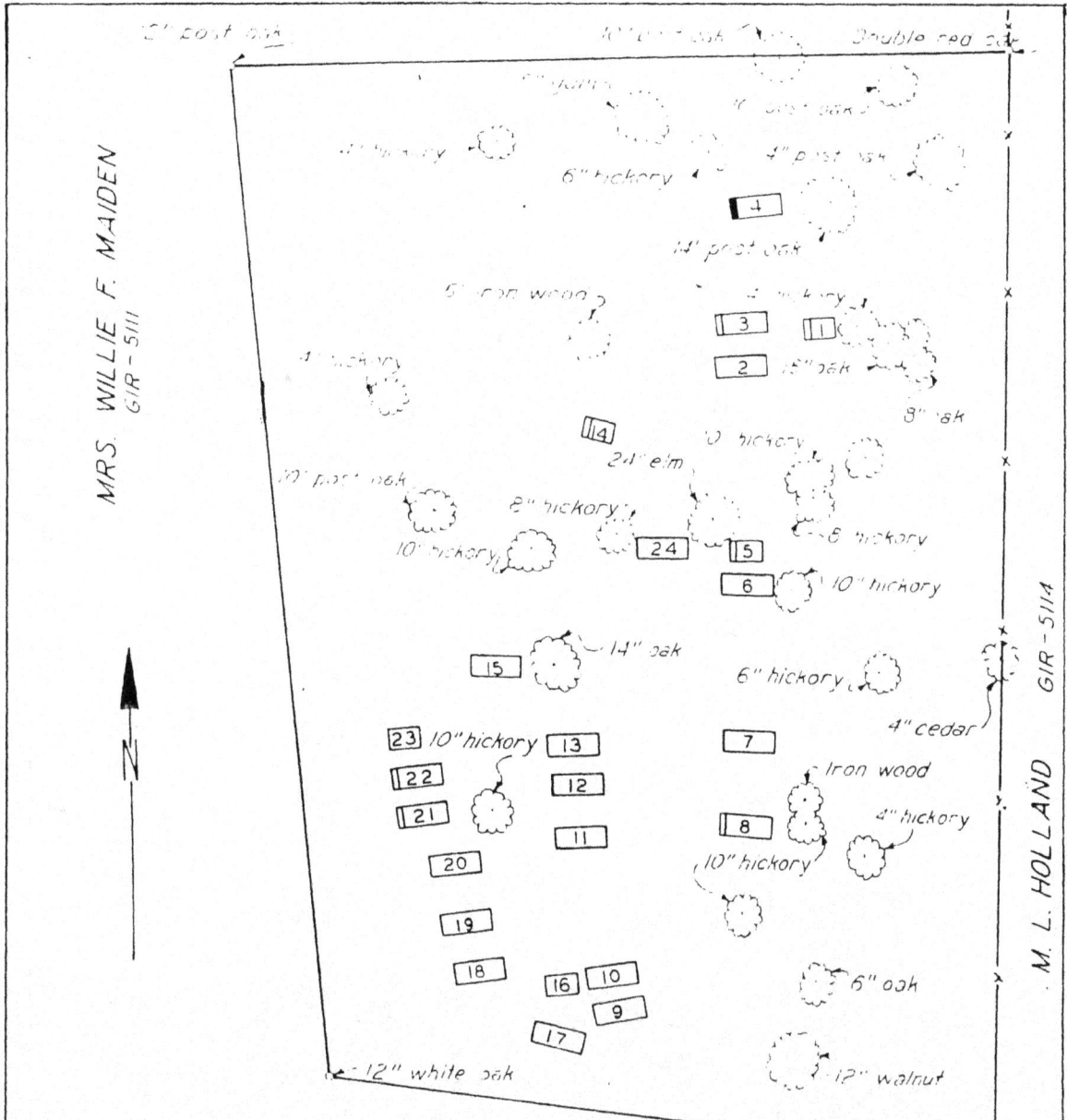

MRS. WILLIE F. MAIDEN
GIR-5III

M. L. HOLLAND
GIR-5II4

DATA

26 graves
Private
L.M. 142, GIR-5II3
L. bank Tenn. R. Mi. 98
Benton County, Tenn.
P.T.S. 6 MS 432 A 608-466

El. 383.4 lowest corner

El. 372.00

MAIDEN
CEMETERY   486
KENTUCKY RESERVOIR

6 MS 432 A 929

* *

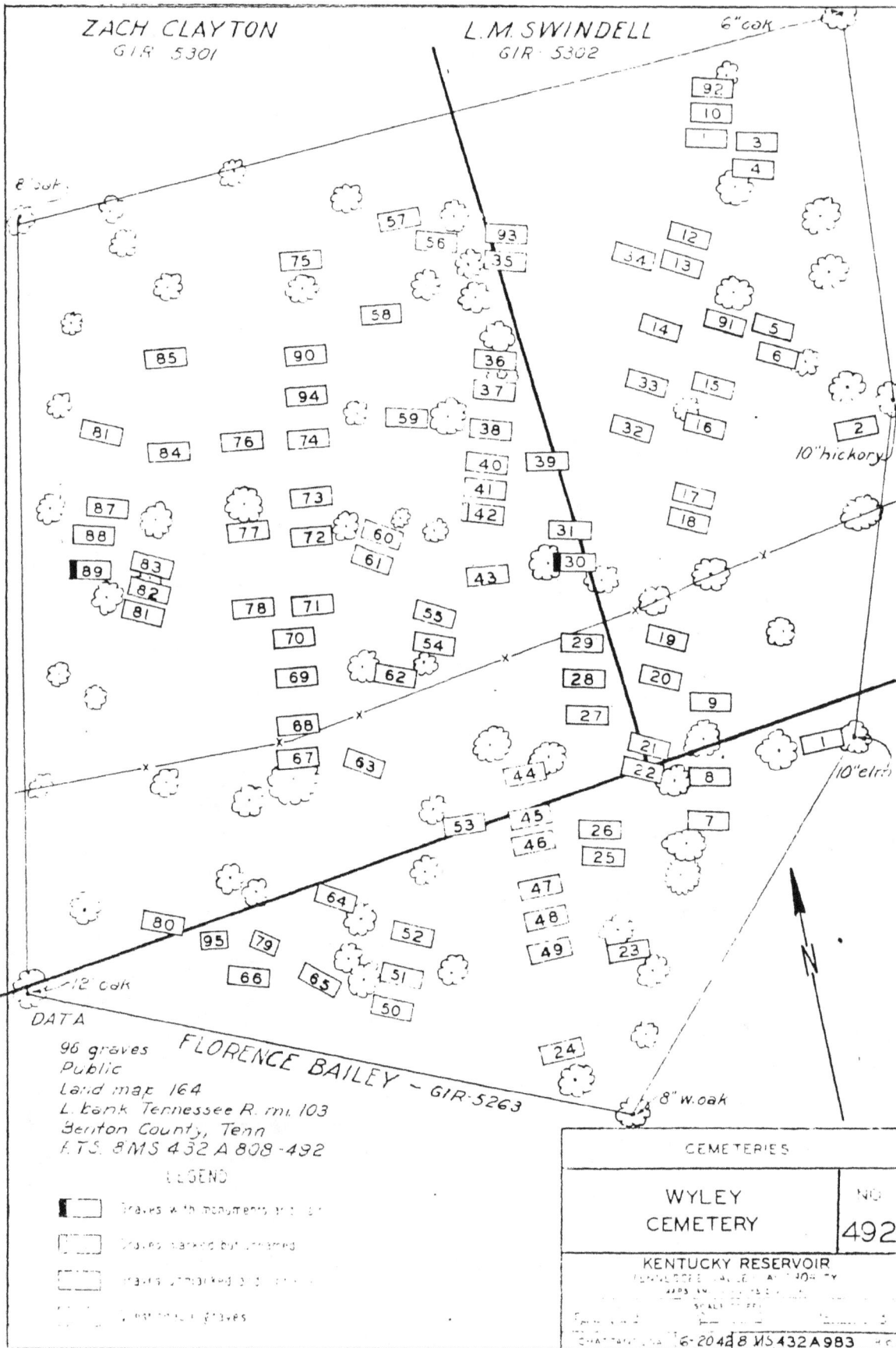

Benton County, Tennessee

* *

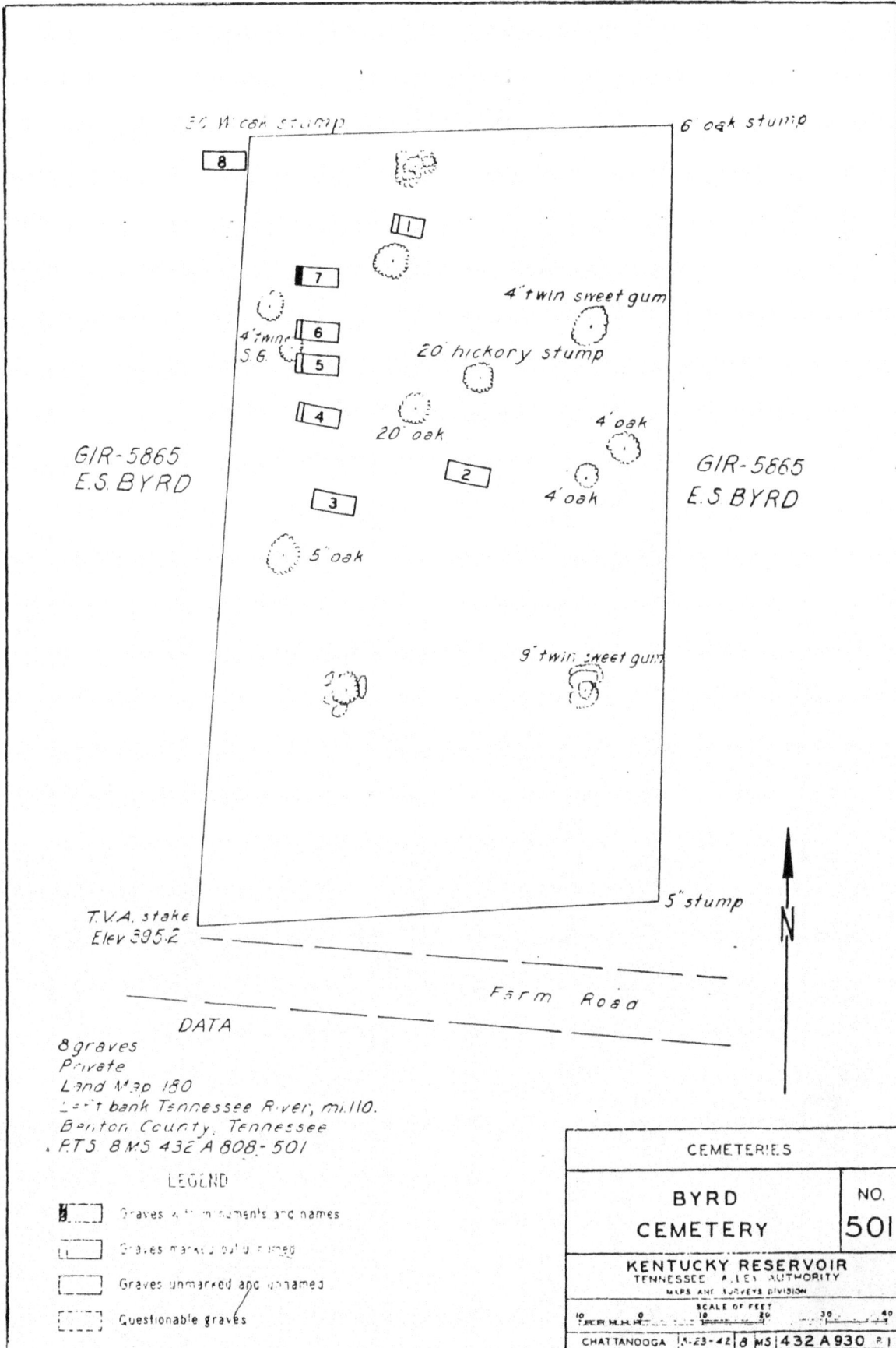

6" W oak stump   6" oak stump

8

1

7

4" twin sweet gum

6

4" twin
S.G.   5   20" hickory stump

4   20" oak   4' oak

GIR-5865   2   GIR-5865
E.S. BYRD   3   4" oak   E.S. BYRD

5" oak

9" twin sweet gum

T.V.A. stake   5" stump
Elev 395.2

Farm Road

DATA

8 graves
Private
Land Map 180
Left bank Tennessee River, mi. 110.
Benton County, Tennessee
F.T.S. 8 MS 432 A 808 - 501

LEGEND

Graves with monuments and names

Graves marked but unnamed

Graves unmarked and unnamed

Questionable graves

CEMETERIES		
BYRD CEMETERY		NO. 501
KENTUCKY RESERVOIR TENNESSEE VALLEY AUTHORITY MAPS AND SURVEYS DIVISION		
SCALE OF FEET		
CHATTANOOGA 5-23-42	8 MS	432 A 930 P.I

* *

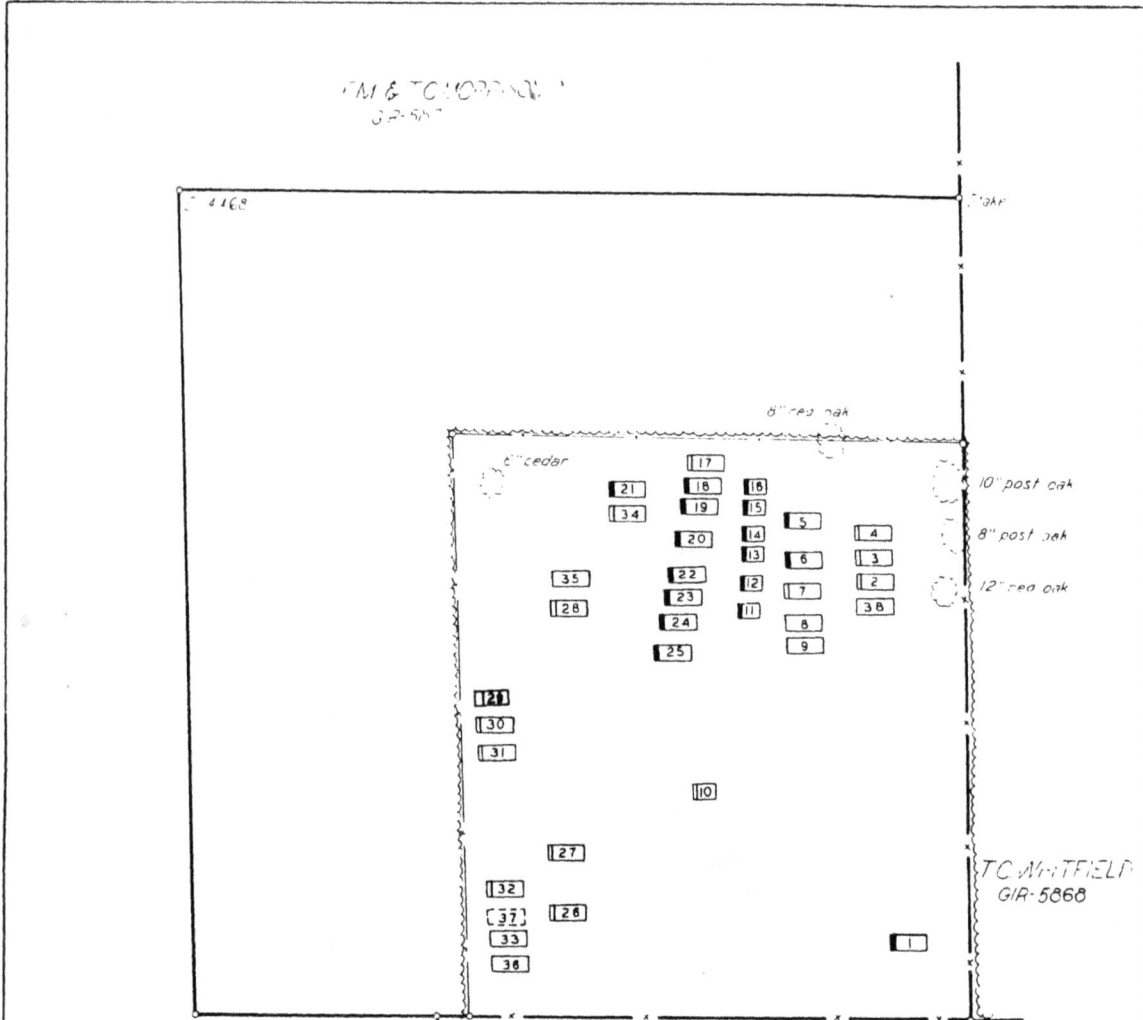

DATA

38 GRAVES

PUBLIC

L M 180, GIR-5870

L BANK TENN R, MI. 112

BENTON COUNTY, TENN

PTS. 8M5432B808-502

LEGEND

GRAVES WITH MONUMENTS

GRAVES MARKED BUT UNNAMED

GRAVES UNMARKED AND UNNAMED

QUESTIONABLE GRAVES

CEMETERIES

PAVATT
CEMETERY

NO.
502

KENTUCKY RESERVOIR
TENNESSEE VALLEY AUTHORITY
MAPS AND SURVEYS DIVISION

SCALE OF FEET
20   0   20   40

CHATTANOOGA 4-8-42 8 MS 432A931

* *

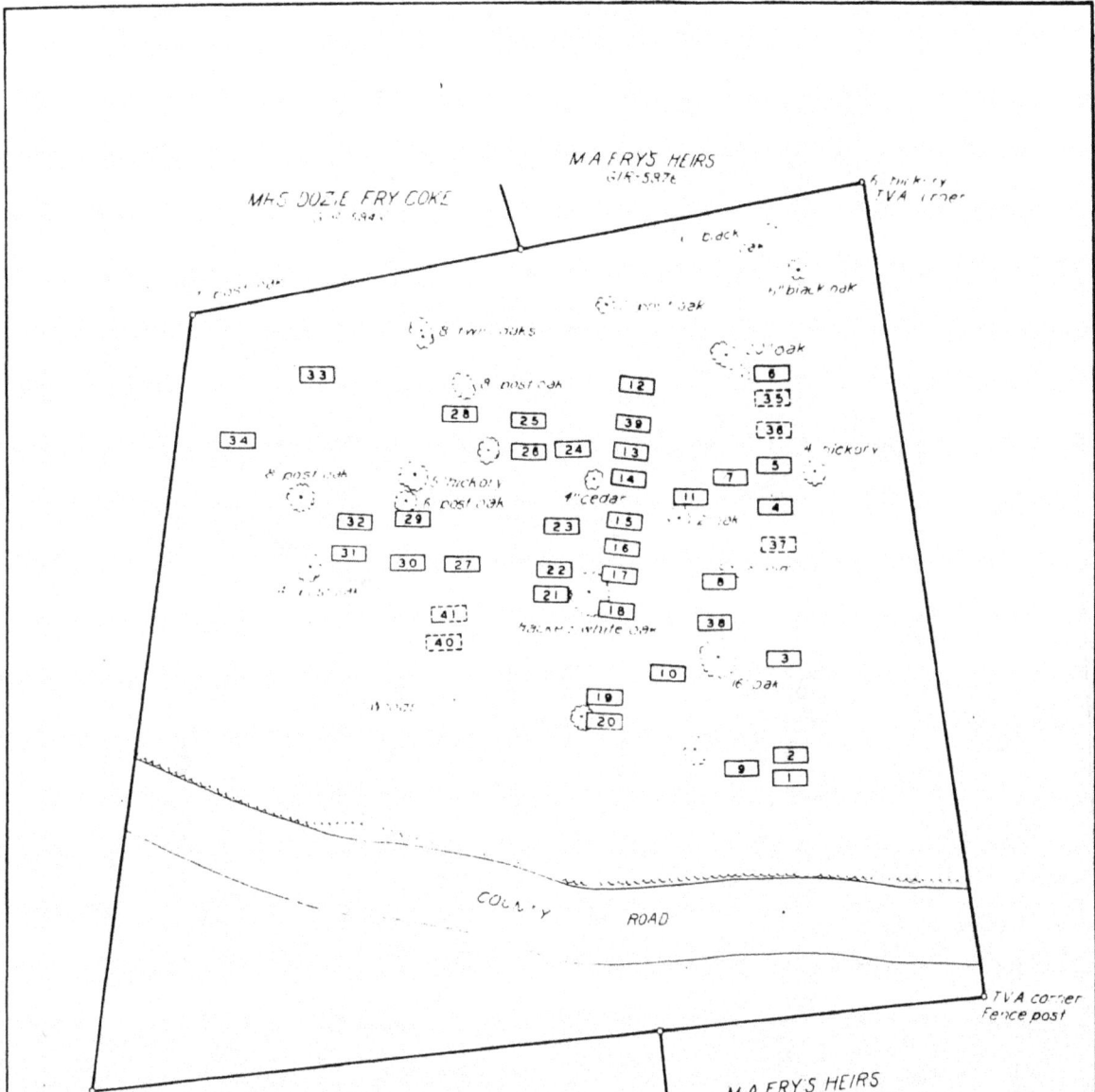

DATA

41 GRAVES

PUBLIC

LAND MAP 180

LEFT BANK TENNESSEE R1, MI. 111

BENTON CO., TENNESSEE

P.T.S BMS432B808-503

N

LEGEND

■ GRAVES WITH MONUMENTS AND NAMES

▯ GRAVES MARKED BUT UNNAMED

▭ GRAVES UNMARKED AND UNNAMED

▭ QUESTIONABLE GRAVES

CEMETERIES

FRY
CEMETERY

NO.
503

KENTUCKY RESERVOIR
TENNESSEE VALLEY AUTHORITY
MAPS AND SURVEYS DIVISION

SCALE OF FEET
20   0   20   40

CHATTANOOGA | 3-19-42 | 8 | MS | 432A915 | R.

* *

D. B. GOSSETT

DATA

60 graves
Public
L.M. 188
L. bank Tenn. R. Mi. 119
Benton County, Tenn.
P.T.S. 6MS432A808-506

Note: Boundaries extended to include all graves visible

BRADLEY
CEMETERY   506

KENTUCKY RESERVOIR

432 A932

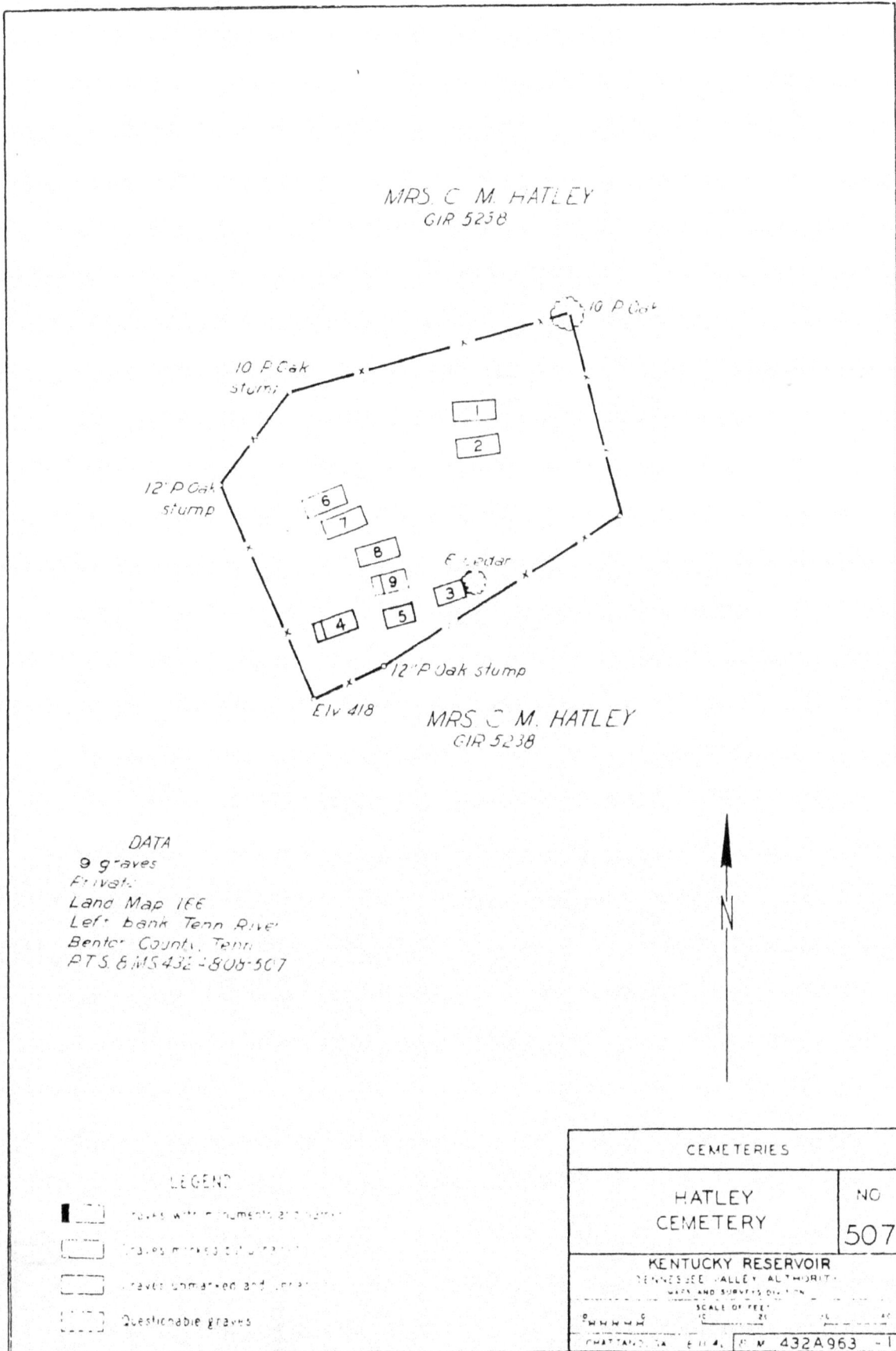

* *

MRS. C M. HATLEY
GIR 5238

10 P Oak

10 P Oak
stump

12' P Oak
stump

1

2

6

7

8

9

3

E cedar

4

5

12 P Oak stump

Elv 418

MRS. C M. HATLEY
GIR 5238

DATA
9 graves
Private
Land Map 166
Left bank Tenn River
Benton County, Tenn
P T S. & MS 432-808-507

N

LEGEND

Graves with monuments and names

Graves marked but unnamed

Graves unmarked and unnamed

Questionable graves

CEMETERIES	
HATLEY CEMETERY	NO 507
KENTUCKY RESERVOIR	

TENNESSEE VALLEY AUTHORITY
MAPS AND SURVEYS DIVISION
SCALE OF FEET

CHATTANOOGA 432A963 -1

* *

J. L. WEAVER
GIR - 3349

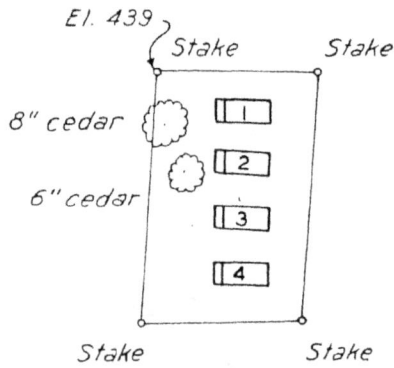

El. 439
Stake   *Stake*

8" cedar | 1 |

| 2 |

6" cedar | 3 |

| 4 |

Stake   *Stake*

N

DATA

4 graves
Private
L. M. 125
R. bank Tenn. R., Mi. 82
Houston County, Tenn.
P.T.S. 8MS 432 A 808-721

LEGEND

▨ Graves with monuments and names

Graves marked but unnamed

Graves unmarked and unnamed

Questionable graves

CEMETERIES	
BEECHAM CEMETERY	NO. 721
KENTUCKY RESERVOIR TENNESSEE VALLEY AUTHORITY MAPS AND SURVEYS DIVISION	
SCALE OF FEET	
CHATTANOOGA 4-1-42 8 MS 432 A 937	

* *

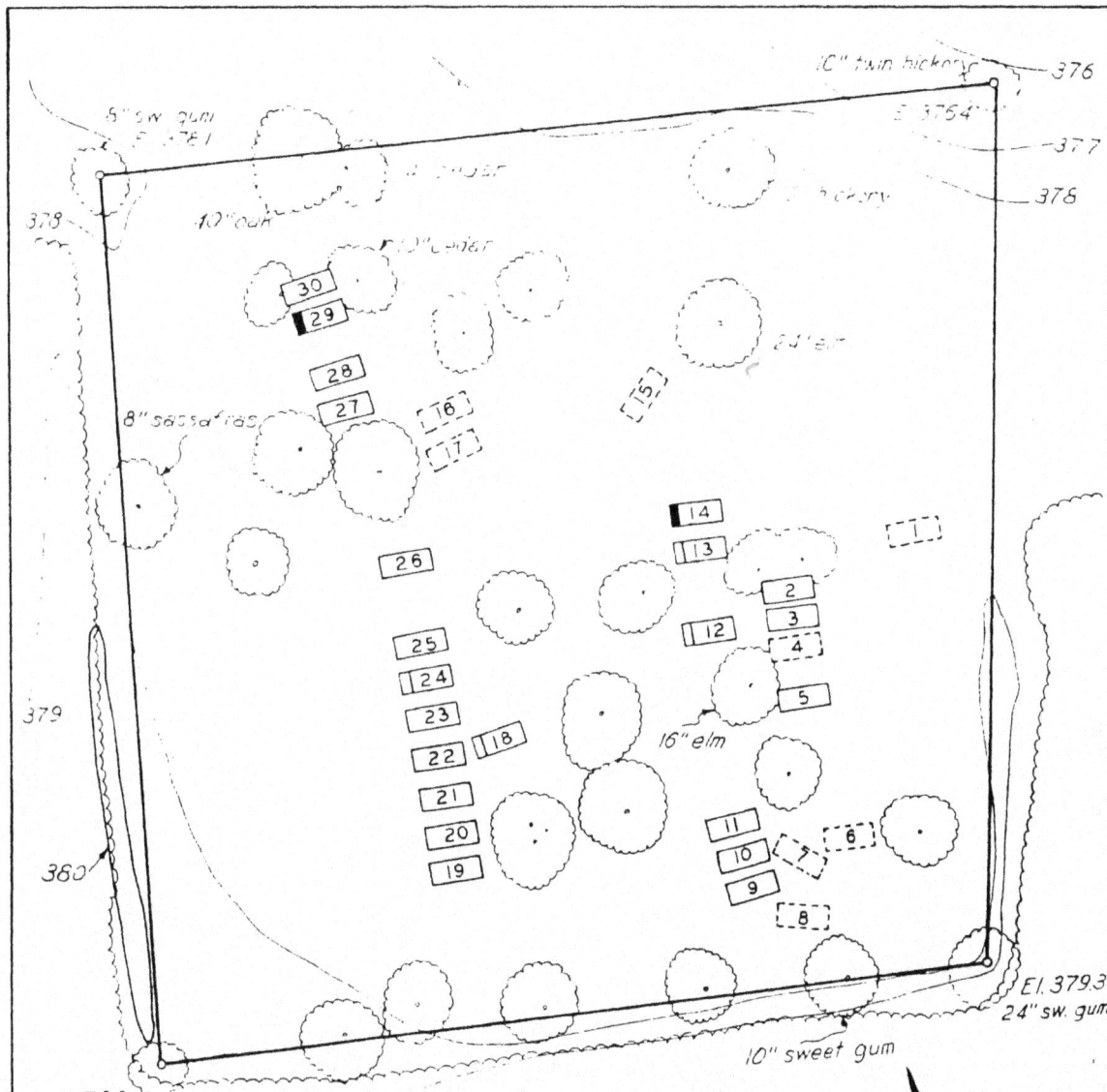

NODLE PEARL JONES
GIR - 5521F

DATA

30 graves
Public
L M. 136
L bank Tenn R., Mi. 89
Benton County, Tenn.
P.T.S. 8MS 432 A 646

LEGEND

▨	Graves with numbers and names
☐	Graves marked - unnamed
☐	Graves unmarked and unnamed
╌╌	Unmarked graves

CEMETERIES	
MELTON CEMETERY	NO 733
KENTUCKY RESERVOIR	
TENNESSEE VALLEY AUTHORITY	

* *

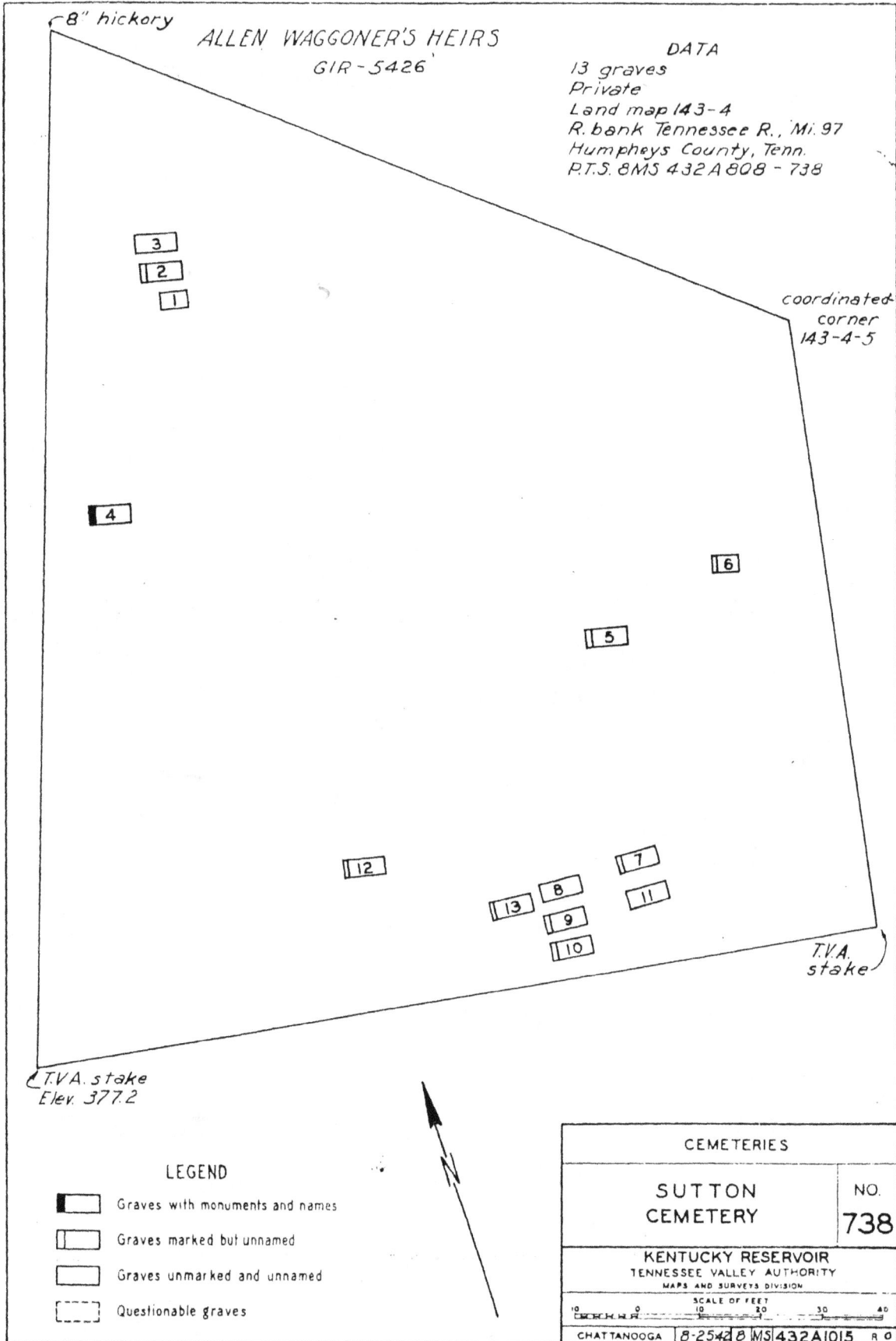

8" hickory

ALLEN WAGGONER'S HEIRS
GIR - 5426

DATA
13 graves
Private
Land map 143-4
R. bank Tennessee R., Mi. 97
Humpheys County, Tenn.
P.T.S. 8MS 432 A 808 - 738

coordinated
corner
143-4-5

T.V.A.
stake

T.V.A. stake
Elev. 377.2

N

LEGEND

Graves with monuments and names

Graves marked but unnamed

Graves unmarked and unnamed

Questionable graves

CEMETERIES

SUTTON
CEMETERY

NO.
738

KENTUCKY RESERVOIR
TENNESSEE VALLEY AUTHORITY
MAPS AND SURVEYS DIVISION

SCALE OF FEET

CHATTANOOGA   8-25-42 8 MS 432A1015   R O

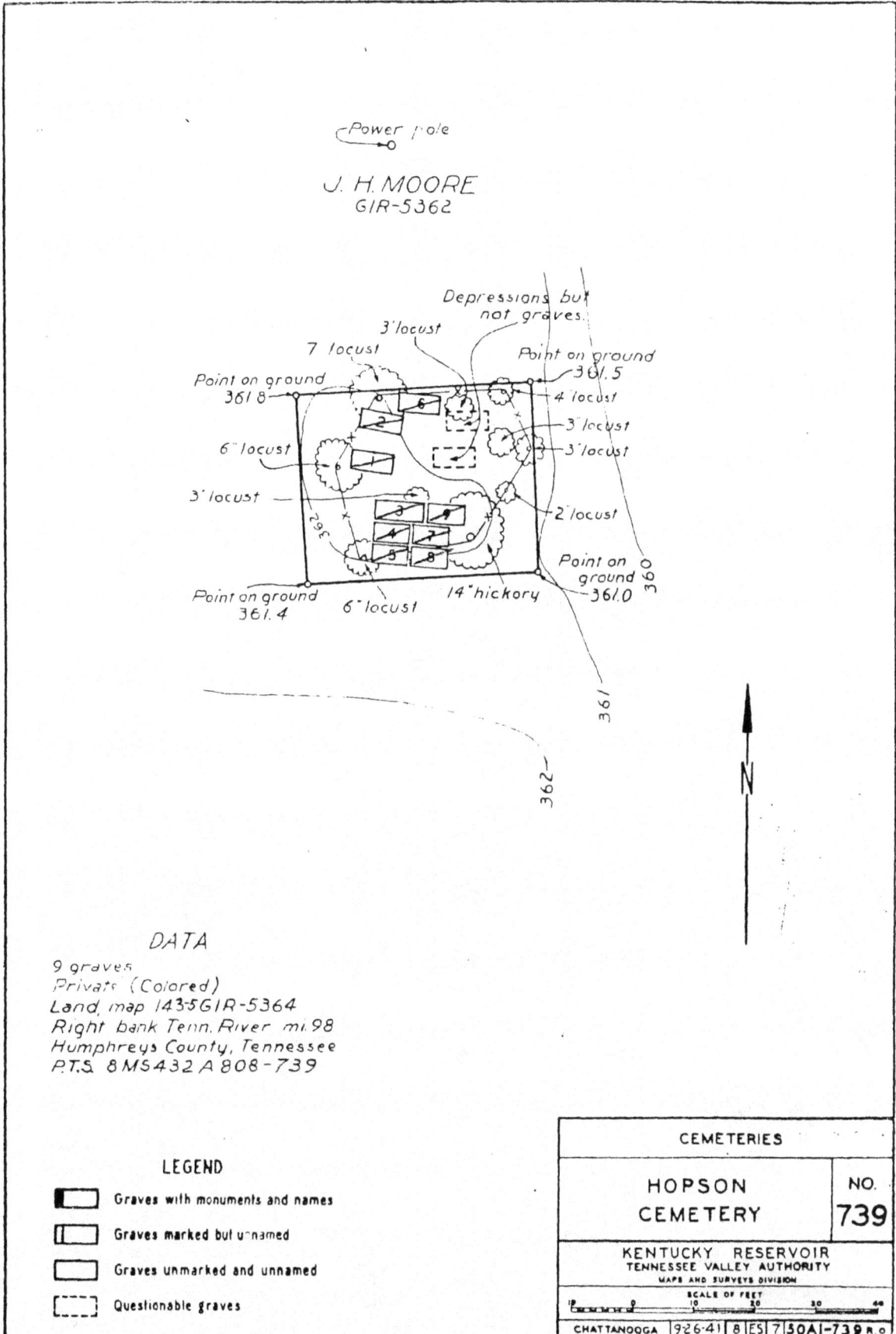

* *

Power pole

J. H. MOORE
GIR-5362

Depressions but
not graves

3" locust

7 locust

Point on ground
361.5

Point on ground
361.8

4 locust

3" locust

6" locust

3" locust

3" locust

2 locust

Point on
ground
361.0

Point on ground
361.4

6" locust

14" hickory

N

DATA

9 graves
Private (Colored)
Land map 1435-GIR-5364
Right bank Tenn. River mi. 98
Humphreys County, Tennessee
P.T.S 8 MS432 A 808-739

LEGEND

▮▯ Graves with monuments and names

▯ Graves marked but unnamed

▭ Graves unmarked and unnamed

⊡ Questionable graves

CEMETERIES		
HOPSON	NO.	
CEMETERY	**739**	
KENTUCKY RESERVOIR		

TENNESSEE VALLEY AUTHORITY
MAPS AND SURVEYS DIVISION

SCALE OF FEET

CHATTANOOGA 9-26-41 8 ES 7 50AI-739 R.0

* *

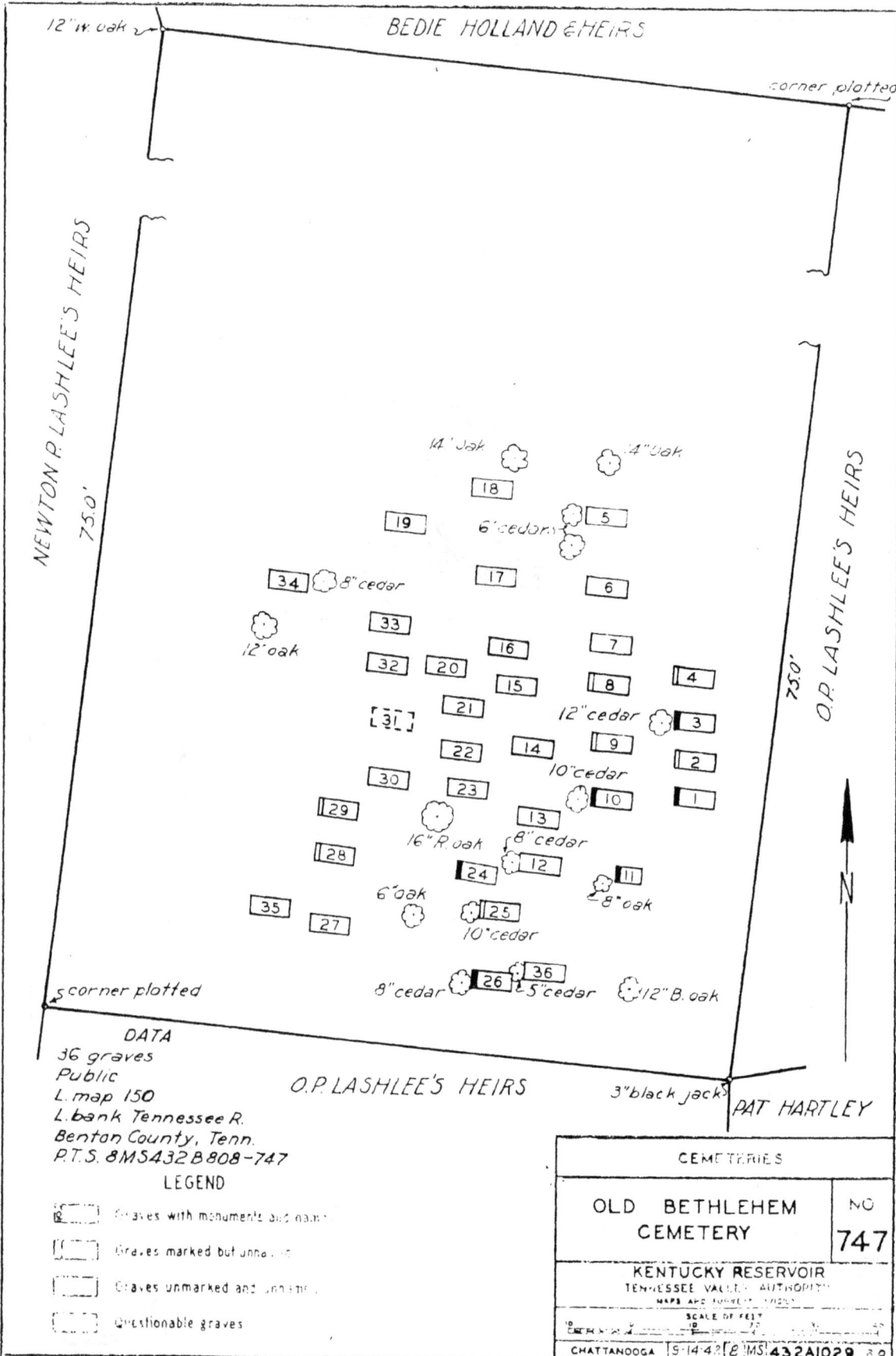

BEDIE HOLLAND & HEIRS

12" w. oak

corner plotted

NEWTON P. LASHLEE'S HEIRS

75.0'

O.P. LASHLEE'S HEIRS

75.0'

14" Oak   14" oak

18

19   6" cedars   5

34   8" cedar   17   6

12" oak   33   7

32   20   16   8   4

15

31   21   12" cedar   3

22   14   9   2

30   23   10" cedar

29   10   1

16" R. oak   13

28   8" cedar

24   12

35   16" R. oak   11

27   6" oak   25   8" oak

10" cedar

s corner plotted   26   36

8" cedar   5" cedar   12" B. oak

N

DATA
36 graves
Public
L. map 150
L. bank Tennessee R.
Benton County, Tenn.
P.T.S. 8 MS 432 B 808-747

O.P. LASHLEE'S HEIRS   3" black jack   PAT HARTLEY

LEGEND

[8___] Graves with monuments and names

[|___] Graves marked but unnamed

[____] Graves unmarked and unnamed

[____] Questionable graves

CEMETERIES

OLD   BETHLEHEM
CEMETERY

NO
747

KENTUCKY RESERVOIR
TENNESSEE VALLEY AUTHORITY
MAPS AND SURVEYS

SCALE OF FEET

CHATTANOOGA   5-14-42   8 MS 432 A 1029

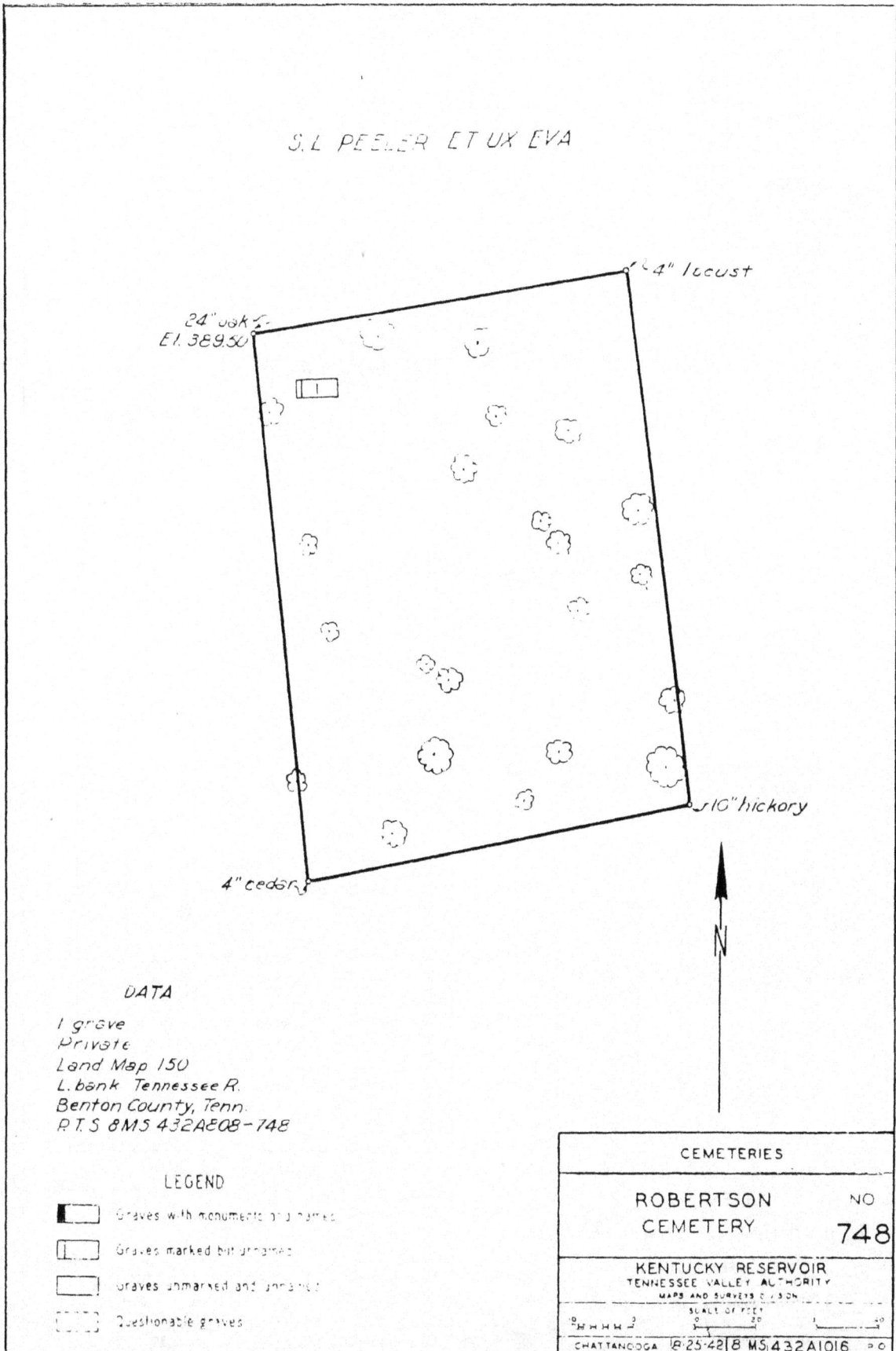

* *

S.L. PEELER ET UX EVA

4" locust

24" oak
El. 389.50

10" hickory

N

4" cedar

DATA

1 grave
Private
Land Map 150
L.bank Tennessee R.
Benton County, Tenn.
R.T.S 8MS 432AE08-748

LEGEND

- Graves with monuments and names
- Graves marked but unnamed
- Graves unmarked and unnamed
- Questionable graves

CEMETERIES	
ROBERTSON CEMETERY	NO 748
KENTUCKY RESERVOIR TENNESSEE VALLEY AUTHORITY MAPS AND SURVEYS DIVISION	
SCALE OF FEET	
CHATTANOOGA 8-25-42 8 MS 432A1016	

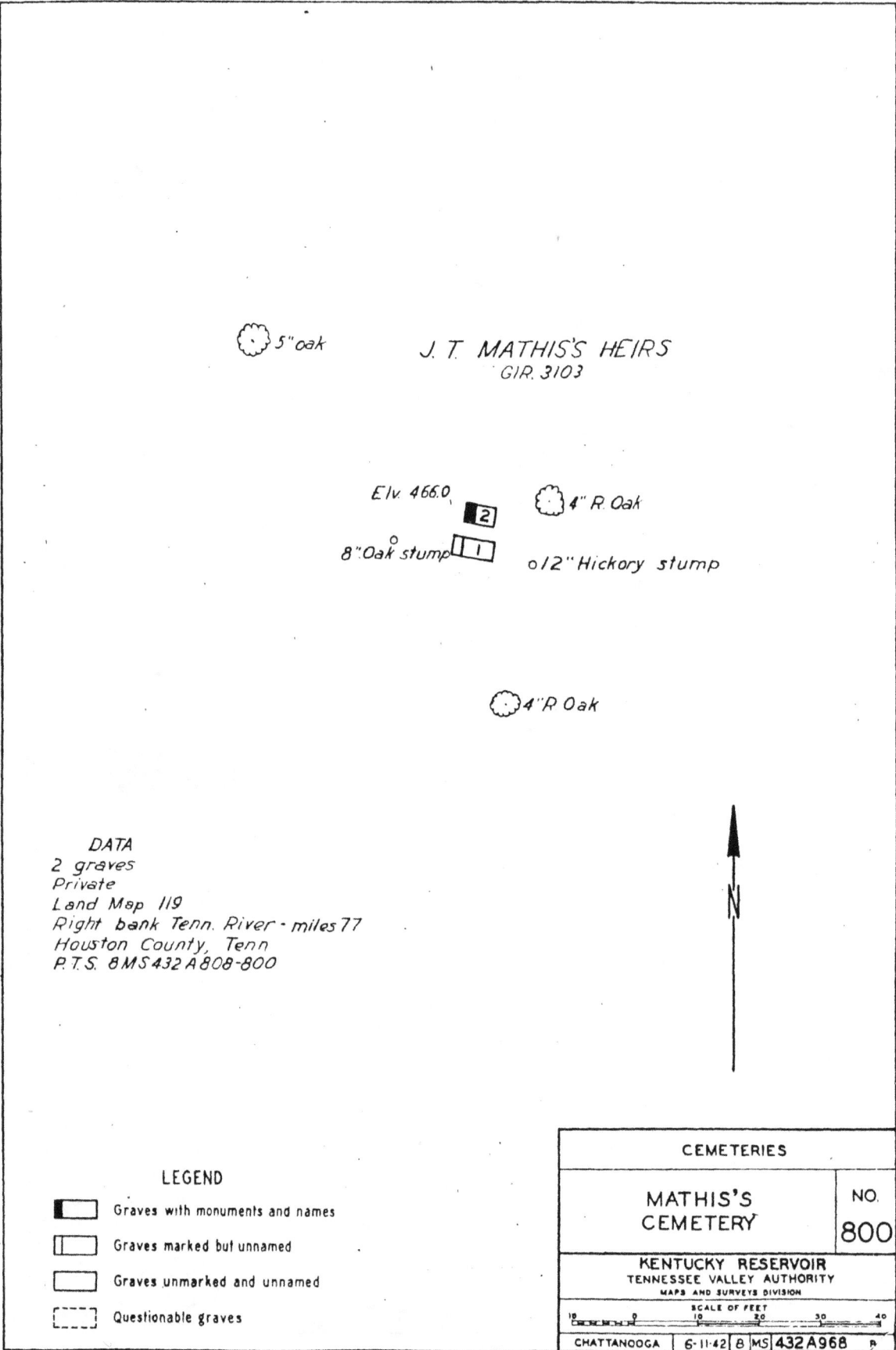

* *

J. T. MATHIS'S HEIRS
GIR. 3103

5" Oak

Elv. 466.0

4" R. Oak

2

8" Oak stump   1

o 12" Hickory stump

4" R. Oak

DATA
2 graves
Private
Land Map 119
Right bank Tenn. River - miles 77
Houston County, Tenn
P.T.S. 8MS 432A808-800

N

LEGEND

■□	Graves with monuments and names
□	Graves marked but unnamed
▭	Graves unmarked and unnamed
⬚	Questionable graves

CEMETERIES	
MATHIS'S CEMETERY	NO. 800
KENTUCKY RESERVOIR TENNESSEE VALLEY AUTHORITY MAPS AND SURVEYS DIVISION	
SCALE OF FEET	
CHATTANOOGA 6-11-42 8 MS 432A968	

* *

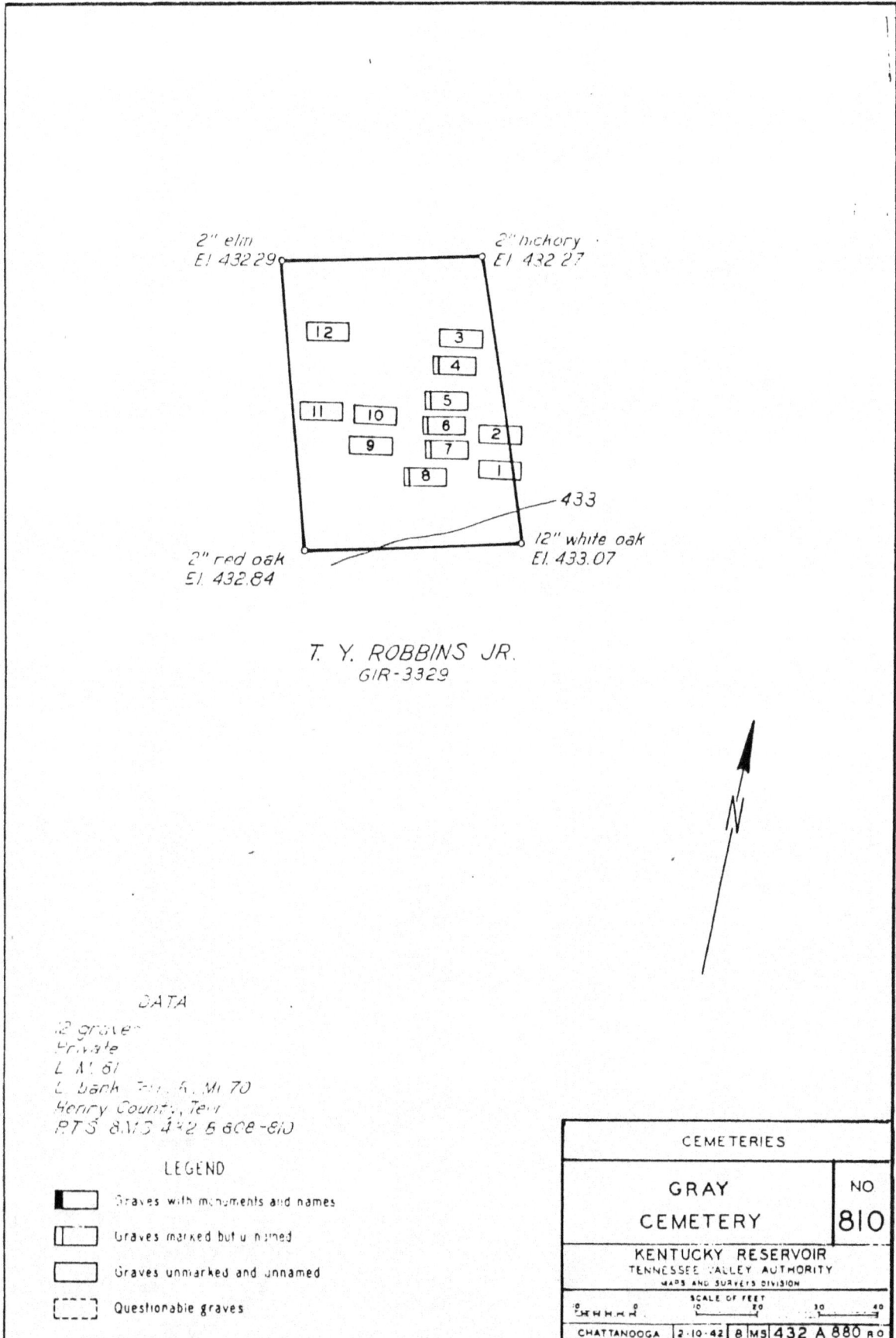

2" elm
El. 432.29

2" hickory
El. 432.27

12

3

4

5

11   10

6

9

7

2

8

1

433

2" red oak
El. 432.84

12" white oak
El. 433.07

T. Y. ROBBINS JR.
GIR-3329

N

DATA

12 graves
Private
L. M. 61
L. bank Trench, Mi. 70
Henry County, Tenn.
R.T.S. B.M.S. 472 B 608-610

LEGEND

Graves with monuments and names

Graves marked but unnamed

Graves unmarked and unnamed

Questionable graves

CEMETERIES

GRAY
CEMETERY

NO
810

KENTUCKY RESERVOIR
TENNESSEE VALLEY AUTHORITY
MAPS AND SURVEYS DIVISION

SCALE OF FEET
0   10   20   30   40

CHATTANOOGA   2-10-42   8 MS   432 A 880 RO

* *

M. H. NEBLETT

Int. foot of bank & old fence row

Point in foot of bank

Int. foot of bank ext. & top of bank of hwy ditch

17

11

12

15

14

18

19

10

9

18" Pine

10" Cedar

12" Hickory

6" Magnolia

8

13

5

7

11

4

18" Cedar

2

6

3

16

18" Cedar

Point in top of bank

Road

County

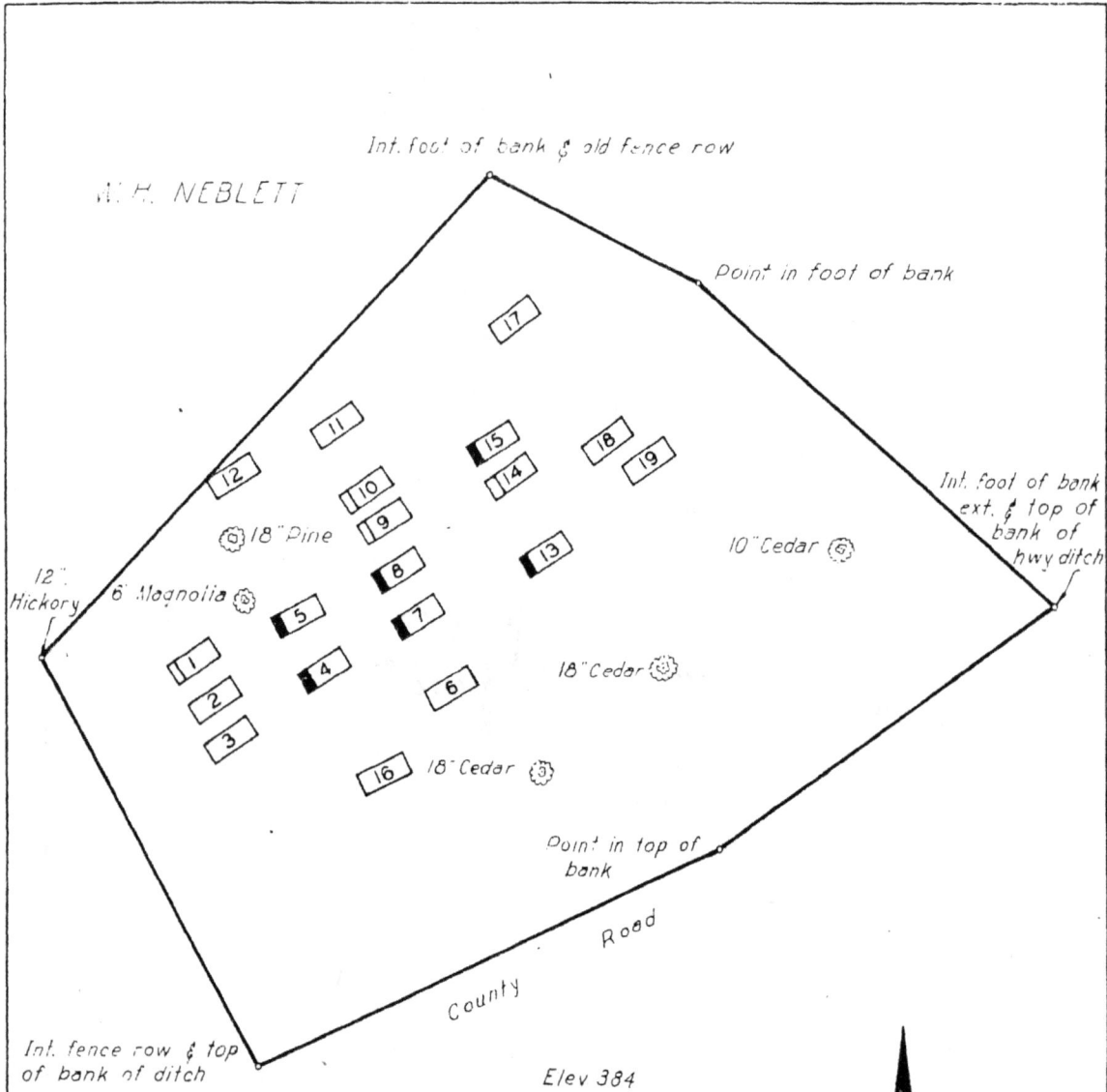

Int. fence row & top of bank of ditch

Elev 384

N

DATA

19 Graves
Private
L.M. 148
Right bank Duck River
Humphreys County, Tenn.
P.T.S. BMS 432 A 806-816

LEGEND

▮▮ Graves with monuments and names

▯▯ Graves marked but unnamed

▭ Graves unmarked and unnamed

⬚ Questionable graves

CEMETERIES

WAGGONER CEMETERY

NO 816

KENTUCKY RESERVOIR
TENNESSEE VALLEY AUTHORITY
MAPS AND SURVEYS DIVISION

SCALE OF FEET
10   0   10   20   30   40

CHATTANOOGA   9-26-42   MS 432 A 1026 - 0

* *

IDA FARMER

GIR - 5562

DATA

1 Grave
Private
Land Map 130
Left bank Tennessee River, Mi. 86
Benton County, Tenn.
P.T.S. 8 MS 432 A 808 -821

N

LEGEND

■□	Graves with monuments and names
□	Graves marked but unnamed
□	Graves unmarked and unnamed
⌐ ¬	Questionable graves

CEMETERIES	
LONE GRAVE CEMETERY	NO. 821
KENTUCKY RESERVOIR TENNESSEE VALLEY AUTHORITY MAPS AND SURVEYS DIVISION	
SCALE OF FEET	
CHATTANOOGA 8-26-42 MS 432A1020 RO	

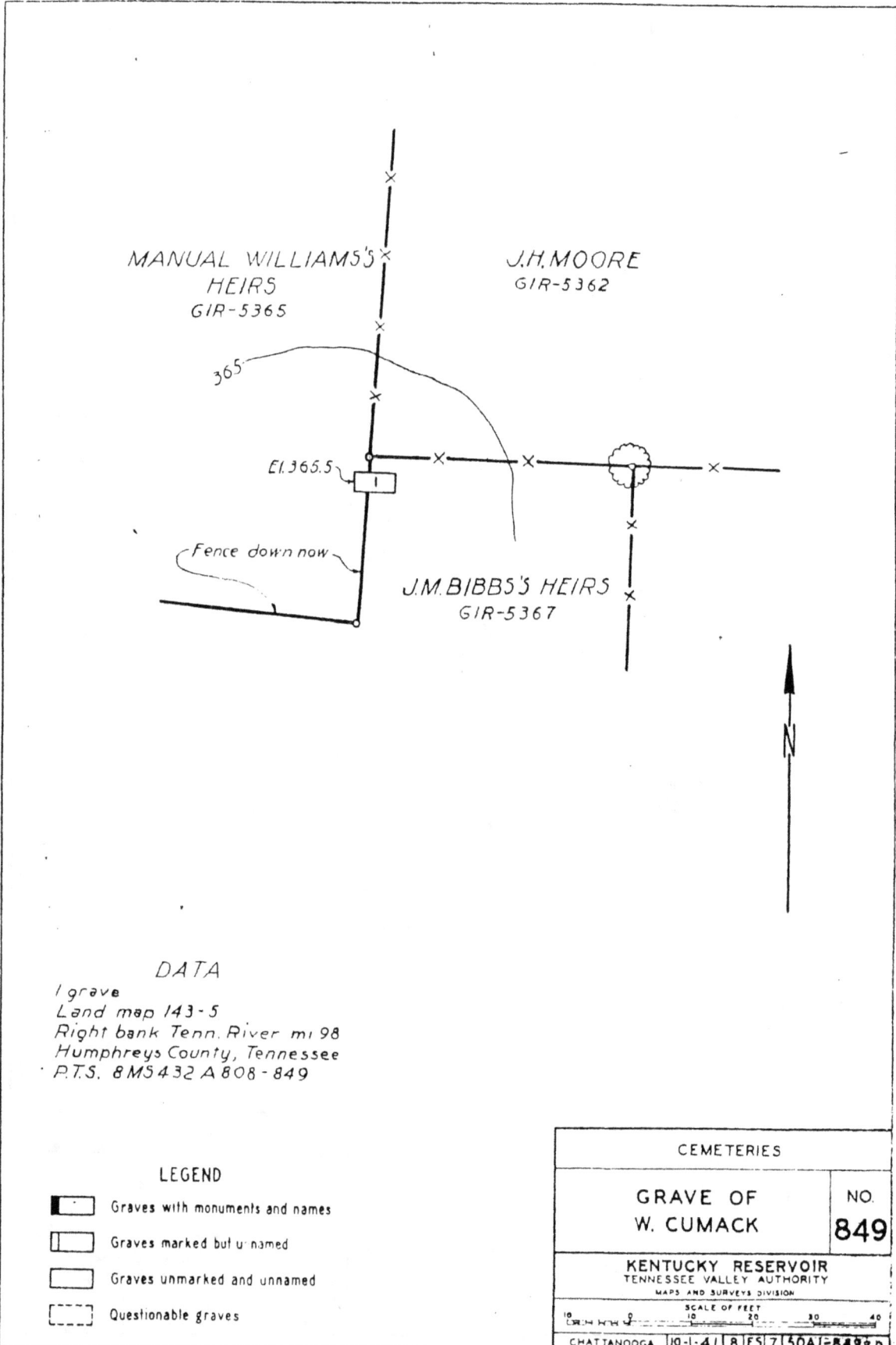

* *

MANUAL WILLIAMS'S
HEIRS
GIR-5365

J.H.MOORE
GIR-5362

365

El.365.5

Fence down now

J.M.BIBBS'S HEIRS
GIR-5367

N

DATA
1 grave
Land map 143-5
Right bank Tenn. River mi 98
Humphreys County, Tennessee
P.T.S. 8MS432 A 808-849

LEGEND

Graves with monuments and names

Graves marked but unnamed

Graves unmarked and unnamed

Questionable graves

CEMETERIES	
GRAVE OF W. CUMACK	NO. 849

KENTUCKY RESERVOIR
TENNESSEE VALLEY AUTHORITY
MAPS AND SURVEYS DIVISION

SCALE OF FEET
10   0   10   20   30   40

CHATTANOOGA | 10-1-41 | 8 | ES | 7 | 50A1-849R0

★ ★

373

375

Sycamore
root 18"Beech

8"Sweet Gum

T.V.A. Stake

18"Beech

24" Sycamore

6   7

5   1

4

3   2

24" Sweet Gum

Sycamore root

T.V.A. Stake

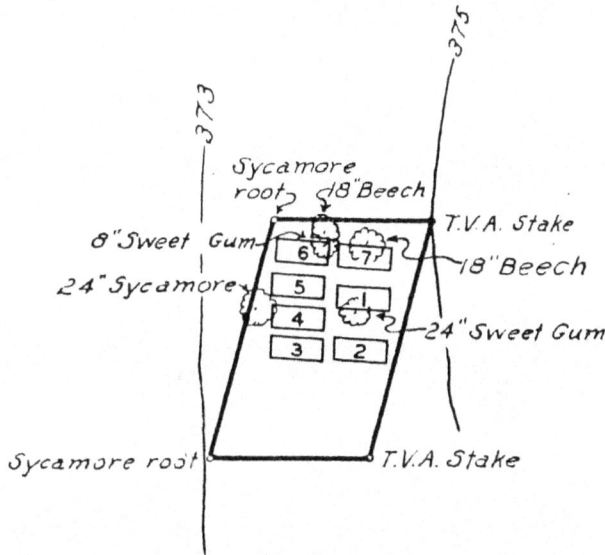

C. D. ASKEW GIR 3478F

Note: Bounds do not agree
with original, but corners
as established are correct.

N

DATA

7 Graves
Private
Land Map 123
Right bank White Oak Creek, Rt. bank Tenn. River mi. 92
Houston County, Tennessee
P.T.S. 8MS 432A808-839

LEGEND

▮▮▭ Graves with monuments and names

▭ Graves marked but unnamed

▭ Graves unmarked and unnamed

⬚ Questionable graves

CEMETERIES	
HOLMES CEMETERY	NO. 839
KENTUCKY RESERVOIR TENNESSEE VALLEY AUTHORITY MAPS AND SURVEYS DIVISION	
SCALE OF FEET	
CHATTANOOGA 4-27-42 8 MS 432A954 R O	

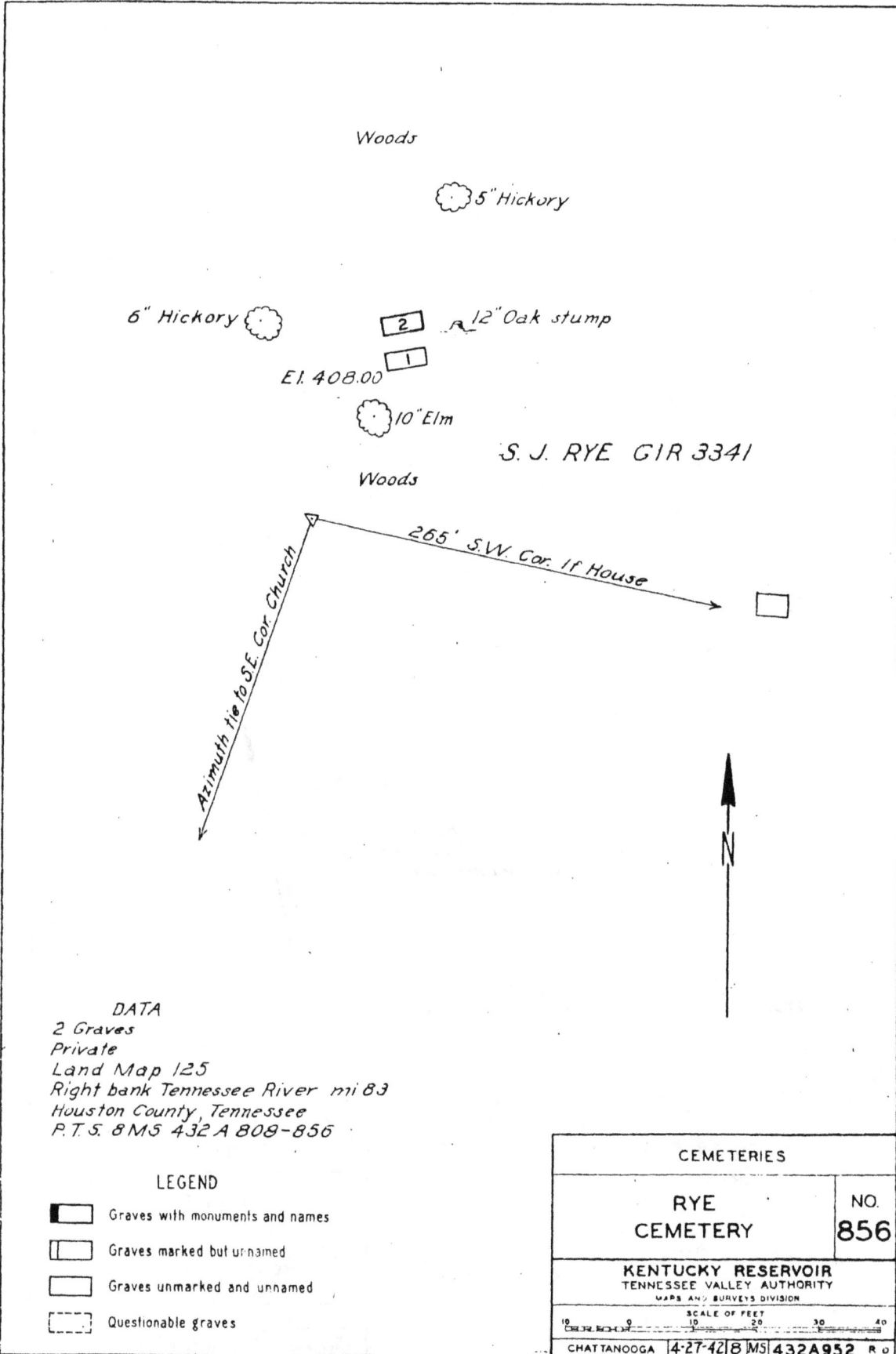

* *

Woods

5" Hickory

6" Hickory

2

12" Oak stump

1

El. 408.00

10" Elm

Woods

S. J. RYE G1R 3341

Azimuth tie to S.E. Cor. Church

265' S.W. Cor. If House

N

DATA
2 Graves
Private
Land Map 125
Right bank Tennessee River mi 83
Houston County, Tennessee
P.T.S. 8 MS 432 A 808-856

LEGEND

Graves with monuments and names

Graves marked but unnamed

Graves unmarked and unnamed

Questionable graves

CEMETERIES	
RYE CEMETERY	NO. 856

KENTUCKY RESERVOIR
TENNESSEE VALLEY AUTHORITY
MAPS AND SURVEYS DIVISION

SCALE OF FEET

CHATTANOOGA | 4-27-42 | 8 MS | 432A952 | R o

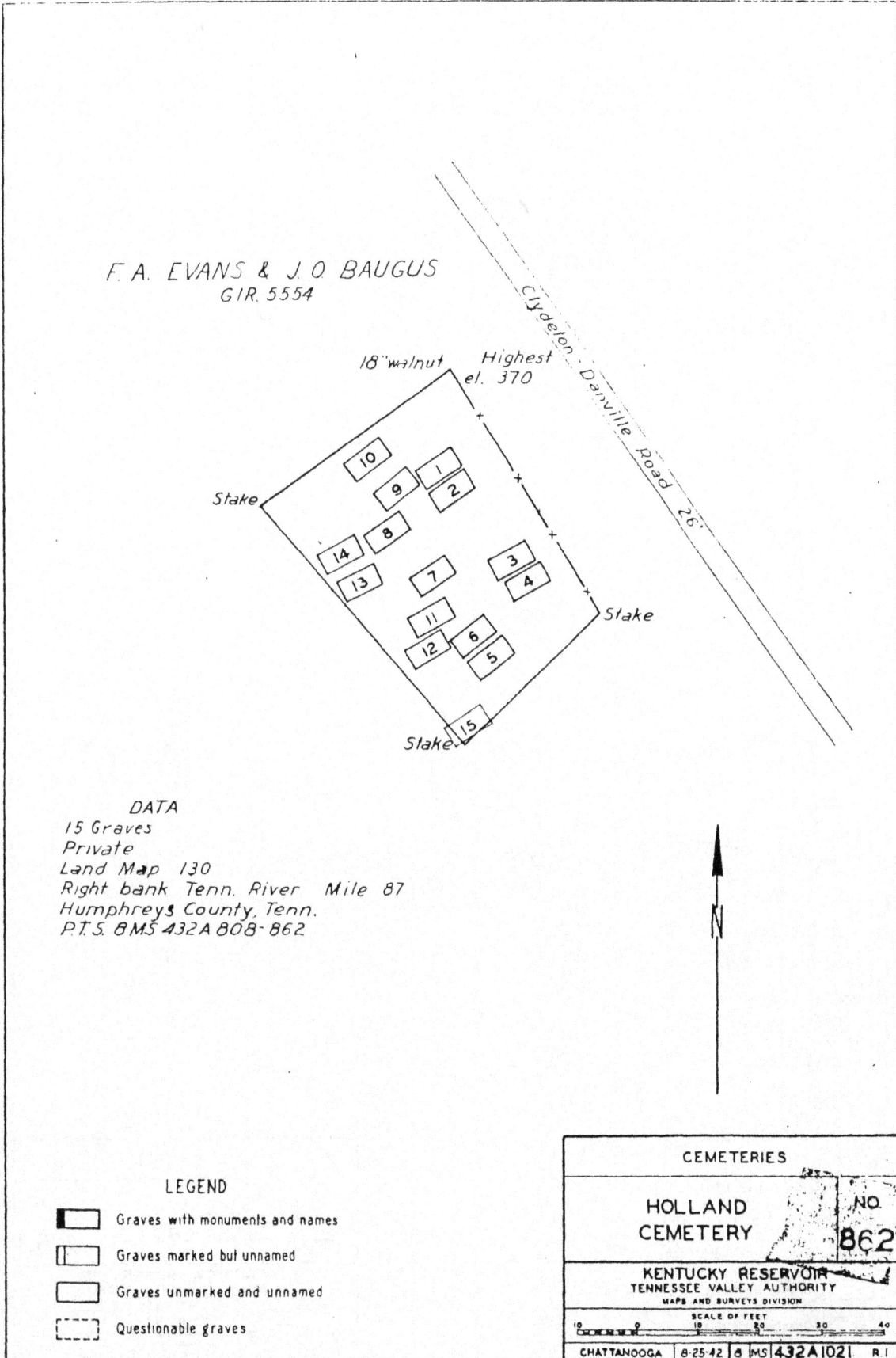

* *

F. A. EVANS & J. O. BAUGUS
GIR. 5554

Clydeton - Danville Road 26

18" walnut   Highest
el. 370

Stake

Stake

Stake

DATA
15 Graves
Private
Land Map 130
Right bank Tenn. River   Mile 87
Humphreys County, Tenn.
P.T.S. 8 MS 432A 808-862

N

LEGEND

▮▬	Graves with monuments and names
▯	Graves marked but unnamed
▭	Graves unmarked and unnamed
⌐⌐	Questionable graves

CEMETERIES

HOLLAND
CEMETERY

NO.
862

KENTUCKY RESERVOIR
TENNESSEE VALLEY AUTHORITY
MAPS AND SURVEYS DIVISION

SCALE OF FEET

CHATTANOOGA   8-25-42 8 MS 432A1021   R.1

* *

LOTTIE RICHARDSON
GIR 3288

all corners staked

C.B. CHRISTOPHER
GIR 3285

Wooded

N

12" white oak
(Sev. corner)

GEORGE SPENCER
CHRISTOPHER
GIR 4555

DATA

1 grave
Private
Land Map 82
L. bank Tenn R. mi 73
Henry County, Tennessee
P.T.S. 8 MS 432N 808-445, 810, & 863

LEGEND

▮▯ Graves with monuments and names

▯ Graves marked but unnamed

▯ Graves unmarked and unnamed

⌐ ⌐ Questionable graves

CEMETERIES	
ALSOP CEMETERY	NO. 863
KENTUCKY RESERVOIR TENNESSEE VALLEY AUTHORITY MAPS AND SURVEYS DIVISION SCALE OF FEET	
CHATTANOOGA 6-15-42 8 MS 432A 971 R O	

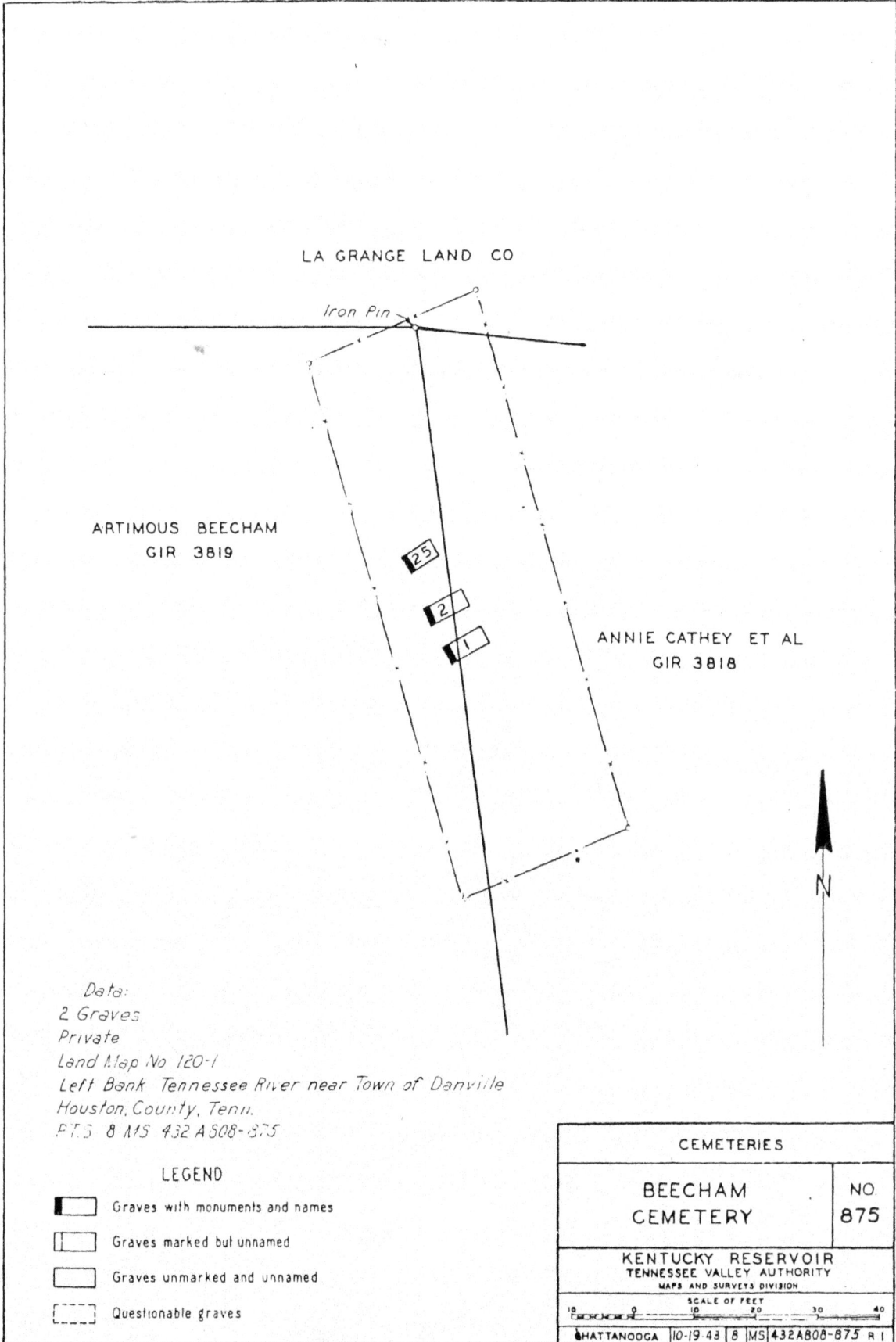

* *

LA GRANGE LAND CO

Iron Pin

ARTIMOUS BEECHAM
GIR 3819

25

2

1

ANNIE CATHEY ET AL
GIR 3818

N

Data:
2 Graves
Private
Land Map No 120-1
Left Bank Tennessee River near Town of Danville
Houston, County, Tenn.
PTS 8 MS 432 A 808-875

LEGEND

■	Graves with monuments and names
▯	Graves marked but unnamed
▭	Graves unmarked and unnamed
⊏⊐	Questionable graves

CEMETERIES	
BEECHAM CEMETERY	NO. 875
KENTUCKY RESERVOIR TENNESSEE VALLEY AUTHORITY MAPS AND SURVEYS DIVISION	

SCALE OF FEET
10 0 10 20 30 40

CHATTANOOGA | 10-19-43 | 8 | MS | 432A808-875 R1

* *

I N D E X

The following is a surname index to Kentucky Lake Reservoir Cemeteries Volume 2. Each name will appear listed in the index only once per page. Read each page carefully.

* * * * * * * * * * * * * *

* *

HALEY 3, 73; HALL 61, 62, 69, 78, 118; HAM 91; HAMBRET 74; HAMLIN 121; HAMPTON 5, 46, 47, 49, 50; HANKINS 52; HANSEL 41; HARDIN 17, 118; HARGROVE 75, 121, 122; HARRISON 15, 99; HARTLEY 13, 15, 208; HARVEY 82, 83; HASSELL 94; HASTINGS 50, 52, 53; HATLEY 20, 21, 70, 203; HAWKINS 142; HAWLEY 5; HAYNES 96; HAZELWOOD 61; HEATH 89, 122; HEATHCOCK 128; HENDERSON 3, 103; HENDON 121, 125; HENDRICKS 123; HERION 102; HERNDON 5, 41, 45, 46, 113; HERRINGTON 78; HICKS 36, 127; HIGGINS 107; HILL 11, 20; HODGES 115, 120, 123; HOLLAND 22, 77, 78, 98, 197, 208; HOLLORAN 157; HOLMES 64; HOOPER 61, 74, 90; HOPKINS 37; HOPSON 92, 96; HORNER 75; HORNEY 9; HORNSBURGER 49; HOSEFORD 111, 113; HOWARD 83, 84, 85; HOWE 94; HUDDLESTON 71; HUDGENS 40; HUDSON 61, 62; HUDSPETH 59; HUGHES 79, 81; HUMBEL 130; HUSTON 34; HUTCHISON 3, 46, 181.

IRVIN 124, 130.

JACKSON 118; JACOBS 62; JENKINS 51, 53; JOHNSON 8, 29, 51, 88; JONES 69, 74, 114, 122, 205.

KEEL 61, 62; KELLY 70, 72, 132; KENDALL 31, 40, 108, 179; KENNEDY 116; KENNERLY 111; KEY 31; KIBBLE 103; KIMBROUGH 59; KING 49, 125, 126; KNIGHT 53, 75, 118, 122, 123, 124, 125, 126, 127, 128; KNIGHTING 62.

LAMASTUS 93; LANCASTER 77, 128; LANE 45, 113; LANGLEY 20; LANKFORD 74; LARGENT 58, 64, 103, 104; LARKINS 89; LASHLEE 17, 36, 37, 90, 91, 99, 176, 208; LASTER 17; LATTIMER 73, 78; LAWRENCE 15, 28; LAWSON 70; LEACH 80; LEAGAN 45; LEDBETTER 94; LEE 30, 37, 54, 87, 93, 175; LEEGON 50; LEMONDS 4, 31, 49, 53, 54; LEMOX 91; LEON 83; LEWIS 21, 85, 88; LILY 52; LIPPS 95; LITTLETON 76, 78; LOCKE 126; LOCKMAN 7, 186; LOERCH 57, 59; LOFTON 95; LOMAX 83; LONG 83, 84, 85; LOVETT 51; LOVE 111, 113; LOWREY 11, 12, 13, 192; LUCAS 79, 81, 82, 83, 136, 140; LUTEN 90; LYELL 96; LYNCH 19; LYONS 116.

McAULEY 63, McBUTGHEN 108; McCRAW 112; McCLAIN 28; McCLURE 70; McCORD 77; McCOWAN 139; McCOY 15; McCULLOUGH 54; McCUTCHEON 109; McDANIEL 13, 16, 18, 45, 47, 104; McDOUGAL 122, 123, 124; McFADDEN 47, 48; McGEE 59, 76, 92; McILWAIN 70, 71; McKEEL 77, 78; McKELVEY 93; McKENZIE 9, 191; McMILLIAN 61, 62, 73; McMULLEN 85; McNEBLETT 71; McNUNN 53; McRAE 185; McSWAIN 3, 6, 44, 173, 180; McWILLIAMS 82, 83, 85.

MADDEN 74; MADISON 83; MAIDEN 197; MANLEY 37, 52; MANNING 62, 118; MANNON 12; MARBERRY 72, 82, 107; MARBLE 83; MARKHAM 3, 4; MARTIN 4, 40, 43, 45, 53, 78, 89, 102, 103, 130;; MASON 82; MASSEY 89, 98; MATHIS 58, 59, 63, 115, 210; MATLOCK 19; MAY 125; MAYBERY 69; MAYNARD 45; MEDLOCK 39, 43, 45, 46; MEIGS 28; MELTON 11, 14, 21, 22, 116, 119, 196; MENZIE 17; MERRELL 3, 4, 5, 6, 11, 40, 47, 69; MIDYETT 31, 163; MILES 115; MILLER 69, 95, 127; MILTON 113; MITCHELL 113; MITCHESON 49; MOBLEY 102, 103, 147; MOFFETT 28; MOODY 27, 30, 50, 51, 52, 111, 112, 118, 130, 171, 182; MOON 3; MOORE 59, 83, 85, 103, 154, 207, 214; MORGAN 50, 113; MORRIS 20, 49, 70, 71, 146, 200; MORTON 52; MOSELY 71; MULLINS 105; MURPHY 9; MURRAY 113; MYERS 22, 40; MYRICK 53.

NAIRON 30; NALLEY 89; NANCE 111; NAPIER 17; NEBLETT 71, 145, 212; NELSON 83; NEWBERRY 112; NEWTON 41; NICHOLS 41, 72, 140; NILES 109; NIX 36, 76, 81; NOBLES 11, 12, 14, 15; NOLAN 105, 116.

ODOM 3, 43, 45, 48, 49, 50; O'GUIN 70, 89; OLIVER 4, 30, 104; OUTLAND 121, 122, 126; OUTLAW 6; OWENS 33, 34, 163, 169.

PACE 28, 31, 41; PAGUE 125; PALMER 108; PARISH 94; PARKER 15, 65, 74, 94, 117; PARLEE 94; PATRICK 12; PATTERSON 76; PAYNE 102, 103, 104, 108, 109; PEAL 118; PEELER 209; PENNINGTON 109; PENNYWITT 59; PENSON 4; PERIGOLD 114; PERKINS 5, 31; PERRY 8, 41, 43, 130; PRESNELL 164; PETTIFORD 8; PHIFER 13, 14, 22, 85, 97, 134, 194; PHILLIPS 19, 49, 83, 104, 113, 116, 117; PIERCE 3, 5, 45; PIERPONT 77; PINO 31; PINSON 183; PLANT 93, 95; POWERS 61; PRESNELL 36; PREWETT 30; PRIMM 96; PULLEY 12.

QUINN 148.

* *

www.ingramcontent.com/pod-product-compliance
Lightning Source LLC
Chambersburg PA
CBHW080419270326
41929CB00018B/3088